HOUSE
OF THE
LORD

THE
HOUSE
OF THE
LORD

*A Study of Holy Sanctuaries,
Ancient and Modern*

James E. Talmage

PUBLISHED BY

DESERET BOOK COMPANY
SALT LAKE CITY, UTAH
1978

Lithographed by

DESERET PRESS

in the United States of America

Preface

Among the numerous sects and churches of the present day, the Latter-day Saints are distinguished as builders of Temples. In this respect they resemble Israel of olden time. It is not surprising that great and widespread interest is manifest respecting this peculiarity of The Church of Jesus Christ of Latter-day Saints, nor that questions are continually arising as to the purpose and motive behind this great labor, and the nature of the ordinances administered in these modern Houses of the Lord. To answer some of these questions, and to place within the reach of earnest inquirers authentic information concerning the doctrine and practise of Temple ministration, this book has been written.

By way of affording means of easy comparison between the Temple-building achievements of past and those of current time, a brief treatment of the sanctuaries of earlier dispensations has been included. While detailed information pertaining to ancient Temples and related sanctuaries is accessible to all, through cyclopedias, Bible dictionaries and works of more special scope, but little concerning the Temples of today and the sacred service therein rendered has been published in separate form. The official "History of the Church of Jesus Christ of Latter-day Saints" contains abundant data on the subject; but the information is distributed through many tomes, and is of access to comparatively few.

Among the special publications in this field, most of which are primarily devoted to the history and description of the Temple at Salt Lake City, are the following:

"Temples: Descriptive and historical sketches of ancient and modern sacred edifices," a pamphlet of 28 pages, by J. M. Sjodahl, Salt Lake City, 1892. This covers the history of the Salt Lake City Temple to the time of the laying of the capstone, April, 1892. The pamphlet contains outline drawings.

"The Salt Lake Temple," an article by James H. Anderson, published in "The Contributor," Vol. XIV, No. 6, April, 1893, 60 pages with numerous illustrations of the Temple at different stages, together with details of construction, and portraits of Church officials and others connected with the erection of the great structure.

"Historical and descriptive sketch of the Salt Lake Temple," an illustrated pamphlet of 36 pages published by the *Deseret News,* Salt Lake City, April, 1893.

"A Description of the Great Temple, Salt Lake City, and a statement concerning the purposes for which it has been built," a pamphlet of 40 pages, by D. M. McAllister, Salt Lake City, 1912. This contains half-tone engravings of both exterior and interior views.

In the present undertaking the author has been the recipient of many courtesies and much assistance from the officials of the several Temples, the Church Historian and his assistants, the general authorities of the Church, and many others. To all who have assisted in the pleasing labor his obligations are respectfully acknowledged.

JAMES E. TALMAGE

Salt Lake City, Utah,
    September 21, 1912.

Contents

CHAPTER I

A Pre-view of the Subject

Both by derivation and common usage the term "temple," in its literal application, is of restricted and specific meaning. The essential idea of a temple is and ever has been that of a *place* specially set apart for service regarded as sacred, and of real or assumed sanctity; in a more restricted sense, a temple is a *building* constructed for and exclusively devoted to sacred rites and ceremonies.

The Latin *Templum* was the equivalent of the Hebrew *Beth Elohim,* and signified the abode of Deity; hence, as associated with Divine worship, it meant literally the HOUSE OF THE LORD.[1]

Structures regarded in their entirety as sanctuaries, or enclosing apartments so designated, have been reared in many different ages, both by worshippers of idols and by the followers of the true and living God. Heathen temples of antiquity were regarded as abiding places of the mythical gods and goddesses whose names they bore, and to whose service the structures were dedicated. While the purlieus of such temples were used as places of gen-

---

[1]In this connection it is interesting and instructive to consider the significance of the name *Bethel,* a contraction of *Beth Elohim,* as applied by Jacob to the place where the presence of the Lord was manifest unto him. Said he, "Surely the Lord is in this place; and I knew it not. And he was afraid, and said, How dreadful is this place! this is none other but the house of God, and this is the gate of heaven. And Jacob rose up early in the morning, and took the stone that he had put for his pillows, and set it up for a pillar, and poured oil upon the top of it. And he called the name of that place Beth-el." (Genesis 28:16-19; read verses 10-22.)

eral assembly and public ceremony, there were always inner precincts, into which only the consecrated priests might enter, and wherein, it was claimed, the presence of the deity was manifest. As evidence of the exclusiveness of ancient temples, even those of heathen origin, we find that the altar of pagan worship stood not within the temple proper, but in front of the entrance. Temples have never been regarded as places of ordinary public assembly, but as sacred enclosures consecrated to the most solemn ceremonials of that particular system of worship, idolatrous or Divine, of which the temple stood as visible symbol and material type.

In olden times the people of Israel were distinguished among nations as the builders of sanctuaries to the name of the living God. This service was specifically required of them by Jehovah, whom they professed to serve. The history of Israel as a nation dates from the exodus. During the two centuries of their enslavement in Egypt, the children of Jacob had grown to be a numerous and powerful people; nevertheless they were in bondage. In due time, however, their sorrows and supplications came up before the Lord, and He led them forth by the outstretched arm of power. No sooner had they escaped from the environment of Egyptian idolatry, than they were required to prepare a sanctuary, wherein Jehovah would manifest His presence and make known His will as their accepted Lord and King.

The Tabernacle, which from the time of its construction in the wilderness and thence onward throughout the period of wandering and for centuries thereafter, was sacred to Israel as the sanctuary of Jehovah, had been built according to revealed plan and specifications. It was a compact and portable structure as the exigencies of migration required. Though the Tabernacle was but a tent, it was made of the best, the most prized, and the costliest materials the people possessed. This condition of excellence was appropriate and fitting, for the finished structure was a nation's offering unto the Lord. Its construction was prescribed in minutest detail, both as to design and material; it was in every respect the best the people could give, and Jehovah sanctified the proffered gift by His divine acceptance. In passing, let us be mindful of the fact that whether it be the gift of a man or a nation, the best, if offered willingly and with pure intent, is always excellent in the sight of God, however poor by other comparison that best may be.

To the call for material wherewith to build the Tabernacle, there was such willing and liberal response that the need was more than met: "For the stuff they had was sufficient for all the work to make it, and too much."[2] Proclamation was made accordingly, and the people were restrained from bringing more. The artificers and workmen engaged in the making of the Tabernacle were designated by direct revelation, or chosen by divinely appointed authority with special reference to their skill and devotion. The completed Tabernacle, viewed in relation to its surroundings and considered in connection with the circumstances of its creation, was an imposing structure. Its frames were of rare wood, its inner hangings of fine linen and elaborate embroideries with prescribed designs in blue, purple, and scarlet; its middle and outer curtains of choice skins; its metal parts of brass, silver, and gold.

Outside the Tabernacle, but within its enclosing court, stood the altar of sacrifice and the laver or font. The first apartment of the Tabernacle proper was an outer room, or Holy Place; and beyond this, screened from observation by the second veil, was the inner sanctuary, the Most Holy Place, specifically known as the Holy of Holies. In the appointed order, only the priests were permitted to enter the outer apartment; while to the inner place, the "holiest of all," none but the high priest might be admitted, and he but once a year, and then only after a long course of purification and sanctification.[3]

---

[2]Exodus 36:7.
[3]Hebrews 9:1-7; Leviticus chap. 16.

Among the most sacred appurtenances of the Tabernacle was the Ark of the Covenant. This was a casket
or chest, made of the best wood obtainable, lined and
overlaid with pure gold, and provided with four rings of
gold to receive the rods or poles used in carrying the Ark
during travel. The Ark contained certain objects of sacred
import, such as the golden pot of manna, preserved as a
remembrance; and to this were afterward added Aaron's
rod that had budded, and the tablets of stone inscribed
by the hand of God. When the Tabernacle was set up in
the camp of Israel, the Ark was placed within the inner
veil, in the Holy of Holies. Resting upon the Ark was
the Mercy Seat, surmounted by a pair of cherubim made
of beaten gold. From this seat did the Lord manifest His
presence, even as promised before either Ark or Tabernacle had been made: "And there I will meet with thee,
and I will commune with thee from above the mercy seat,
from between the two cherubims which are upon the ark
of the testimony, of all things which I will give thee in
commandment unto the children of Israel."[4]

No detailed description of the Tabernacle, its appurtenances or furniture, will be attempted at this place; it is
sufficient for our present purpose to know that the camp of
Israel had such a sanctuary; that it was constructed
according to revealed plan; that it was the embodiment of
the best the people could give both as to material and
workmanship; that it was the offering of the people to
their God, and was duly accepted by Him.[5] As shall yet
be shown, the Tabernacle was a prototype of the more
stable and magnificent Temple by which in course of time
it was superseded.

After Israel had become established in the land of
promise, when, after four decades of wandering in the
wilderness, the covenant people possessed at last a Canaan
of their own, the Tabernacle with its sacred contents was

[4]Exodus 25:22.
[5]Exodus 40:34-38.

given a resting place in Shiloh; and thither came the tribes to learn the will and word of God.[6] Afterward it was removed to Gibeon[7] and yet later to the City of David, or Zion.[8]

David, the second king of Israel, desired and planned to build a house unto the Lord, declaring that it was unfit that he, the king, should dwell in a palace of cedar, while the sanctuary of God was but a tent.[9] But the Lord spake by the mouth of Nathan the prophet, declining the proposed offering, and making plain the fact that to be acceptable unto Him it was not enough that the gift be appropriate, but that the giver must also be worthy. David, king of Israel, though in many respects a man after God's own heart, had sinned; and his sin had not yet found atonement. Thus spake the king: "I had in mine heart to build an house of rest for the ark of the covenant of the Lord, and for the footstool of our God, and had made ready for the building: But God said unto me, Thou shalt not build an house for my name, because thou hast been a man of war, and hast shed blood."[10] Nevertheless, David was permitted to gather material for the House of the Lord, which edifice not he, but Solomon, his son, should build.

Soon after Solomon's accession to the throne he set about the labor, which, as heritage and honor, had come to him with his crown. He laid the foundation in the fourth year of his reign, and the building was completed within seven years and a half. With the great wealth accumulated by his kingly father and specifically reserved for the building of the Temple, Solomon was able to put the known world under tribute, and to enlist the co-operation of nations in his great undertaking. The temple workmen numbered scores of thousands, and every depart-

---

[6]Joshua 18:1; see also 19:51; 21:2; Judges 18:31; I Samuel 1:3, 24; 4:3, 4.
[7]I Chron. 21:29; II Chron. 1:3.
[8]II Samuel 6:12; II Chron. 5:2.
[9]II Samuel 7:2.
[10]I Chron. 28:2, 3; compare II Samuel 7:1-13.

ment was in charge of master craftsmen. To serve on the great structure in any capacity was an honor; and labor acquired a dignity never before recognized. Masonry became a profession, and the graded orders therein established have endured until this day. The erection of the Temple of Solomon was an epoch-making event, not alone in the history of Israel, but in that of the world.

According to commonly accepted chronology, the Temple was finished about 1005 B. C. In architecture and construction, in design and costliness, it is known as one of the most remarkable buildings in history. The dedicatory services lasted seven days—a week of holy rejoicing in Israel. With fitting ceremony, the Tabernacle of the Congregation and the sacred Ark of the Covenant were brought into the Temple; and the Ark was deposited in the inner sanctuary, the Most Holy Place. The Lord's gracious acceptance was manifest in the cloud that filled the sacred chambers as the priests withdrew: "So that the priests could not stand to minister by reason of the cloud: for the glory of the Lord had filled the house of God."[11] Thus did the Temple supersede and include the Tabernacle, of which, indeed, it was the gorgeous successor.

A comparison of the plan of Solomon's Temple with that of the earlier Tabernacle shows that in all essentials of arrangement and proportion the two were so nearly alike as to be practically identical. True, the Tabernacle had but one enclosure, while the Temple was surrounded by courts, but the inner structure itself, the Temple proper, closely followed the earlier design. The dimensions of the Holy of Holies, the Holy Place, and the Porch, were in the Temple exactly double those of the corresponding parts in the Tabernacle.

The glorious pre-eminence of this splendid structure was of brief duration. Thirty-four years after its dedication, and but five years subsequent to the death of

---

[11]II Chron. 5:14; see also 7:1, 2, and compare Exodus 40:35.

Solomon, its decline began; and this decline was soon to develop into general spoliation, and finally to become an actual desecration. Solomon the king, the man of wisdom, the master-builder, had been led astray by the wiles of idolatrous women, and his wayward ways had fostered iniquity in Israel. The nation was no longer a unit; there were factions and sects, parties and creeds, some worshipping on the hill-tops, others under green trees, each party claiming excellence for its own particular shrine. The Temple soon lost its sanctity. The gift became depreciated by the perfidy of the giver, and Jehovah withdrew His protecting presence from the place no longer holy.

The Egyptians, from whose bondage the people had been delivered, were again permitted to oppress Israel. Shishak, king of Egypt, captured Jerusalem—the city of David and the site of the Temple—"and he took away the treasures of the house of the Lord."[12] Part of the aforetime sacred furniture left by the Egyptians was taken by others, and bestowed upon idols.[13] The work of desecration continued through centuries. Two hundred and sixteen years after the Egyptian spoliation, Ahaz, king of Judah, robbed the Temple of some remaining treasures, and sent part of its remnant of gold and silver as a present to a pagan king whose favor he sought to gain. Furthermore, he removed the altar and the font, and left but a house where once had stood a Temple.[14] Later, Nebuchadnezzar, king of Babylon, completed the despoiling of the Temple, and carried away its few remaining treasures. He then destroyed the building itself by fire.[15]

Thus, about six hundred years before the earthly advent of our Lord, Israel was left without a Temple. The people had divided; there were two kingdoms—Israel and Judah—each at enmity with the other; they had become idolatrous and altogether wicked; the Lord had

[12]I Kings 14:25, 26.
[13]II Chron. 24:7.
[14]II Kings 16:7-9, 17 and 18; see also II Chron. 28:24, 25.
[15]II Chron. 36:18, 19; see also II Kings 24:13; 25:9.

rejected them and their sanctuary. The Kingdom of
Israel, comprising approximately ten of the twelve tribes,
had been made subject to Assyria about 721 B. C., and a
century later the Kingdom of Judah was subdued by the
Babylonians. For seventy years the people of Judah—
thereafter known as Jews—remained in captivity, even as
had been predicted.[16] Then, under the friendly rule of
Cyrus[17] and Darius[18] they were permitted to return to
Jerusalem, and once more to rear a Temple in accordance
with their faith. In remembrance of the director of the
work, the restored Temple is known in history as the Temple of Zerubbabel. The foundations were laid with solemn
ceremony; and on that occasion living veterans who remembered the earlier Temple, wept with joy.[19] In spite
of legal technicalities[20] and other obstructions, the work
continued, and within twenty years after their return from
captivity the Jews had a Temple ready for dedication.
The Temple of Zerubbabel was finished 515 B. C., specifically on the third day of the month of Adar, in the
sixth year of the reign of Darius the king. The dedicatory
services followed immediately.[21] While this Temple was
greatly inferior in richness of finish and furniture as compared with the splendid Temple of Solomon, it was nevertheless the best the people could build, and the Lord
accepted it as an offering typifying the love and devotion
of His covenant children. In proof of this Divine acceptance, witness the ministrations of such prophets as Zech-
ariah, Haggai, and Malachi, within its walls.

About sixteen years before the birth of Christ, Herod
I, king of Judea, commenced the reconstruction of the
then decayed and generally ruinous Temple of Zerubbabel. For five centuries that structure had stood, and

[16]Jeremiah 25:11, 12; 29:10.
[17]Ezra, chaps. 1 and 2.
[18]Ezra, chap. 6.
[19]Ezra 3:12, 13.
[20]Ezra 4:4-24.
[21]Ezra 6:15-22.

doubtless it had become largely a wreck of time. Many
incidents in the earthly life of the Savior are associated
with the Temple of Herod. It is evident from scripture
that while opposed to the degraded and commercial uses
to which the Temple had been betrayed, Christ recognized
and acknowledged the sanctity of the temple precincts.
The Temple of Herod was a sacred structure; by what-
soever name it might have been known, it was to Him the
House of the Lord. And then, when the sable curtain
descended upon the great tragedy of Calvary, when at last
the agonizing cry, "It is finished," ascended from the
cross, the veil of the Temple was rent, and the one-time
Holy of Holies was bared. The absolute destruction of the
Temple had been foretold by our Lord, while yet He
lived in the flesh.[22] In the year 70 A.D. the Temple was
utterly destroyed by fire in connection with the capture
of Jerusalem by the Romans under Titus.

The Temple of Herod was the last temple reared on
the eastern hemisphere. From the destruction of that
great edifice onward to the time of the re-establishment
of the Church of Jesus Christ in the nineteenth century,
our only record of temple building is such mention as is
found in Nephite chronicles. Book of Mormon scriptures affirm that temples were erected by the Nephite
colonists on what is now known as the American continent; but we have few details of construction and fewer
facts as to administrative ordinances pertaining to these
western temples. The people constructed a Temple about
570 B. C. and this we learn was patterned after the
Temple of Solomon, though greatly inferior to that gorgeous structure in grandeur and costliness.[23] It is of interest
to read that when the resurrected Lord manifested Himself
to the Nephites on the western continent, He found them
assembled about the Temple.[24] The Book of Mormon,

---

[22]Matt. 24:2; Mark 13:2; Luke 21:6.
[23]See Book of Mormon, II Nephi 5:16.
[24]See Book of Mormon, III Nephi 11:1.

however, makes no mention of temples even as late as
the time of the destruction of the Temple at Jerusalem;
and moreover the Nephite nation came to an end within
about four centuries after Christ. It is evident, therefore,
that on both hemispheres temples ceased to exist in the
early period of the apostasy and the very conception of a
Temple in the distinctive sense perished amongst mankind.

For many centuries no offer of a sanctuary was made
unto the Lord; indeed, it appears that no need of such was
recognized. The apostate church declared that direct
communication from God had ceased; and in place of
Divine administration a self-constituted government
claimed supreme power. It is evident that, as far as the
Church was concerned, the voice of the Lord had been
silenced; that the people were no longer willing to listen
to the word of revelation, and that the government of the
Church had been abrogated by human agencies.[25]

When, in the reign of Constantine, a perverted Christianity had become the religion of state, the need of a
place wherein God would reveal Himself was still utterly
unseen or ignored. True, many edifices, most of them
costly and grand, were erected. Of these some were dedicated to Peter and Paul, to James and John; others to the
Magdalene and the Virgin; but not one was raised by
authority and name to the honor of Jesus, the Christ.
Among the multitude of chapels and shrines, of churches
and cathedrals, the Son of Man had not a place to call His
own. It was declared that the pope, sitting in Rome, was
the vicegerent of Christ, and that without revelation he
was empowered to declare the will of God.[26]

Not until the Gospel was restored in the nineteenth
century, with its ancient powers and privileges, was the
Holy Priesthood manifest again among men. And be it
remembered that the authority to speak and act in the
name of God is essential to a Temple, and a Temple is

[25]See the author's "The Great Apostasy," chap. IX.
[26]See the author's "The Great Apostasy," chap. X.

void without the sacred authority of the Holy Priesthood. In the year of our Lord 1820, Joseph Smith, the prophet of the latest dispensation, then a lad in his fifteenth year, received a Divine manifestation,[27] in which both the Eternal Father and His Son, Jesus Christ, appeared and instructed the youthful suppliant. Through Joseph Smith, the Gospel of old was restored to earth, and the ancient law was re-established. In course of time, through the ministry of the prophet, The Church of Jesus Christ of Latter-day Saints was organized, and its establishment was marked by manifestations of Divine power.[28]

It is a significant fact that this Church, true to the distinction it affirms—that of being the Church of the living God as its name proclaims—began in the very early days of its history to provide for the erection of a temple.[29] The Church was organized as an earthly body-corporate on the sixth of April, A. D. 1830; and, in July of the year following, a revelation was received designating the site of a future temple near Independence, Missouri. The construction of a temple on this chosen spot is yet delayed, as is also the case with another temple-site in Far West Missouri,[30] on which the cornerstones were laid in 1838. The Church holds as a sacred trust the commission to build the temples so located, but as yet the way has not been opened for the consummation of the plan. In the meantime temples in other places have been reared, and already the modern dispensation is marked by the erection of six such sacred edifices.

On the first day of June, 1833, in a revelation to the Prophet Joseph Smith, the Lord directed the immediate building of a holy house, in which He promised to endow His chosen servants with power and authority.[31] The

---

[27]See the author's "The Articles of Faith," Lecture I, and references thereto.
[28]See the author's "The Articles of Faith," specifically Lecture I, and notes thereon.
[29]See Doctrine and Covenants 36:8; 42:36; 133:2.
[30]See Doctrine and Covenants 115:7-16.
[31]See Doctrine and Covenants, Section 95.

people responded to the call with willingness and devotion. In spite of dire poverty and in the face of unrelenting persecution, the work was carried to completion, and in March, 1836, the first Temple of modern times was dedicated at Kirtland, Ohio.[32] The dedicatory services were marked by Divine manifestations comparable to those attending the offering of the first Temple of olden times; and on later occasions heavenly beings appeared within the sacred precincts with revelations of the Divine will to man. In that place the Lord Jesus was again seen and heard.[33] Within two years from the time of its dedication the Kirtland Temple was abandoned by the people who built it; they were forced to flee because of persecution, and with their departure the sacred Temple became an ordinary house, disowned of the Lord to whose name it had been reared. The building still stands and is used as a meeting-house by a small and comparatively unknown sect.

The migration of the Latter-day Saints was to the west; and they established themselves first in Missouri, and later in Illinois with Nauvoo as the central seat of the Church. Scarcely had they become settled in their new abode when the voice of revelation was heard calling upon the people to again build a house sacred to the name of God.

The corner-stones of the Nauvoo Temple were laid April 6, 1841, and the capstone was placed in position May 24, 1845; each event was celebrated by a solemn assembly and sacred service. Though it was evident that the people would be forced to flee again, and though they knew that the Temple would have to be abandoned soon after completion, they labored with might and diligence to finish and properly furnish the structure. It was dedicated April 30, 1846, though certain portions, such as the baptistry, had been previously dedicated and used in

---

[32]See Doctrine and Covenants, Section 109.
[33]See Doctrine and Covenants, 110:1-10.

ordinance work. Many of the Saints received their blessings and holy endowments in the Nauvoo Temple, though, even before the completion of the building, the exodus of the people had begun. The Temple was abandoned by those who in poverty and by sacrifice had reared it. In November, 1848, it became a prey to incendiary flames, and in May, 1850, a tornado demolished what remained of the blackened walls.

On the 24th of July, 1847, the "Mormon" pioneers entered the valleys of Utah, while yet the region was Mexican territory, and established a settlement where now stands Salt Lake City. Four days later Brigham Young, prophet and leader, indicated a site in the sagebrush wastes, and, striking the arid ground with his staff, proclaimed, "Here will be the Temple of our God." That site is now the beautiful Temple Block, around which the city has grown. In February, 1853, the area was dedicated with sacred service, and on the 6th of April following, the corner stones of the building were laid to the accompaniment of solemn and imposing ceremony. The Salt Lake City Temple was forty years in building; the capstone was laid on the 6th of April, 1892, and the completed Temple was dedicated one year later.

Of the four Temples already erected in Utah, the one in Salt Lake City was the first begun and the last finished. During its course of construction three other Temples were built by the Latter-day Saints, one at St. George, one at Logan, and one at Manti, Utah. Add to these the two earlier Temples—at Kirtland, Ohio, and at Nauvoo, Illinois—and we have six of these sacred structures already erected in the present and last dispensation of the Priesthood—the dispensation of the fulness of times.

It is not the purpose of the present chapter to consider in detail any particular Temple, either ancient or modern; but rather to show the essential and distinguishing features of Temples, and to make plain the fact that in both ancient and modern times the covenant people have regarded the building of Temples as a labor specifically required at their hands. From what has been said it is plain that a Temple is more than chapel or church, more than synagogue or cathedral; it is a structure erected as the House of the Lord, sacred to the closest communion between the Lord Himself and the Holy Priesthood, and devoted to the highest and most sacred ordinances characteristic of the age or dispensation to which the particular Temple belongs. Moreover, to be indeed a holy Temple—accepted of God, and by Him acknowledged as His House—the offering must have been called for, and both gift and giver must be worthy.

The Church of Jesus Christ of Latter-day Saints proclaims that it is the possessor of the Holy Priesthood again restored to earth, and that it is invested with Divine commission to erect and maintain Temples dedicated to the name and service of the true and living God, and to administer within those sacred structures the ordinances of the Priesthood, the effect of which shall be binding both on earth and beyond the grave.

CHAPTER II

Sanctuaries in Earlier Dispensations

As understood and applied herein, the designation "temple" is restricted to mean an actual structure, reared by man, hallowed and sanctified for the special service of Deity, such service including the authoritative administration of ordinances pertaining to the Holy Priesthood, and not merely a place, however sacred the spot may have become. If sacred places were to be classed with sacred buildings as essentially temples, the category would include many a holy Bethel rarely considered as such. In the more extended application of the term, the Garden in Eden was the first sanctuary of earth, for therein did the Lord first speak unto man and make known the Divine law. So too, Sinai became a sanctuary, for the mount was consecrated as the special abode of the Lord while He communed with the prophet, and issued His decrees. The sanctity of such places was as that of Horeb, where God spake unto Moses from the midst of the flame; and where, as the man approached he was halted by the command: "Draw not nigh hither: put off thy shoes from off thy feet, for the place whereon thou standest is holy ground."[1] A temple, however, is characterized not alone as the place where God reveals Himself to man, but also as the House wherein prescribed ordinances of the Priesthood are solemnized.

---

[1]Exodus 3:5.

The "Testimony"

Prior to the construction of the Tabernacle in the wilderness, and indeed during the early stages of the memorable journey from Egypt, the people of Israel had a certain depository for sacred things, known as the Testimony. This is definitely mentioned in connection with the following incident. Under Divine direction a vessel of manna was to be preserved, lest the people forget the power and goodness of God, by which they had been fed:

> "And Moses said, This is the thing which the Lord commandeth, Fill an omer of it to be kept for your generations; that they may see the bread wherewith I have fed you in the wilderness, when I brought you forth from the land of Egypt.
>
> "And Moses said unto Aaron, Take a pot, and put an omer full of manna therein, and lay it up before the Lord, to be kept for your generations.
>
> "As the Lord commanded Moses, so Aaron laid it up before the Testimony, to be kept."[2]

There appears little room for doubt that the Testimony here referred to was a material structure, and that its name is suggestive of Divine witness as to its sacred character. Inasmuch as the account of the exodus contains no mention of the making of such a structure, and moreover as its existence and use were definitely affirmed before the people had had time or opportunity to shape it in the wilderness, it would seem that they must have brought the sacred Testimony with them from Egypt. This incident is of interest and importance as indicating the existence of a holy sanctuary during the formative stages of Israel's growth as a nation, and while the people were in subjection to idolatrous rulers. This application of the term Testimony must not be confused with later usage by which the tables of stone bearing the divinely inscribed Decalogue are so designated.[3] It is to be noted further that the Tabernacle, wherein was housed the Ark of the Covenant containing the sacred tables of stone, is

---

[2]Exodus 16:32-34.

[3]See Exodus 31:18; 25:16; 32:15; 34:28, 29.

distinctively called the Tabernacle of Testimony. These several uses of the term lead to no ambiguity if the context be duly considered in each case.

The Provisional Tabernacle

While Moses communed with the Lord on Sinai, the people, left for a time to themselves, set up a golden calf in imitation of Apis, an Egyptian idol; and in consequence of their idolatrous orgies, the Lord's anger was kindled against them. During the period of their consequent estrangement, before a reconciliation had been effected between Jehovah and His people, Divine manifestations ceased within the camp and only afar off could the Lord be found. In connection with this condition we read of the establishment of a temporary place of meeting —possibly the dwelling tent of Moses, which became sanctified by the Divine Presence. Thus runs the record:

"And Moses took the tabernacle, and pitched it without the camp, afar off from the camp, and called it the Tabernacle of the congregation. And it came to pass, that every one which sought the Lord went out into the tabernacle of the congregation, which was without the camp.

"And it came to pass, when Moses went out unto the tabernacle, that all the people rose up, and stood every man at his tent door, and looked after Moses, until he was gone into the tabernacle.

"And it came to pass, as Moses entered into the tabernacle, the cloudy pillar descended, and stood at the door of the tabernacle, and the Lord talked with Moses.

"And all the people saw the cloudy pillar stand at the tabernacle door: and all the people rose up and worshipped, every man in his tent door.

"And the Lord spake unto Moses face to face, as a man speaketh unto his friend. And he turned again into the camp: but his servant Joshua, the son of Nun, a young man, departed not out of the tabernacle."[4]

That the tent here called the Tabernacle of the Congregation[5] is not the elaborate and costly structure specially built as the Lord directed, is evident from the fact that the greater and more enduring Tabernacle had not been constructed at the time referred to in the scripture

---

[4]Exodus 33:7-11.

[5]In the Authorized Version of the Holy Bible this sanctuary is called the Tabernacle of the Congregation; in the Revised Version it is designated the Tent of Meeting; preponderance of authority is in favor of the latter reading.

last cited. Unlike the later Tabernacle, which was set up in the center of the camp with the tribes massed about it in specified order, this Provisional Tabernacle was pitched outside the camp—afar off—perhaps as an indication of the Lord's withdrawal following Israel's idolatrous turning away from Him. That the Provisional Tabernacle was, however, a holy sanctuary is attested by the personal communion therein between Jehovah and His servant Moses.

The Tabernacle of the Congregation

From amidst the clouds, and to the accompaniments of thunders and lightnings on Sinai, the Lord gave unto Moses the law and the testimony. Not alone did Moses there talk with the Lord in person, but by Divine command, Aaron and his sons Nadab and Abihu, together with seventy of the elders of Israel, went up upon the mountain and did see God, even the God of Israel. Over Sinai the glory of the Lord abode for many days: "And Moses went into the midst of the cloud, and gat him up into the mount; and Moses was in the mount forty days and forty nights."[6]

When he descended Moses bore with him the commission to call upon the children of Israel for contributions and offerings of their substance and all their precious things, such as would be suitable for the construction of a sanctuary for service in the wilderness.

"And the Lord spake unto Moses, saying,

"Speak unto the children of Israel, that they bring me an offering: of every man that giveth it willingly with his heart ye shall take my offering.

"And this is the offering which ye shall take of them; gold, and silver, and brass,

"And blue, and purple, and scarlet, and fine linen, and goats' hair,

"And rams' skins dyed red, and badgers' skins, and shittim wood,

"Oil for the light, spices for anointing oil, and for sweet incense,

"Onyx stones, and stones to be set in the ephod, and in the breastplate.

"And let them make me a sanctuary; that I may dwell among them.

---

[6]Exodus 24:9, 10, 18; read the entire chapter.

"According to all that I shew thee, after the pattern of the tabernacle, and the pattern of all the instruments thereof, even so shall ye make it."[7]

The response of the people was so liberal and prompt that a surplus of material was soon amassed.

"And they spake unto Moses, saying, The people bring much more than enough for the service of the work, which the Lord commanded to make.

"And Moses gave commandment, and they caused it to be proclaimed throughout the camp, saying, Let neither man nor woman make any more work for the offering of the sanctuary. So the people were restrained from bringing.

"For the stuff they had was sufficient for all the work to make it, and too much."[8]

Divine direction was manifest in the appointment of men who should be in charge of the labor. Bezaleel, the son of Uri, and Aholiab, the son of Ahisamach, were designated by revelation as the master craftsmen under whose direction the other workers should labor until all had been finished in direct accord with the revealed pattern and plan. And when so finished it was the embodiment of the best in material and workmanship.

The Tabernacle stood in an outer enclosure or court, walled in by canvas screens with entrance curtains finely embroidered. The curtains that formed the walls of the court were suspended from pillars, which stood at intervals along the sides of an oblong. The longer walls ran east and west, with the main entrance to the enclosure on the eastern side. Of the two squares within the curtains, the easterly was reserved for assemblies of the people, while the square to the west constituted the more sacred area pertaining to the Tabernacle itself.

The entire space so enclosed covered one hundred cubits east and west and fifty cubits north and south, or approximately one hundred and fifty feet by seventy-five

---

[7]Exodus 25:1-9. For details of the building and furnishings of the Tabernacle of the Congregation see Exodus chapters 25-31, more particularly chapter 25, which account is in part repeated in 36:8-38.

[8]Exodus 36:5-7.

feet.[9] In the easterly section, and therefore removed
from the Tabernacle, stood the altar of burnt-offerings.
Between the altar and the Tabernacle stood the laver; this
was a large vessel of brass standing upon a pedestal and
containing water for the ceremonial cleansing of the hands
and feet of the priests. It is interesting to note that the
laver and its supporting pedestal were made by special
contribution of the women, who gave their brazen mirrors
for this purpose. The Tabernacle stood with its longer
axis east and west, and with its entrance on the easterly
side. The structure was but thirty cubits long by ten
cubits broad, or forty-five by fifteen feet; these are the
dimensions given by Josephus, and they are practically
in accord with the description in Exodus, which states
that the walls comprised twenty boards on a side, each
board one and a half cubits wide; at the west end there
were six boards, each one and a half cubits wide or nine
cubits in all; these with the angle posts would make the
entire breadth equal to that given by Josephus, ten cubits.
The boards of the walls were held together by tenon-
joints having sockets of silver, two to each board; the
boards themselves were overlaid with gold and were provided with rings of the same metal to receive the bars,
which also were overlaid with gold.

It will be seen that the Tabernacle was but a small
structure, entirely unsuited to the accommodation of large
assemblies, but it is to be remembered that for such it
was never intended. Within the Tabernacle, only the appointed bearers of the Priesthood officiated; and of these
none but the few actually engaged in the service of the
day could be admitted.

The Tabernacle was divided by a curtain, specifically
called the Veil, into two compartments, the outer of which

---

[9]The cubit is an ancient measure of length, the value of which varied in different countries and at different times. As the term occurs in the Bible, it denotes
varying lengths. In line with modern encyclopedias, Bible dictionaries, etc., the
length herein adopted is one foot six inches. See Encyclopaedia Britannica. Smith's
Bible Dictionary, etc.

was known as the Holy Place, and the inner as the Most Holy Place or Holy of Holies. Josephus and some others state that the Tabernacle comprised three parts; the third division, however, was really outside the main tent and appeared as a porch at the east end, five cubits deep, and extending across the entire front. The Veil, which separated the Holy Place from the Holy of Holies, was of fine workmanship, "of blue, and purple, and scarlet, and fine twined linen of cunning work," and was embroidered with cherubim. It was hung upon four pillars of wood overlaid with gold; the hooks were of gold and the sockets of silver. The wood used for these pillars, as indeed that used in other parts of the structure, was the rare, costly, and durable shittim or acacia, sometimes known as thorn-wood. Beyond the Veil the enclosure was most holy, and therein was placed the Ark of the Covenant with its Mercy Seat bearing the sacred cherubim, the description of which appears in the record as follows:

"And Bezaleel made the ark of shittim wood: two cubits and a half was the length of it, and a cubit and a half the breadth of it, and a cubit and a half the height of it:

"And he overlaid it with pure gold within and without, and made a crown of gold to it round about.

"And he cast for it four rings of gold, to be set by the four corners of it; even two rings upon the one side of it, and two rings upon the other side of it.

"And he made staves of shittim wood, and overlaid them with gold.

"And he put the staves into the rings by the sides of the ark, to bear the ark.

"And he made the mercy seat of pure gold: two cubits and a half was the length thereof, and one cubit and a half the breadth thereof.

"And he made two cherubims of gold, beaten out of one piece made he them, on the two ends of the mercy seat:

"One cherub on the end on this side, and another cherub on the other end on that side: out of the mercy seat made he the cherubims on the two ends thereof.

"And the cherubims spread out their wings on high, and covered with their wings over the mercy seat, with their faces one to another; even to the mercy seatward were the faces of the cherubims."[10]

Outside the Veil, yet within the Tabernacle, was the

---

[10]Exodus 37:1-9; compare 25:10-22.

Holy Place; in this were placed the table of shewbread, the altar of incense, and the golden seven-branched candlestick.[11]

The rich fabrics of delicate workmanship forming the walls and roof of the Tabernacle were protected by coarser hangings of goats' hair, and these in turn by a covering of skins. The structure as completed is referred to in the scripture sometimes as the Tent of the Congregation and at others as the Tabernacle of the Congregation; the former expression occurs thirteen times, the latter one hundred and thirty-three times; yet notwithstanding this difference, the original in each case was *Ohel Moed,* the best authenticated translation of which is the Tent of Meeting. Let it not be supposed, however, that this means in the ordinary sense a meeting-house, for the meeting here expressed is not that of a concourse of worshippers, but the place of communion between God and His Priesthood. The Tent of Meeting, or the Tabernacle of the Congregation, in Israel, was the Lord's tent wherein He met the authorized representatives of His people.

On the first day of the second year following Israel's exodus from Egypt, the Tabernacle was set up for the first time, and all the sacred furniture was disposed according to the direct commands of the Lord. The veil was hung, and the place was consecrated as a most holy spot, ineffably sacred as the dwelling place of Jehovah. Then, even as on Sinai a cloud had shrouded the temporary abiding place of God, so was it with the Tabernacle:

"Then a cloud covered the tent of the congregation, and the glory of the Lord filled the tabernacle.

"And Moses was not able to enter into the tent of the congregation, because the cloud abode thereon and the glory of the Lord filled the tabernacle.

"And when the cloud was taken up from over the tabernacle, the children of Israel went onward in all their journeys:

---

[11]See Exodus 37:10-29; compare 25:23-40.

"But if the cloud were not taken up, then they journeyed not till the day that it was taken up.

"For the cloud of the Lord was upon the tabernacle by day, and fire was on it by night, in the sight of all the house of Israel, throughout all their journeys."[12]

The all-pervading and all-controlling thought in the erection of this portable sanctuary was that of expressing the close association between Jehovah and His people. The people were to consider themselves specifically the people of God, and amongst them should be His dwelling, surpassing in a transcendent degree the presence of the gods of wood and stone housed among the idolatrous nations with whom Israel had to contend. This thought was expressed in the earliest commandment respecting the building of the Tabernacle: "And let them make me a sanctuary; that I may dwell among them."[13]

Even more truly indispensable than Tabernacle or Temple, in the maintenance of close relationship with Deity, is the Priesthood. It was therefore to be expected that with the establishment of a holy sanctuary, appointments and ordinations should be made whereby men would be truly set apart to the sacred offices of the Priesthood. While Moses was the great high priest of Israel, standing at the head of a distinctive dispensation of Divine authority and power, there were many priestly functions pertaining to the less exalted orders, and unto these Aaron and his four sons, Nadab, Abihu, Eleazer, and Ithamar, were set apart. As the Tabernacle had been built under express direction extending even into minute detail, so the ministrations of the Priesthood were prescribed and the order of worship was established, whereby the people should be reminded that amongst them dwelt Jehovah, before whom they should set none other gods.[14]

The Tabernacle was prepared primarily for migratory service; its parts therefore were separately finished and

---

[12]Exodus 40:34-38.
[13]Exodus 25:8.
[14]See Exodus chapter 28.

so fitted as to permit of easy putting together or taking apart. When set up within its court, the Tabernacle occupied the place of honor in the center of the camp.

On the east, and therefore immediately before the entrance to the court, were the tents of the Priests; while on the other three sides the Levites were encamped. These, being closest in attendance have been likened to the body-guard of the Great King[15] whose throne was within the sanctuary; and beyond them were stationed the other tribes in order of established precedence. While dismantled and in transit, when the people were on the march, the Tabernacle still held the central place; its bearers were the Levites, and the whole army of Israel was its guard.

Until Israel had become permanently established in the land of promise, the Tabernacle of the Congregation had but temporary resting places. As the people moved the sanctuary was carried, until it found a somewhat more permanent home at Shiloh. There, at the door of the Tabernacle, the final apportionment of Canaan among the tribes was made.[16] There it remained during the period of the Judges, and until after the Ark of God had been allowed to pass from the custody of Israel to that of the Philistines, because of sin.[17] The glory of the sanctuary was largely lost, and though the Tabernacle continued in existence its sacred service was in abeyance. Sadly was the truth declared, "The glory is departed from Israel: for the ark of God is taken."[18] There is evidence that for a short time during the reign of Saul, the Tabernacle was established at Nob; for there we find the priest Ahimelech maintaining the service of the shew-bread,[19] but the Ark of the Covenant was certainly not there.[20] We next

[15]See Smith's Dictionary of the Bible (Barnum's ed.), art. "Tabernacle."
[16]Joshua 18:1-3; 19:51; see also 21:2; Judges 18:31; I Sam. 1:3, 24; 4:3, 4.
[17]See I Samuel 4:10-18.
[18]I Samuel 4:22.
[19]See I Samuel 21:1-6.
[20]See I Samuel 7:1, 2.

learn of the Tabernacle having been set up at Gibeon, though the conditions resulting in its removal thither are not fully stated.[21] The Ark was housed in another tent, and finally both were brought into the splendid Temple of Solomon by which all earlier sanctuaries were superseded.

The Third Tabernacle

Yet another tent of sanctuary was made and used in Israel prior to the erection of the great Temple. This we may call for convenience the Third Tabernacle; it was erected by David the king, in his own city, as a shelter for the Ark of the Covenant. As already cited, the scriptural record tells of the capture of the Ark by the Philistines, and of its return to Israel. This incident occurred during the latter part of the administration of the Judges, before Israel had bowed to a king in Canaan.[22]

Throughout the reign of Saul, the Ark remained under the roof of a private dwelling; wherein, however, a priest was maintained for its care and ministry. One of the early acts of David after he became king, was to plan the removal of the Ark to a more suitable situation. In the course of this removal, Uzzah was stricken, because without authority he essayed to take hold of the sacred vessel; and this manifestation of Divine displeasure so affected David that he delayed his purpose of setting up the Ark in his own city and placed it in another private house—that of Obed-edom the Gittite.[23] While the Ark remained beneath that roof the household was blessed and prospered. In course of time the original plan was carried into effect and the Ark was set up in a tent specially prepared for its reception in the City of David: "And they brought in the ark of the Lord, and set it in his place, in the midst of the tabernacle that David had

---

[21]See I Chron. 21:28-30; compare II Chron. 1:3-6.
[22]I Samuel 4:10-22; also chapters 5 and 6; and 7:1-2.
[23]II Samuel 6:1-12; see also I Chron. chapter 13.

pitched for it: and David offered burnt offerings and peace offerings before the Lord."[24]

Thus, during the reign of David there were two places regarded as sanctuaries; and the worship of the people was divided. Solomon appears to have acknowledged the sanctity of both places—the resting place of the Ark at Jerusalem and the place of the Tabernacle of the Congregation at Gibeon.[25] Through him both shrines were again brought together.[26]

The Temple of Solomon

Scarcely had the Ark of the Covenant been deposited at the capital of the kingdom—the City of David,—when the king became desirous of erecting for its accommodation a more enduring shelter than the tent in which it had been installed with pomp and ceremony. It appears that the conscience of the king was troubled by the thought that he was better housed than was the sanctuary of the Lord: "Now it came to pass, as David sat in his house, that David said to Nathan the prophet, Lo, I dwell in an house of cedars, but the ark of the covenant of the Lord remaineth under curtains."[27] It was David's desire to build a suitable House for the Lord and Nathan the prophet at first encouraged the undertaking. The Lord spake to Nathan however, and directed him to decline the king's proffered gift. Although Jehovah had been without a fixed place recognized by the people as His, though as He said He had not dwelt in a house amongst Israel, but had gone from tent to tent and from one tabernacle to another,[28] though as the context implies, the Lord had been neglected in the long delay attending the erection of a house to His name, nevertheless David could not be

[24]II Samuel 6:17; see also I Chron. 15:1, and 16:1.
[25]See I Kings 3:15 and II Chron. 1:3, 4.
[26]See I Kings 8:1-4.
[27]I Chron. 17:1; see also II Samuel 7:1, 2.
[28]I Chron. 17:4, 5.

honored with the commission or even the permission to build such a house for he was accounted a man of blood.[29] Let us not undertake to judge the extent of David's offending; to do so would be to usurp the Divine prerogative; it is enough for us to know that even the gift of royalty may be declined if there be aught requiring reconciliation between the mortal and his God. David, however, was permitted to provide means and to gather material which afterward should be used in the erection of the Temple,[30] moreover, the very site on which the great building was subsequently erected was chosen and sanctified through his agency. A great pestilence had fallen upon Israel, and the Angel of the Lord, sent forth with the warrant of destruction, was seen by David, standing, sword in hand, on Mount Moriah at the threshing floor of Araunah the Jebusite.[31] That spot, hallowed by the presence of a heavenly messenger, though that messenger was the Angel of Death, was marked by the erection of an altar, as the Lord directed through the prophet Gad.[32]

As David realized that his years of life were few, he laid upon Solomon, his son and chosen successor, the solemn charge to build the house he had been forbidden to build. The king dwelt pathetically upon his own disqualification, and then repeated the Lord's promise of acceptance at the hand of Solomon. The scriptural record runs thus:

"So David prepared abundantly before his death.
"Then he called for Solomon his son, and charged him to build an house for the Lord God of Israel.
"And David said to Solomon. My son, as for me, it was in my mind to build an house unto the name of the Lord my God:
"But the word of the Lord came to me, saying, Thou hast shed blood abundantly, and hast made great wars: thou shalt not build an house unto my name, because thou hast shed much blood upon the earth in my sight.
"Behold, a son shall be born to thee, who shall be a man of rest; and

---

[29]See I Chron. 22:8; compare 28:3; and I Kings 5:3.
[30]See I Chron. 22:1-5.
[31]II Samuel 24:15-25; see also I Chron. 21:15-17; and II Chron. 3:1.
[32]See I Chron. 21:18-30; compare II Samuel 24:18-25.

I will give him rest from all his enemies round about: for his name shall be Solomon, and I will give peace and quietness unto Israel in his days.

"He shall build an house for my name; and he shall be my son, and I will be his father: and I will establish the throne of his kingdom over Israel for ever.

"Now, my son, the Lord be with thee; and prosper thou, and build the house of the Lord thy God, as he hath said of thee.

"Only the Lord give thee wisdom and understanding, and give thee charge concerning Israel, that thou mayest keep the law of the Lord thy God.

"Then shalt thou prosper, if thou takest heed to fulfill the statues and judgments which the Lord charged Moses with concerning Israel: be strong, and of good courage; dread not, nor be dismayed.

"Now, behold, in my trouble I have prepared for the house of the Lord an hundred thousand talents of gold, and a thousand thousand talents of silver; and of brass and iron without weight; for it is in abundance: timber also and stone have I prepared; and thou mayest add thereto.

"Moreover there are workmen with thee in abundance, hewers and workers of stone and timber, and all manner of cunning men for every manner of work.

"Of the gold, the silver, and the brass, and the iron, there is no number. Arise therefore, and be doing, and the Lord be with thee.

"David also commanded all the princes of Israel to help Solomon his son, saying,

"Is not the Lord your God with you? and hath he not given you rest on every side? for he hath given the inhabitants of the land into mine hand; and the land is subdued before the Lord, and before his people.

"Now set your heart and your soul to seek the Lord your God; arise therefore, and build ye the sanctuary of the Lord God, to bring the ark of the covenant of the Lord, and the holy vessels of God, into the house that is to be built to the name of the Lord."[33]

David gave Solomon detailed instructions as to the design and specifications of the house and its appurtenances, the plan of the porch and that of both the main structure and the accessory buildings, "and the pattern of all that he had by the Spirit." Furthermore he gave directions as to the ministry of the various courses of Priests and Levites, "and for all the work of the service of the house of the Lord, and for all the vessels of service in the house of the Lord.[34]

The actual work of construction was begun in the fourth year of Solomon's reign, and the Temple was

---

[33]I Chron. 22:5-19; see also 28:1-8; 29:1-7.

[34]I Chron. 28:11-13.

ready for dedication in the twelfth, or about 1005 B. C. At the inception of the labor, Solomon entered into an agreement with Hiram, a neighboring king, whereby the resources of Tyre and Sidon were annexed in the great undertaking. Through this alliance the splendid forests of Lebanon were made accessible; cedar, and fir, and other trees were felled and floated by the thousand to the most convenient point for land transportation to Jerusalem. It had been previously explained to Hiram that the demand would be a heavy one, for, as Solomon had said: "The house which I build is great: for great is our God above all gods."[35] Sidonian hewers were put to work,—the most skilful of all known woodmen; and the timbers of Lebanon were supplied in abundance. The extent of the demand may be judged from the enormous payment proffered and made by Solomon.[36]

Israelitish workmen were employed in great numbers, both in co-operation with the Sidonians and at home. Thus we read:

"And King Solomon raised a levy out of all Israel; and the levy was thirty thousand men.

"And he sent them to Lebanon, ten thousand a month by courses: a month they were in Lebanon, and two months at home: and Adoniram was over the levy.

"And Solomon had threescore and ten thousand that bare burdens, and fourscore thousand hewers in the mountains;

"Beside the chief of Solomon's officers which were over the work, three thousand and three hundred, which ruled over the people that wrought in the work.

"And the king commanded, and they brought great stones, costly stones, and hewed stones, to lay the foundation of the house.

"And Solomon's builders and Hiram's builders did hew them, and the stonesquarers: so they prepared timber and stones to build the house."[37]

For the successful employment of such great numbers of workmen an effective system of organization was necessary; we are not surprised, therefore, in reading that

---

[35]II Chron. 2:5; see also the entire chapter.
[36]See I Kings 5:11; and II Chron. 2:10, 15.
[37]I Kings 5:13-18.

thirty-three hundred overseers were in service. The efficiency of the system is attested by the success attending the great undertaking. The Israelites and the men of Tyre and Sidon worked in harmony, and much of the building material was shaped by pattern and measurement in forest and quarry; therefore "the house, when it was in building, was built of stone made ready before it was brought thither; so that there was neither hammer nor ax nor any tool of iron heard in the house, while it was in building."[38]

Our primary source of information relating to the erection of the great Temple is the scriptural record contained in I Kings, chapters 6 and 7; a later account appears in II Chronicles, chapter 3 and 4, which account as well as the description given by Josephus[39] appears to have been derived from the record first cited.

In general, the design of Solomon's Temple was that of the specially constructed Tabernacle of the Congregation, though the dimensions of the Temple were double those of the Tabernacle. It will be remembered that the porch of the Tabernacle was five cubits deep; that of the Temple measured ten cubits in depth; in each case the porch extended across the full width of the house. The Holy Place, or first compartment within the walls, was twenty cubits long, ten cubits wide and ten high in the Tabernacle; that of the Temple was forty by twenty cubits and twenty cubits high. The inner sanctuary, Oracle, or Holy of Holies, in the Tabernacle was cubical and measured ten cubits each way; in the Temple this sacred enclosure was a cube of twenty cubits. Thus the ground plan of the Tabernacle covered thirty-five by twenty cubits, and that of the Temple seventy cubits by forty. These measurements do not take into account the side chambers, which in the Tabernacle were five cubits wide; those connected with the Temple measured ten cubits in

[38]I Kings 6:7; compare Deuteronomy 27:5, 6.
[39]Josephus, Antiquities of the Jews, Book VIII: chaps. 2, 3, 4.

extreme width; with these included, the entire area of the Tabernacle was forty by twenty cubits, and that of the Temple eighty by forty cubits; or, at the usually accepted equivalent for the cubit, sixty by thirty feet for the Tabernacle, and one hundred and twenty feet by sixty feet for the Temple. In height the same relation was maintained; the Tabernacle rose fifteen cubits and the Temple thirty cubits. The Temple porch appears to have towered above the height of the main structure.[40]

In the porch, standing as a guard at the threshold of the Temple, were two brazen pillars, of elaborate design, and doubtless of emblematical significance. They were regarded as of such importance as to merit detailed description, and the name of their maker was inscribed in the Temple archives. They were wrought by Hiram of Tyre,—not the king who bore the same name—but a master-artisan, skilled in the working of brass. Hiram fashioned the pillars, each twelve cubits in circumference and eighteen cubits high exclusive of the massive chapiters, which were ornamented with pomegranates and lily work. The pillar at the right of the entrance was named Jachin, meaning "He shall establish," and that at the left was called Boaz, signifying "In it is strength."[41] Whatever deeper meaning may have been attached to these massive columns, their suggestive symbolism of strength and firmness is plainly apparent. As to whether they actually supported the roof of the porch, or were free, standing as embellishments and symbols alone, the scriptural text is not definite.

The walls of the great Temple were of hewn stone, yet on the inside no stone was visible; for the walls were wainscotted from floor to ceiling with cedar, richly decorated with carvings of flowers, trees, and other designs, and the flooring was of fir.[42] Moreover, the interior was

---

[40]See II Chron. 3:4.
[41]See I Kings 7:13-22.
[42]I Kings 6:15-18, 29.

richly embellished with overlaid work in pure gold. The
partition by which the Oracle or Holy of Holies was
divided off, corresponding to the veil in the Tabernacle,
was thus overlaid, and was hung with chains of gold.[43]
The cherubim that stood as the symbol of guardianship
over the Oracle were of olive wood, covered with gold,
the precious metal being fitted upon the carved work.[44]

The vestibule or porch stood at the east end; and this
constituted the only entrance to the Temple proper. On
the other three sides, therefore surrounding both the Holy
Place and the Oracle, were numerous small chambers,
built in three tiers or stories. The width of these was
five cubits in the lowest story, six cubits in the middle, and
seven cubits in the top story; this peculiarity in width
increasing with height was made possible by the decrease
in the thickness of the walls. By this rebatement of the
walls, the cedarn chambers were well supported yet they
formed no part of the main structure; it was so designed
"that the beams should not be fastened in the walls of
the house."[45] These small apartments were therefore
"chambers round about, against the walls of the house,"
yet of independent construction. From the mention made
by Ezekiel[46] these chambers are supposed to have numbered thirty, though no precise specification is found.
They were probably used for service required of the priests
aside from the ceremonial labor connected with the general ritual. Entrance to these chambers was provided on
the right side of the building with winding stairs leading
to the upper rooms. Above the level of the upper chambers were windows by which the outer apartment or Holy
Place was lighted; the Holy of Holies, however, was
without natural light.

The furniture within the Temple comprised but few
objects, yet every piece was of special design and for

[43]Verses 19-22.
[44]Verse 35.
[45]Verses 5, 6.
[46]Ezekiel 41:6, 7.

exclusive use. In the Holy Place stood the table, or a series of tables to bear the sacred shew-bread. Mention is made also of an altar of gold, and of ten candlesticks of pure gold set in front of the entrance to the Oracle, five on either side; furthermore there were tongs of gold, bowls and snuffers, basins and spoons. The Oracle was prepared for the reception of the Ark of the Covenant, and to overshadow that holy vessel there were prepared the two great cherubim, each ten cubits high; these were of olive wood overlaid with gold.

The Temple stood within walled enclosures, generally spoken of as outer and inner courts respectively. The wall of the inner court is described as consisting of three courses of hewn stone, in which was set a course of cedar beams. This corresponded to the single enclosure of the ancient Tabernacle. Inasmuch as all the specified measurements show the Temple to have been double the size of the Tabernacle, this court may have been of corresponding proportion; it is therefore generally believed to have extended one hundred cubits north and south and two hundred cubits east and west.[47]

Within the court, "before the porch of the Lord" stood the altar of sacrifice. This was of brass twenty cubits square and ten cubits high. To the service of the altar belonged many of the utensils such as basins, pots, and shovels, specially made under the direction of the master craftsman, Hiram of Tyre. Another prominent object within the court was the molten sea, called also the brazen sea.[48] This great font measured thirty cubits in circumference and stood five cubits high, and was richly ornamented. The walls were a hand-breadth in thickness, and the brim was embellished with flower work. It was mounted on twelve brazen oxen, arranged in groups of three, the groups facing respectively north, south, east

---

[47]For specifications as to the courts, see I Kings 6:36; compare 7:12; see also II Kings 23:12; II Chron. 4:9; 33:5.

[48]I Kings 7:23-26; II Chron. 4:2; see also II Kings 25:13; compare Jeremiah 52:17.

and west. The great font stood between the altar and
the porch "on the right side of the house, eastward, over
against the south."[49] Associated with the molten sea
were ten smaller vessels called lavers, mounted on bases
of special construction and provided with wheels to facil-
itate removal.[50] The lavers were used in connection with
the service of the altar, for the washing of the offerings;
but the main font or molten sea was reserved for the
ceremonial cleansing of the priests.

When the House of the Lord was completed, elaborate
preparations were made for its dedication. First came
the installation of the Ark of the Covenant and its appurtenances, the Tabernacle of the Congregation, and the
holy vessels. With great solemnity and to the accompaniment of ceremonial sacrifice, the Ark was brought by
the priests and placed within the Holy of Holies beneath
the wings of the cherubim. At this time the Ark contained only the two tables of stone "which Moses put
there." The staves by which the Ark was borne were so
drawn out as to be visible from within the Holy Place,
and then "it came to pass, when the priests were come out
of the holy place, that the cloud filled the house of the
Lord, So that the priests could not stand to minister because of the cloud: for the glory of the Lord had filled
the house of the Lord."[51]

Then Solomon addressed the assembled multitude, re-
citing the circumstances under which the building of the
Temple had been conceived by his father David and executed by himself, and proclaiming the mercy and goodness
of Israel's God. Standing before the altar of the Lord, in
the court of the Temple, the king spread forth his hands
toward heaven, and offered the dedicatory prayer. The
king then blessed the people, saying "Blessed be the
Lord, that hath given rest unto his people Israel, accord-

---

[49]I Kings 7:39.
[50]I Kings 7:27-39; compare II Chron. 4:6.
[51]I Kings 8:10, 11.

ing to all that he promised: there hath not failed one word of all his good promise, which he promised by the hand of Moses his servant. The Lord our God be with us, as he was with our fathers: let him not leave us, nor forsake us."[52]

The principal services with the attendant festivities lasted seven days, and "on the eighth day he sent the people away: and they blessed the king, and went unto their tents joyful and glad of heart for all the goodness that the Lord had done for David his servant, and for Israel his people."[53]

For only a third of a century did this splendid edifice maintain its supremacy and glory. In the later years of his reign Solomon had done wickedly in the sight of God and the people had not been slow to follow their king in evil paths. Israel had grown weak in their allegiance to Jehovah and had gone after strange gods. Following the death of Solomon the nation was disrupted. In the fifth year of the reign of Rehoboam, Shishak king of Egypt besieged the City of David and even despoiled the Temple and carried away part of the sacred treasures. Next, Jehoash, king of one part of the divided nation, took away gold and silver and sacred vessels from the House of the Lord and carried them into Samaria.[54] It is thus shown that the desecration of the Temple was not effected wholly by the enemies of Israel; the people to whom the House had once been sacred contributed to its profanation. Ahaz, the wicked king of Judah, removed the altar from its place and substituted therefor another fashioned by his own order after the pattern of the altars of the heathen; moreover he took down the molten sea and dismantled the lavers.[55] Mannasseh, another evil king who reigned in Judah, followed after Baal and set up idola-

---

[52] I Kings 8:56, 57; for the dedicatory services in full see the entire chapter.
[53] Verse 66.
[54] II Kings 14:13, 14.
[55] II Kings 16:10-18: see also II Chron. 28:24.

trous shrines within the very precincts of the Temple.[56]
The precious things of the House of the Lord were used
as barter between kings. So, Asa king of Judah purchased the aid of Ben-hadad, to fight against Israel;[57] so
also did Jehoash purchase peace from Hazael king of
Syria;[58] and so did Hezekiah strip the House of the Lord
for plunder wherewith to pay tribute to the Assyrians.[59]

Some attempts were made to repair the worst of the
ravages upon and within the Temple[60] but it seemed
that the House had been abandoned to its fate. In the
year 586 B. C., Nebuchadnezzar, king of Babylon, completed the destruction of the Temple in connection with
his conquest of the kingdom of Judah. Whatever of value
was yet there he carried away, and the building was destroyed by fire.[61]

There occurs yet one later mention of some of the
vessels that had been made for the service of Jehovah,—
when they were brought out to crown the triumph of
Belshazzar in his heathenish feast. Then was manifest
the displeasure of the Lord, and the trembling king heard
from the lips of Daniel his doom,—for he had been un-
mindful of the fate that had overtaken his father, and had
lifted up himself against the Lord of heaven; and had
brought out the vessels of the house of God that he and
his lords, his wives and his concubines might drink wine
therefrom; and he had praised the gods of silver, and
gold, of brass, iron, wood, and stone, which see not, nor
hear, nor know; but the God in whose hand was his
breath and whose were all his ways had he not glorified.
He had been weighed in the balances and was found
wanting; and his kingdom was taken from him. That
night, Belshazzar the king was slain.[62]

---

[56]II Kings 21:1-7; see also II Chron. 33:1-7.

[57]I Kings 15:18.

[58]II Kings 12:18.

[59]II Kings 18:15, 16.

[60]See II Kings 12:2-14; compare II Chron. 24:7-14; see also II Kings 22:3-7;
compare II Chron. 34:8-13.

[61]II Kings 24:13; 25:9-17; II Chron. 36:7, 19; compare Isaiah 64:11; Jeremiah
27:16, 19-22; 28:3; 52:13, 17-23; Lamentations 2:7; 4:1; and Ezra 1:7.

[62]See Daniel, chapter 5.

The Temple of Ezekiel's Vision

In the twenty-fifth year of the Babylonian captivity, while yet the people of Israel were in exile in a strange land, the word of the Lord came to the prophet Ezekiel; the power of God rested upon him; and he saw in vision a glorious Temple, the plan of which he minutely described.[63] As to whether the prophet himself considered the design so shown as one to be subsequently realized, or as but a grand yet unattainable ideal, is not declared. Certain it is that the Temple of the vision has not yet been builded.

In most of its essential features Ezekiel's ideal followed closely the plan of Solomon's Temple; so close, indeed, is the resemblance, that many of the details specified by Ezekiel have been accepted as those of the splendid edifice destroyed by Nebuchadnezzar. A predominant characteristic of the Temple described by Ezekiel was the spaciousness of its premises and the symmetry of both the Holy House and its associated buildings. The area was to be a square of five hundred cubits, walled about and provided with a gateway and arches on each of three sides; on the west side the wall was to be unbroken by arch or portal. At each of the gateways were little chambers regarded as lodges,[64] and provided with porches. In the outer court were other chambers. The entire area was to be elevated, and a flight of steps led to each gateway. In the inner court was seen the great altar, standing before the House, and occupying the center of a square of one hundred cubits.[65] Ample provision was made for every variety of sacrifice and offering, and for the accommodation of the priests, the singers, and all engaged in the holy ritual.[66] The main structure comprised a Porch, a Holy Place, and an inner sanctuary or Most Holy Place,

---

[63]See Ezekiel, chapters 40 to 43.
[64]So designated in the Revised Version.
[65]Ezekiel 40:47.
[66]Verses 44-46.

the last named elevated above the rest and reached by
steps. The plan provided for even greater exclusiveness
than had characterized the sacred area of the Temple of
Solomon; the double courts contributed to this end. The
service of the Temple was prescribed in detail; the ordinances of the altar, the duties of the priests, the ministry
of the Levites, the regulations governing oblations and
feasts were all set forth.[67]

The immediate purpose of this revelation through the
vision of the prophet appears to have been that of awak-
ening the people of Israel to a realization of their fallen
state and a conception of their departed glory. The
prophet was thus commanded:

"Thou son of man, shew the house to the house of Israel, that they
may be ashamed of their iniquities: and let them measure the pattern.

"And if they be ashamed of all that they have done, show them the
form of the house, and the fashion thereof, and the goings out thereof, and
the comings in thereof, and all the forms thereof, and all the ordinances
thereof, and all the forms thereof, and all the laws thereof: and write it in
their sight, that they may keep the whole form thereof, and all the ordinances thereof, and do them.

"This is the law of the house; Upon the top of the mountain the
whole limit thereof round about shall be most holy. Behold, this is the law
of the house."[68]

The Temple of Zerubbabel

For three score years and ten the Jews had grieved
and groaned under Babylonian rule. The greater part
of the once proud Kingdom of Judah had been carried
away captive, and such as remained in the land of their
fathers had lost their national status and had become
largely merged with the Gentiles. With dreadful exactness
had been fulfilled the dire prediction of Jeremiah. Through
that prophet the Lord had spoken, saying:

"Therefore thus saith the Lord of hosts; Because ye have not heard
my words,

"Behold, I will send and take all the families of the north, saith the

[67]Ezekiel, chapters 44-48.
[68]Ezekiel 43:10-12.

Lord, and Nebuchadrezzar [Nebuchadnezzar] the king of Babylon, my servant, and will bring them against this land, and against the inhabitants thereof, and against all these nations around about, and will utterly destroy them, and make them an astonishment, and an hissing, and perpetual desolations.

"Moreover I will take from them the voice of mirth, and the voice of gladness, the voice of the bridegroom, and the voice of the bride, the sound of the millstones, and the light of the candle.

"And this whole land shall be a desolation, and an astonishment; and these nations shall serve the king of Babylon seventy years."[69]

However, the gloom of the saddening prophecy had been lightened by one ray of hope and promise—the assurance that when the seventy years of the Lord's chastisement had been completed, the people should return to the land of their inheritance, and once again be recognized as the Lord's own.[70] In the encouragement of that hope the people had lived; by its inspiration their prophets, even while in captivity, had sought the Lord, and declared His will to the people; by its light Ezekiel had seen in the vision of seership the re-establishment of his people and the possibility of a Temple greater and grander than the first. In due time the God of Israel made good His word, and vindicated anew His power as King of kings; He ruled and overruled the passions of nations and the acts of earthly rulers, and once again brought His people from the land of their bondage. Persia had become the controlling power among the nations, and by decree of the Persian king, Judah was emancipated. Behold the power of God in directing the rulers among mortals:

"Now in the first year of Cyrus king of Persia, that the word of the Lord by the mouth of Jeremiah might be fulfilled, the Lord stirred up the spirit of Cyrus king of Persia, that he made a proclamation throughout all his kingdom, and put it also in writing, saying,

"Thus saith Cyrus king of Persia, The Lord God of heaven hath given me all the kingdoms of the earth; and he hath charged me to build him an house at Jerusalem, which is in Judah.

"Who is there among you of all his people? his God be with him, and let him go up to Jerusalem, which is in Judah, and build the house of the Lord God of Israel, (he is the God,) which is in Jerusalem.

---

[69]Jeremiah 25:8-11; see also 29:10.

[70]See Jeremiah 25:12-14. See also the author's "The Articles of Faith," Lecture XVII, "The Dispersion of Israel."

"And whosoever remaineth in any place where he sojourneth, let the men of his place help him with silver, and with gold, and with goods, and with beasts, beside the freewill offering for the house of God that is in Jerusalem."[71]

Under this gracious permission the people returned to the land of their fathers, and set about the work of building anew a House to the Lord. Cyrus had issued his royal decree that the structure be worthy the great Name to which it was to be reared—the foundations were to be strongly laid; the height was to be three score cubits, and the breadth the same; there were to be set three rows of great stones and a row of new timber; moreover, the expenses were to be met by the royal treasury.[72] The king restored to the people the vessels that had been taken by Nebuchadnezzar from the first Temple,—all these, numbering many thousands, were formally delivered by the king's treasurer.[73]

So great was the enthusiasm of the people, so strong their desire to have individual part in the holy undertaking, that many who had been careless of their heritage now claimed priestly standing; but, as their genealogy had not been preserved, they were debarred from the priesthood, though permitted to return with the rest. The prerogatives of the priestly order were denied them until one would arise with power to declare their genealogy through Urim and Thummim.[74]

Zerubbabel and Jeshua had charge of the work; and without delay they builded anew the altar of the God of Israel and re-established the ritual of sacrifice, and the observance of the sacred festivals.[75] Masons and carpenters, workmen and artisans of all kinds and degrees were brought into service; again were Tyre and Sidon put under friendly tribute, and once more the wealth of

---

[71]Ezra 1:1-4.
[72]Ezra 6:3-4.
[73]Ezra 1:7-11.
[74]See Ezra 2:61-63.
[75]Ezra 3:1-6.

the forests of Lebanon was brought to Jerusalem. Priests and Levites were marshalled in order as of old, and the sound of trumpets and cymbals was mingled with the voices of the singers. Is there cause for wonder that as the foundations were laid, old men who remembered the first House and its glory wept aloud and shouted in their tearful joy?[76]

But adversaries arose who put obstacles in the way of the builders. The people of Canaan—Israelites who had forgotten their allegiance to God, and had mingled with idolaters, took offense at the activity of the returned Jews. At first they offered to assist in the work, but being refused recognition because of their idolatrous associations, they became obstructionists, and "weakened the hands of the people of Judah, and troubled them in building; and hired counsellors against them, to frustrate their purpose, all the days of Cyrus king of Persia, even until the reign of Darius king of Persia."[77] The claim was made that of old the people of Judah had been a trouble to other nations, and that with the restoration of their Temple they would again become seditious. At last the protests and charges reached Darius, the reigning monarch; and he, having investigated the whole matter, issued a decree, that not only should the Jews be free from interruption in the building of the Temple, but that a portion of the king's tribute, the regular taxes of the land, should be devoted to the work; and, said the king:

"Also I have made a decree, that whosoever shall alter this word, let timber be pulled down from his house, and being set up, let him be hanged thereon; and let his house be made a dunghill for this. And the God that hath caused his name to dwell there destroy all kings and people, that shall put to their hand to alter and to destroy this house of God which is at Jerusalem. I Darius have made a decree; let it be done with speed."[78]

With such support the people soon completed the building. Though nearly twenty years elapsed between

---

[76]Ezra 3:8-13.
[77]Ezra 4:1-6; see also verses 7-24, and chapter 5.
[78]Ezra 6:11, 12; see also verses 7-10.

the laying of the foundation and the finishing, the greater part of the labor was done during the last four years. The dedicatory services were solemn and inspiring. For seven days the Feast of Unleavened Bread was observed; the Passover was eaten by those who had returned from captivity and by such others as had "separated themselves unto them from the filthiness of the heathen of the land, to seek the Lord God of Israel."[79]

This, the second Temple, was finished in the year 515 B. C.; it is known in history as the Temple of Zerubbabel. In general plan it was patterned after the Temple of Solomon, though in many of its dimensions it exceeded its prototype. The court was divided into a section for priests only and another for the public; according to Josephus the division was effected by a wooden railing.[80] An altar of unhewn stone was erected in place of the great brazen altar of old.[81] The Holy Place was graced by but one candlestick instead of ten; and by a single table for the shew-bread instead of the ten tables overlaid with gold which stood in the first Temple. We read also of a golden altar of incense, and of some minor appurtenances. The Most Holy Place was empty, for the Ark of the Covenant had not been known after the people had gone into captivity.

In many respects the Temple of Zerubbabel appeared poor in comparison with its splendid predecessor and in certain particulars, indeed, it ranked lower than the ancient Tabernacle of the Congregation—the sanctuary of the nomadic tribes. Critical scholars specify the following features characteristic of the Temple of Solomon and lacking in the Temple of Zerubbabel: (1) the Ark of the Covenant; (2) the sacred fire; (3) the Shekinah, or glory of the Lord, manifested of old as the Divine Presence; (4) the Urim and Thummim, by which Jehovah

---

[79]Ezra 6:21.
[80]Josephus, Antiquities of the Jews: XIII, 13:5.
[81]Compare Exodus 20:25; Deut. 27:5; Joshua 8:31.

made plain His will to the priests of the Aaronic order; (5) the genius or spirit of prophecy, indicative of the closest communion between mortals and their God. Notwithstanding these differences the Temple of Zerubbabel was recognized of God and was undoubtedly the site or seat of Divine revelation to duly constituted prophets.

The inferiority of the second Temple as compared with the first is generally conceded; the difference, however, was rather in matter of splendor than in point of size.[82] But even such glory as it did possess was not to be long maintained. Again the people became recreant to their God, and the voice of the prophet was unheeded. Again did Jehovah permit the heathen to oppress Judah. Of the later history of this Temple the Biblical record gives but few details; but from other sources we learn of its vicissitudes. In connection with the Maccabean persecution the House of the Lord was profaned. A Syrian king, Antiochus Epiphanes, captured Jerusalem (168 to 165 B. C.) and perpetrated blasphemous outrage against the religion of the people. He plundered the Temple and carried away its golden candlestick, its golden altar of incense, its table of shewbread, and even tore down the sacred veils, which were of fine linen and scarlet. His malignity was carried so far that he purposely desecrated the altar of sacrifice by offering swine thereon, and erected a heathen altar within the sacred enclosure. Not content with the violation of the Temple, this wicked monarch had altars erected in the towns and ordered the offering of unclean beasts upon them. The rite of circumcision was forbidden on pain of death, and the worship of Jehovah was declared a crime.[83] As a result of this persecution many of the Jews apostatized, and declared that they belonged to the Medes and Persians—the nations from whose dominion they had been delivered by the power of God.

---

[82]See Haggai 2:1-4; compare Zech. 4:10.

[83]See Josephus, Antiquities of the Jews, Book XII, 5:3-5.

Among those who remained true to the religion of their fathers was Mattathias, who was a priest, and a man of prominence. He was besought to offer heathen sacrifice; not only did he refuse but in righteous indignation he slew those who did attempt the sacrilege. This act led to further strife and for three years the struggle continued. Judas, son of Mattathias, came into prominence and is known as Judas Maccabeus,—the first of the Maccabees. Under his leadership the people returned to Jerusalem and found the Temple deserted, as it had been left by the army of Antiochus. Its gates had been broken down and burned; and within the walls weeds were growing. Judas tried to cleanse and rehabilitate the House; he brought in new vessels, and replaced the candlestick, the altar of incense, the table of shewbread, and the veils, and built a new altar for burnt offerings. Then in the year 163 B. C. the House was rededicated; and the occasion was remembered in annual festival thereafter under the name of the Feast of Dedication.[84]

In the interest of self-preservation the Jews entered into an alliance with the Romans, who eventually became their masters. During the reign of the Maccabees the Temple fell into decay, and when the last of that dynasty had been succeeded by Herod the Great, the House was little more than a ruin. Nevertheless the priestly orders had been maintained; and some semblance of ritualistic worship had continued. The history of the Temple of Zerubbabel is merged with that of the Temple of Herod.

The Temple of Herod

In the year 37 B. C. Herod I, known in history as Herod the Great, was established on the throne as King of Judea. He had already served successively as procurator and tetrarch, and, indeed, had been king in name for some time prior to his enthronement, during which period

---

[84]See Josephus, Antiquities of the Jews, Book XII, chaps. 6 and 7; and II Maccabees 2:19; 10:1-8; see also John 10:22.

he had been in hostile conflict with the people over whom the decree of the Roman Senate had made him ruler. He came to the throne noted for arrogance and cruelty; and his reign was one of tyranny, in which even family relationship and the closest ties of blood proved unavailing to protect the victims of his displeasure. In the early part of his reign he put to death nearly all the members of the Sanhedrin, the great Jewish Council, and throughout he ruled with increasing severity. Nevertheless he was successful in maintaining peace with other governments, and by his Roman masters was accounted an able ruler. Among his acts of cruelty was the slaughter of the babes of Bethlehem, a murder planned and executed in the hope of including among the victims the Child Jesus.[85]

Such is the character of the man who proposed to replace the time-worn Temple of Zerubbabel by a new and more splendid structure. Can it be thought that a proffered gift from such a donor could be acceptable to the Lord? David had aforetime offered to build a House to the Lord, but had been restrained, for he was a man of blood. Herod's purpose in the great undertaking was that of aggrandizing himself and the nation, rather than the rendering of homage to Jehovah. His proposition to rebuild or restore the Temple on a scale of increased magnificence was regarded with suspicion and received with disfavor by the Jews, who feared that were the ancient edifice demolished, the arbitrary monarch might abandon his plan and the people would be left without a Temple. To allay these fears the king proceeded to reconstruct and restore the old edifice, part by part, directing the

---

[85]See Matt. 2:1-10, 16-18. "A little child made the great Herod quake upon his throne. When he knew that the magi were come to hail their King and Lord, and did not stop at his palace, but passed on to a humbler roof, and when he found that they would not return to betray this child to him, he put to death all the children in Bethlehem that were under two years old. The crime was great; but the number of the victims, in a little place like Bethlehem, was small enough to escape special record among the wicked acts of Herod from Josephus and other historians, as it had no political interest."—Smith's Comprehensive Dictionary of the Bible, art. "Jesus Christ," page 466.

work so that at no time was the Temple service seriously interrupted. So little of the ancient structure was allowed to stand, however, that the Temple of Herod must be regarded as a new creation. The work was begun about sixteen years before the birth of Christ; and while the Holy House itself was practically completed within a year and a half, this part of the labor having been performed by a body of one thousand priests specially trained for the purpose, the temple area was a scene of uninterrupted building operations down to the year 63 A. D. We read that in the time of Christ's ministry the Temple had been forty-six years in building;[86] and at that time it was unfinished.

The Biblical record gives us little information regarding this the last and the greatest of ancient temples; for what we know concerning it we are indebted mainly to Josephus, with some corroborative testimony found in the Talmud. In all essentials the Holy House or Temple proper was similar to the two earlier houses of sanctuary, though externally far more elaborate and imposing than either; but in the matter of surrounding courts and associated buildings, the Temple of Herod preeminently excelled. In proceeding from the outer wall to the innermost enclosure occupied by the Holy House one would traverse successive courts, each at a higher level than the last, to which arrangement the slopes of Mount Moriah were favorable. The courts extended as enormous platform-terraces, supported by foundations of massive masonry, which rose vertically in some places seven hundred feet from the foot of the hill.

The outer wall enclosing the entire temple area, which approximated the form of a square, measured four hundred cubits, or one stadium, (about six hundred feet) along each side. The east wall, constituting the principal defense of the city on that side, was unbroken by gates; on each of the other three sides one or more large and

---

[86]John 2:20.

beautiful portals afforded passage through the fortress-like wall. The four sides of the great enclosure, immediately within the outer wall, were occupied by a series of magnificent porticoes, of Grecian design, forming a covered colonnade in which every pillar was a massive monolith of white marble. This colonnade was interrupted at the north-west corner, where the continuity of the wall was broken by the Tower of Antonia, in reality a fortified castle, from which a subterranean passage led into the inner enclosure where stood the Holy House. The colonnade or line of porticoes along the south side was particularly elaborate, and was known as the Royal Porch. Here were four rows of huge columns, and consequently three corridors, of which the inner was forty-five feet wide and one hundred feet high, while each of the side corridors measured thirty feet in width and sixty feet in height. The imposing effect of the Royal Porch is dwelt upon by Josephus, who states that its beauty was incredible to those who had not seen it, and amazing to those who beheld.

The east colonnade or row of porticoes was known as Solomon's Porch,[87] the name having reference to a tradition that the porch covered and included part of the original wall erected by the builder of the first Temple. Within the colonnade was a spacious area, to which general admission was allowed; this was the Court of the Gentiles. It was in this court that money-changers and traffickers in animals used for sacrifice had established their stalls at the time of our Lord's ministry, and from which they were expelled through His righteous indignation, the while He declared: "It is written, My house shall be called the house of prayer; but ye have made it a den of thieves."[88]

Between the Court of the Gentiles and the inner courts rose a wall twenty-five cubits high; this marked

[87]See John 10:23; Acts 3:11; 5:12.
[88]Matt. 21:12-13; see also Mark 11:15; Luke 19:45; John 2:14.

the boundary of the more sacred precincts within which no Gentile could be lawfully admitted. At intervals along the wall were inscription tablets, warning all who were not of Israel to enter not on pain of death. A literal translation of such inscription reads: "Let no alien enter within the balustrade and embankment about the sanctuary. Whoever is caught makes himself responsible for his death which will follow."

The inner courts were accessible from the Court of the Gentiles through nine gates, of which one was on the east, and four were on the north and south respectively; as in the earlier Temples the west wall was without a gate. Of these portals the principal one was on the east; this was an elaborate structure built of the costly Corinthian brass, and known as the Corinthian Gate, though sometimes called from the name of its donor, the Gate of Nicanor; furthermore this is held by many authorities to be the Beautiful Gate, before which sat the lame man who was healed through the ministrations of Peter and John.[89]

Part of the space within the inner courts was open to Israelites of both sexes, and was known distinctively as the Court of the Women. This was a colonnaded enclosure, and constituted the place of general assembly in the prescribed course of public worship. Chambers used for ceremonial purposes occupied the four corners of this court; and between these and the houses at the gates, were other buildings, of which one series constituted the Treasury wherein were set trumpet-shaped receptacles for gifts.[90]

Beyond the Court of the Women and really a continuation thereof, was a section sufficiently described by its name, the Court of the Men; these two courts are sometimes referred to as one and designated the Court of Israel. Within this court were numerous buildings re-

[89]See Acts 3:2, 10.
[90]See Mark 12:41-44.

served for the storage of sacred things or devoted to special assemblies. Within and above the Court of Israel was the Court of the Priests, wherein was placed the great altar of sacrifice, and to which were admitted none but duly appointed priests and laymen who came to make offerings. The altar was a large structure of unhewn stones, forty-seven feet square at the base, and diminishing upward to the hearth which was a square of thirty-six feet. The inclined way of approach was on the south side.[91] A laver or font, reserved for the prescribed ablutions of the officiating priests, stood nearby on the west.

Within the Court of the Priests, on an elevation reached by twelve steps, stood the Holy House, the Temple itself. In comparison with its many and massive outliers, this was a small edifice, but in the architectural plan it was made the most impressive, if not the most imposing feature of the whole. It has been properly described as "a glittering mass of white marble and gold."[92] Like the earlier Temples, this comprised Porch, Holy Place, and Most Holy Place or Holy of Holies. The Porch measured one hundred cubits both in width and height. The Holy Place was forty by twenty cubits, as in the Temple of Zerubbabel, but its height was increased to forty cubits. By adding side chambers, with a passage between them and the main building, Herod made the new Temple greater and grander than either of its predecessors. The Holy of Holies retained the original form and dimensions, making it a cube, twenty cubits in each measurement. Between this and the Holy Place hung a double veil, of finest material, elaborately embroidered. The outer of the two veils was open at the north end, the inner at the south; so that the high priest who entered at the appointed time once a year could pass between the veils without exposing the Holy of Holies. The sacred chamber was empty save for a large stone upon which

[91]Compare Exodus 20:26.
[92]See Encyclopaedia Britannica, 11th ed., art. "Temple."

the high priest sprinkled the sacrificial blood on the Day
of Atonement; this stone occupied the place of the Ark
and its Mercy Seat. Outside the veil, in the Holy Place,
stood the altar of incense, the seven-branched candlestick, and the table of shewbread.

That the Temple of Herod was by far the grandest
structure ever erected as a Temple in any age is generally
admitted; yet its beauty and grandeur lay in architectural excellence rather than in the sanctity of its worship
or in the manifestation of the Divine Presence within its
walls. Its ritual and service were largely man-prescribed;
for while the letter of the Mosaic Law was professedly
observed, the law had been supplemented and in many
features supplanted by rule and priestly prescription. The
Jews professed to consider it holy, and by them it was
proclaimed as the House of the Lord. Devoid though it
was of the Divine accompaniments of earlier shrines accepted of God, and defiled as it was by priestly arrogance
and usurpation, as also by the selfish interest of traffic
and trade, it was nevertheless recognized even by our
Lord the Christ as His Father's House.[93] Therein the
Boy Jesus was presented as required by the Law,[94] thereto
came He with His people at the time of the Passover;[95]
within its precincts He declared Himself and the Father
who sent Him.[96] When at last, rejected by His own, and
by them brought to the cross, He wrought the sacrifice
through which salvation was made possible to man, the
veil of the Temple was rent by an unseen power and the
last vestige of supreme sanctity departed from the place.[97]

As long as it stood, however, the Temple was held by
the Jews in high veneration. An utterance of the Savior,
construed by the dark-minded as an aspersion upon the

[93]Matt. 21:12; compare Mark 11:15; Luke 19:45.
[94]See Luke 2:22-38.
[95]Luke 2:42-50. See also John 2:13-23; 5:1; 12:12-20.
[96]Luke 19:47; John 10:22-39.
[97]Matt. 27:51; Mark 15:38; Luke 23:45.

Temple, was used against Him as one of the chief accusations on which His death was demanded. When the Jews clamored for a sign of His authority He predicted His own death and subsequent resurrection, saying, "Destroy this temple, and in three days I will raise it up."[98] They blindly regarded this remark as a disrespectful allusion to their Temple, a structure built by human hands, and they refused to forget or forgive. That this veneration continued after the crucifixion of our Lord is evident from accusations brought against Stephen, and still later against Paul. In their murderous rage the people accused Stephen of disrespect for the Temple, and brought false witnesses who uttered perjured testimony saying, "This man ceaseth not to speak blasphemous words against this holy place."[99] And Stephen was numbered with the martyrs. When it was claimed that Paul had brought with him into the temple precincts, a Gentile, the whole city was aroused, and the infuriated mob dragged Paul from the place and sought to kill him.[100]

For thirty or more years after the death of Christ, the Jews continued the work of adding to and embellishing the temple buildings. The elaborate design conceived and projected by Herod had been practically completed; the Temple was well-nigh finished, and, as soon afterward appeared, was ready for destruction. Its fate had been definitely foretold by the Savior Himself. Commenting on a remark by one of the disciples concerning the great stones and the splendid buildings on the Temple hill, Jesus had said, "Seest thou these great buildings? There shall not be left one stone upon another that shall not be thrown down."[101]

This dire prediction soon found its literal fulfilment. In the great conflict with the Roman legions under Titus, many of the Jews had taken refuge within the temple

[98]John 2:19-22; see also Matt. 26:61; 27:40; Mark 14:58; 15:29.
[99]Acts 6:13.
[100]See Acts 21:26-40.
[101] Mark 13:1, 2. See also Matt. 24:1, 2; Luke 21:5, 6.

courts, seemingly hoping that there the Lord would again fight the battles of His people and give them victory. But the protecting presence of Jehovah had long since departed therefrom and Israel was left a prey to the foe. Though Titus would have spared the Temple, his legionaries, maddened by the lust of conflict, started the conflagration and everything that could be burned was burned. The slaughter of the Jews was appalling; thousands of men, women and children were ruthlessly butchered within the walls, and the temple courts were literally flooded with human blood. This event occurred in the year 70 A. D.; and according to Josephus, in the same month and on the same day of the month as that on which the once glorious Temple of Solomon had fallen a prey to the flames kindled by the king of Babylon.[102] Of the temple furniture the golden candlestick and the table of shewbread from the Holy Place were carried by Titus to Rome as trophies of war; and representations of these sacred pieces are to be seen on the arch erected to the name of the victorious general.

Since the destruction of the splendid Temple of Herod no other structure of the kind, no Temple, no House of the Lord as the terms are used distinctively, has been reared on the eastern hemisphere. Sometime between 361 and 363 A. D. the Roman emperor Julian, surnamed because of his reversion from Christianity to paganism Julian the Apostate, attempted to reconstruct the Temple at Jerusalem. His purpose was not that of devotion to nor love for God; but that of controverting prophecy, and thus proving false the Christian belief.[103] So ends the category of Temples reared to the name of the living God prior to the dispensation of the fulness of times.

---

[102]Josephus, Wars of the Jews, Book VI; 4:5, 8. For a detailed and graphic account of the destruction of the Temple see chapters 4 and 5 in their entirety.

[103]He actually began excavations, but his workmen were driven in great panic from the spot, by terrific explosions and bursts of flame. The Christians regarded the occurrence as miraculous; and Julian himself, it is certain, was so dismayed by it that he desisted from the undertaking."—P. V. N. Meyers, General History, page 334.

CHAPTER III

Need of Temples in the Present Dispensation

Among the numerous sects and churches professing Christianity, The Church of Jesus Christ of Latter-day Saints stands alone in the teaching and practise of temple ministration. The devotion of this people to the sacred labor of building temples and administering therein the saving ordinances of the Gospel has attracted the attention and aroused the wonder of both philosopher and layman. It is not enough to attempt an explanation of this singular and stupendous sacrifice by ascribing it to assumed and unproved fanaticism; the earnest investigator, the careful observer, and even the cursory reader, indeed, if he be honest, admits that beneath this devotion is a deeply-seated and an abiding faith. It cannot be affirmed that the Latter-day Saints build temples as monuments of communal wealth nor in the pride of human aggrandisement; for we find them thus arduously engaged even while bread was scarce and clothing scant among them; and throughout their history the people have looked upon their temples as edifices belonging to the Lord, and upon themselves as stewards entrusted with the custody of the consecrated properties. Nor can it be said that this Church builds temples as other sects erect chapels, churches, cathedrals, and synagogues; for the Church has the equivalent of these, and indeed the meeting-houses and places of public worship maintained by the Latter-

day Saints are proportionately greater in number than
are those of other denominations. Moreover, as already
stated, these temples are not used as places of common
assembly, nor as houses of general and congregational
service.

Why, then, does The Church of Jesus Christ of Latter-
day Saints build and maintain temples? In answer let
the following pertinent facts be carefully considered.

Necessity of obedience to the laws and ordinances of the Gospel

As part of its declaration of faith, the Church proclaims:

*"We believe that through the atonement of Christ, all mankind may be
saved, by obedience to the laws and ordinances of the Gospel."*[1]

While professing belief in the possibility of a universal salvation, the Church affirms that salvation is assured only on condition of individual compliance with the
requirements established by the Redeemer, without whose
atoning sacrifice none could be saved. The atonement
wrought by the Christ on Calvary was a vicarious offering, in the beneficent results of which all mankind are
made partakers. As to redemption from the thrall of
mortality incident to the transgression in Eden, the sacrificial death of Christ met in full the exactions incident to
the broken law; and none but Adam shall be held account-
able for Adam's disobedience, nor for any results thereof.
In the just judgment to which every mortal shall come,
all conditions of inherited weakness, temptation due to
environment, the capacity to choose and to act, the measure of knowledge to which the subject has attained, the
meed of truth he has accepted or rejected, the opportunities he has used aright or wrongly spurned, the fidelity
with which he walked in the light or the depravity
through which he wandered in the forbidden paths of

[1]See the author's "The Articles of Faith," Lecture IV; and references therein
given.

darkness,—these and every other fact and circumstance entering into the individual life will be duly weighed and considered. At the bar of God the distinguishing feature of Divine mercy will be, as in the affairs of mortal life it now is, not an arbitrary forgiveness of sin nor unearned annulment of the debts of guilt, but the providing of a way whereby the sinner may be enabled to meet the requirements of the Gospel, and so in due course pass from the prison house of sin to the glorious freedom of a righteous life.

There is but one price set on forgiveness for individual transgression, and this is alike to all,—to poor and rich, to bond and free, to illiterate and learned; it knows no fluctuations, it changes not with time; it was the same yesterday as today it is, and even so shall be forever,—and that price, at which may be bought the pearl beyond all price, is *obedience to the laws and ordinances of the Gospel.*

Hear this further declaration of faith taught by the restored Church:

"*We believe that the first principles and ordinances of the Gospel are:—(1) Faith in the Lord Jesus Christ; (2) Repentance; (3) Baptism by immersion for the remission of sins; (4) Laying-on of hands for the Gift of the Holy Ghost.*"[2]

Faith in the Lord Jesus Christ is the fundamental principle of the Gospel, the first letter in the alphabet of salvation with which are spelled the words of life eternal. Yet who can have faith in aught of which he knows nothing? Knowledge is essential to faith, and faith impels its possessor to seek further knowledge, and to make of that knowledge, wisdom, which is but knowledge applied and put to use. To preach Christ and Him crucified[3] is the one and only way by which faith in Him may be taught through the medium of either precept or example.

---

[2]See the author's "The Articles of Faith," Lectures V—VIII with references therein given.

[3]I Cor. 1:23; 2:2.

While knowledge and faith are thus closely associated,
the two are not identical, nor is the one an assured out-
growth of the other. A man may have learned the truth,
and yet may ignore it. His knowledge, far from develop-
ing within his soul the faith that leads to right action, may
but add to his condemnation, for he sins without even the
mitigation of ignorance. Evil spirits have testified of their
knowledge that Jesus is the Christ, nevertheless they remain the fallen followers of Satan.[4] As living faith de-
velops within the soul of man it leads its possessor to
seek a means whereby he may rise from the thraldom of
sin; and the very thought of such emancipation inspires a
loathing for the evil contamination of the past. The
natural fruitage of that glorious growth is repentance.

Repentance, as a requirement made of all men, constitutes the second principle of the Gospel of Christ. It
comprises a sincere sorrow for the sins of the past, and a
resolute turning away therefrom with the solemn determination to endeavor by Divine assistance to return
thereto no more. Repentance comes as a gift from God
to him who has treasured and nurtured the earlier gift of
faith. It is not to be had for the careless asking; it may
not be found upon the highway; it is not of earth, but a
treasure of heaven, and is given with care, yet with
boundless liberality unto those who have brought forth
works that warrant its bestowal. That is to say, all who
prepare themselves for repentance will, by the humbling
and softening influence of the Holy Spirit, be brought to
the actual possession of this great gift. When Peter was
charged by his fellow-worshippers with a breach of law in
that he had associated with Gentiles, he told his hearers
of the Divine manifestations he had so recently received;
they believed and declared "Then hath God also to the
Gentiles granted repentance unto life." Paul also, in
writing to the Romans, teaches that repentance comes
through the goodness of God.[5]

[4]See Mark 1:24; 3:11; 5:1-18; and Matt. 8:28-34.
[5]Acts 11:18; Rom. 2:4; see also the author's "The Articles of Faith," Lecture
V:19-30 and references therein given.

Wilful persistency in sin may lead to the loss and forfeiture of the ability to repent; and for man to procrastinate the day of repentance is to invite and eventually to insure such forfeiture. The Divine word through the mouth of a modern prophet is thus explicit:

"For I the Lord cannot look upon sin with the least degree of allowance;

"Nevertheless, he that repents and does the commandments of the Lord shall be forgiven;

"And he that repents not, from him shall be taken even the light which he has received, for my Spirit shall not always strive with man, saith the Lord of Hosts."[6]

The Latter-day Saints believe and teach that repentance will be possible, and indeed required to the yet unrepentant, even after death; and they affirm that this doctrine is supported by scripture both ancient and modern. We read that while the body of our Lord lay in the tomb, between the evening of the day of crucifixion and the glorious resurrection morn, He was engaged in ministerial labor in the world of disembodied spirits. Peter specifically declares that our Lord "went and preached unto the spirits in prison; which sometime were disobedient, when once the long-suffering of God waited in the days of Noah."[7] The context with which appear these words of the inspired apostle, shows that the event referred to occurred prior to the Savior's resurrection. Furthermore, it will be remembered that one of the condemned malefactors, whose cross of death stood alongside that of Jesus, manifested faith and even some degree of repentance, and received from the suffering Christ the benediction and assurance "Today shalt thou be with me in Paradise."[8] It cannot be maintained that this promise implied the passing of the repentant sinner directly from the cross into Heaven—the abode of the redeemed in the presence of God; for surely there had been no opportunity for the

---

[6]Doctrine and Covenants 1:31-33.
[7]I Peter 3:19-20; compare 4:6.
[8]See Luke 23:39-43.

suffering penitent to put his repentance into effect by complying with the established laws and ordinances of the Gospel, and without such compliance, even as to the single requirement of water-baptism alone, the man could neither enter nor see the Kingdom of God, or the word of Christ would have been proven false.[9] Moreover, as conclusive proof of the fact that between the time of Christ's death and resurrection, neither He nor the contrite sinner had gone to the abode of God, we have the words of the Risen Lord to the sorrowing Magdalene: "I am not yet ascended to my Father."[10]

In view of scriptural affirmation that the disembodied Christ did visit and minister among the spirits who had been disobedient, and who, because of unpardoned sin were still held in duress, it is pertinent to inquire as to the scope and object of our Savior's ministry among them. His preaching must have been purposeful and positive; moreover, it is not to be assumed that His message was other than one of relief and mercy. Those to whom He went were already in prison, and had been there long. To them came the Redeemer, to preach, not to further condemn, to open the way that led to light, not to intensify the darkness of despair in which they languished. Had not that visit of deliverance been long predicted? Centuries before that fateful time Isaiah had prophesied of proud and wicked spirits: "And they shall be gathered together, as prisoners are gathered in the pit, and shall be shut up in the prison, and after many days shall they be visited."[11] And again, referring to the appointed ministry of the Christ, the same inspired voice of prophecy declared part of that work to be "to open the blind eyes, to bring out the prisoners from the prison, and them that sit in darkness out of the prison house."[12] David, filled with

---

[9]Consider our Lord's declaration to Nicodemus, John 3:1-5.
[10]John 20:17.
[11]Isaiah 24:22.
[12]Isaiah 42:6, 7.

the emotions of contrition and hope, sang in measures of mingled sadness and joy: "Therefore my heart is glad, and my glory rejoiceth: my flesh also shall rest in hope. For thou wilt not leave my soul in hell."[13]

From these and other scriptures we learn that the ministry of Christ was not confined to the few who lived in mortality during the short period of His earthly life, nor to them and the generations then future; but to all, dead, living, and yet unborn. It cannot be denied that myriads had lived and died before the meridian of time, and of these multitudes, as of the many since born, unnumbered hosts have died without a knowledge of the Gospel and its prescribed plan of salvation. What is their condition, as indeed what shall be the state of the present inhabitants of earth, and of the multitudes yet future, who shall die in ignorance and without the faith that saves? Let us ask again, how can those who know not Christ have faith in Him, and how, while lacking both knowledge and faith can they avail themselves of the provision made for their salvation?

The Church of Jesus Christ of Latter-day Saints affirms that the plan of salvation is not bounded by the grave; but that the Gospel is deathless and everlasting, reaching back into the ages that have gone, and forward into the eternities of the future. The ministry of the Savior among the dead doubtless included the revelation of His own atoning death, the inculcation of faith in Himself and in the divinely-appointed plan He represented, and the necessity of a repentance acceptable unto God. It is reasonable to believe that the other essential requirements comprised within the *laws and ordinances of the Gospel* were made known.

To the less thoughtful reader it may appear that to teach the possibility of repentance beyond the grave may tend to weaken belief in the absolute necessity of re-

---

13Psalms 16:9-10.

pentance and reformation in this life. A careful consideration of the matter, however, will show that this doctrine affords no reason for such objection. To reject or ignore in any degree a gift of God is to forfeit to the corresponding extent one's claim upon that gift. To the soul that has wilfully neglected the opportunities for repentance here offered, repentance in the hereafter may be, and indeed it is reasonable to believe will be, so difficult as to be long unattainable. This conception is justified by scripture, as witness the words of Amulek, a Nephite prophet, who thus admonished the Church on the western continent four score years before the birth of Christ:

"For behold, this life is the time for men to prepare to meet God; * * * therefore, I beseech of you, that ye do not procrastinate the day of your repentance until the end; * * * Ye cannot say, when ye are brought to that awful crisis, that I will repent, that I will return to my God. Nay, ye cannot say this; for that same spirit which doth possess your bodies at the time that ye go out of this life, that same spirit will have power to possess your body in that eternal world. For behold, if ye have procrastinated the day of your repentance, even until death, behold, ye have become subjected to the spirit of the devil, and he doth seal you his."[14]

Baptism by water is taught by the Church in this dispensation as an essential ordinance of the Gospel. Baptism is the gateway leading into the fold of Christ, the portal to the Church, the established rite of naturalization in the Kingdom of God. The candidate for admission into the Church, having obtained and professed faith in the Lord Jesus Christ, and having sincerely repented of his sins, is properly required to give evidence of this spiritual sanctification by some outward ordinance, prescribed by authority as the sign or symbol of the new profession. The initiatory ordinance is baptism by water, to be followed by the higher baptism of the Holy Spirit; and, as a result of this act of obedience, remission of sins is granted.[15]

---

[14]Book of Mormon, Alma 34:32-35.
[15]"The Articles of Faith," Lecture VI:1. For a general treatment of Baptism see Lectures VI and VII.

That baptism is essential to salvation is attested by many specific scriptures; yet even without such its essentiality appears in view of the unconditional requirement of repentance, and the evident fact that to be of value and effect repentance must imply obedience to the Divine requirements, which include baptism by water. Be it remembered that Jesus, the Christ, though untouched by the taint of sin, submitted in person to this ordinance, which was administered by the Baptist in the waters of Jordan. The burden of John's teaching was "Repent ye; for the kingdom of heaven is at hand," and to such as came to him professing repentance he administered baptism by water immersion. Then came Jesus unto John, to be baptized of him; and the Baptist, regarding Him as one without sin, demurred, saying:

"I have need to be baptized of thee, and comest thou to me?

"And Jesus answering said unto him, Suffer it to be so now: for thus it becometh us to fulfil all righteousness. Then he suffered him.

"And Jesus, when he was baptized, went up straightway out of the water: and, lo, the heavens were opened unto him, and he saw the Spirit of God descending like a dove, and lighting upon him:

"And lo a voice from heaven, saying, This is my beloved Son, in whom I am well pleased."[16]

It is evident from the foregoing that the baptism of Jesus was acceptable unto the Father, and was by Him characterized as an act of humility and obedience on the part of the Son, with which He was well pleased. Some time after His own baptism Jesus affirmed, in words at once forceful and unequivocal, that baptism is required of all men as a condition of entrance into the kingdom of God. To Nicodemus, a ruler among the Jews, who came by night professing some measure of faith, Jesus said: "Verily, verily, I say unto thee, Except a man be born of water and of the Spirit, he cannot enter into the kingdom of God."[17] When in the resurrected state He manifested Himself to the apostles, He instructed them by way of final and special commission: "Go ye therefore, and

---

[16]Matt. 3:13-17.
[17]See John 3:1-7.

teach all nations, baptizing them in the name of the Father, and of the Son, and of the Holy Ghost."[18] The necessity and purpose of the ordinance appear in His further words on the same solemn occasion: "He that believeth and is baptized shall be saved; but he that believeth not shall be damned."[19]

The Apostles, inspired by that Divine commission, ceased not to teach the necessity of baptism, even as long as their ministry endured among mortals.[20]

The elders of the Church in the present dispensation have been directed and empowered by the same authority, and almost in the same words: "Go ye into all the world, preach the Gospel to every creature, acting in the authority which I have given you, baptizing in the name of the Father, and of the Son, and of the Holy Ghost; and he that believeth and is baptized shall be saved, and he that believeth not shall be damned."[21] On another occasion the Lord added, in a revelation through the modern prophet, Joseph Smith: "Therefore, as I said unto mine apostles I say unto you again, that every soul who believeth on your words, and is baptized by water for the remission of sins, shall receive the Holy Ghost." And further, "Verily, verily, I say unto you they who believe not on your words, and are not baptized in water, in my name, for the remission of their sins, that they may receive the Holy Ghost, shall be damned, and shall not come into my Father's kingdom, where my Father and I am."[22]

The Gift of the Holy Ghost follows baptism by water, and its authoritative bestowal constitutes the next essential ordinance of the Gospel.[23] In both ancient and modern times this endowment has been regarded as a higher

---

[18]Matt. 28:19.
[19]Mark 16:16.
[20]See Acts 2:38; 9:1-18; 10:30-48; 22:1-16; I Peter 3:21.
[21]Doctrine and Covenants 68:8, 9.
[22]Doctrine and Covenants, 84:64, 74; see also 112:28, 29.
[23]See "The Articles of Faith," Lecture VIII.

baptism, lacking which the baptism of water is incomplete. John, distinctively known as the Baptist, so taught on the very eve of our Savior's personal ministry. Consider well his words: "I indeed baptize you with water unto repentance: but he that cometh after me is mightier than I, whose shoes I am not worthy to bear: he shall baptize you with the Holy Ghost, and with fire."[24] John testifies further that the One who should thus inaugurate the higher baptism was Jesus, Himself. Not until after he had administered the ordinance of water baptism to Jesus, did John recognize Him as the Christ; but immediately after that recognition, the Baptist fearlessly proclaimed his testimony:

"Behold the Lamb of God * * * This is he of whom I said, After me cometh a man which is preferred before me * * * And I knew him not: but he that sent me to baptize with water, the same said unto me, Upon whom thou shalt see the Spirit descending, and remaining on him, the same is he which baptizeth with the Holy Ghost."[25]

Jesus repeatedly promised the apostles that the "Comforter" or the "Spirit of Truth"[26] should be given unto them; and this assurance was made specific and final immediately prior to the ascension. He "commanded them that they should not depart from Jerusalem, but wait for the promise of the Father, which, saith he, ye have heard of me. For John truly baptized with water; but ye shall be baptized with the Holy Ghost not many days hence. * * * Ye shall receive power, after that the Holy Ghost is come upon you: and ye shall be witnesses unto me."[27] The promise was fulfilled at the succeeding Pentecost when the apostles received power never before known to them, the endowment being marked by an outward manifestation of fiery tongues.[28] The apostles thereafter promised the Holy Ghost to those who sought

---

[24]Matt. 3:11; compare Mark 1:7, 8; Luke 3:16.
[25]John 1:29-33.
[26]John 14:16, 17, 26; 15:26; 16:7, 13.
[27]Acts 1:4, 5, 8.
[28]Acts 2:1-4.

salvation. Peter's exhortation to the multitude, on that same memorable day of Pentecost, is particularly explicit and forceful. In answer to the inquiry, "Men and brethren, what shall we do?" the chief of the apostles replied: "Repent, and be baptized every one of you in the name of Jesus Christ for the remission of sins, and ye shall receive the gift of the Holy Ghost."[29]

A similar assurance as to the higher endowment of the Holy Ghost following the ordinance of water-baptism was made by Nephite prophets,[30] and by the resurrected Christ in His visit to the people of the western continent.[31] And later still this has been repeated through the Church in the current dispensation, that of the fulness of times: "I say unto you again," said the Lord in a revelation to certain elders of the Church, "that every soul who believeth on your words, and is baptized by water for the remission of sins, shall receive the Holy Ghost."[32]

By way of summary let it be repeated: The Church of Jesus Christ of Latter-day Saints holds as a fundamental doctrine, attested and proved by scripture both ancient and modern, that compliance with *the laws and ordinances of the Gospel* is an absolute and irrevocable requirement for admission into the Kingdom of God, or in other words, for the securing of individual salvation to the souls of men, and that this requirement is universal, applying alike to every soul that has attained to age and powers of accountability in the flesh, in whatever period or dispensation that soul has lived in mortality. It follows as a necessary consequence that if any soul has failed, either through ignorance or neglect, to render obedience to these requirements, the obligation is not removed by death.

---

[29]Acts 2:37, 38.
[30]For an instance, see Book of Mormon, II Nephi 31:8, 12-14, 17.
[31]III Nephi 11:35; 12:2.
[32]Doctrine and Covenants 84:64.

Vicarious Service of the Living for the Dead

A question now arises as to how it is possible for the dead to comply with the terms of the Gospel and do in the spirit what they had failed to do in the flesh. The exercise of faith and the manifestation of repentance by disembodied spirits may offer no great difficulty to human understanding; but that the dead shall obey the ordinances of the Gospel requiring water-baptism and the baptism of the Spirit by the authorized laying-on of hands, appears to many as truly impossible as seemed the new birth to Nicodemus. He listened in amazement to the Savior's words: "Except a man be born again he cannot see the kingdom of God;" and asked: "How can a man be born when he is old? Can he enter the second time into his mother's womb, and be born?" At last he learned that the new birth referred to was baptism by water and the baptism of the Spirit. With equal pertinency it may now be asked: How can a man be baptized when he is dead? Can he enter the second time into his body of flesh and be immersed in water by human agency? The answer is that the necessary ordinances may be performed for the dead by their living representatives, the mortal subject acting as proxy for the departed one. Thus, even as a man may be baptized in his own person for himself, he may be baptized as proxy for and in behalf of the dead.

The validity of vicarious service, in which one person acts in behalf of another, is generally recognized as an element of human institutions; and that such service may be acceptable unto God is attested by the written word. Ancient and modern scripture, the record of history other than sacred, the traditions of tribes and nations, the rites of bloody sacrifice, and even the sacrificial abominations of pagan idolatry, involve the essential conception of vicarious propitiation and of service rendered by proxy. The scape-goat[33] and the altar victim[34] in the Mosaic

[33]Lev. 16:20-22.
[34]Lev. chap. 4.

dispensation, when offered by constituted authority and with due accompaniment of acknowledgment and repentance, were accepted by the Lord as sacrifices in mitigation of the sins of His people.

The most significant sacrifice of all, the greatest work ever wrought amongst mankind, the pivotal event in human history, the supreme achievement which was at once the most glorious consummation and the most blessed beginning, is the Atonement of Christ; and this was pre-eminently a vicarious offering. No one who believes that Jesus died for man can doubt the validity and efficacy of vicarious ministration. He gave His life as a fore-ordained sacrifice, voluntarily offered and duly accepted as a propitiation for broken law, and the means by which salvation was made possible unto man. That His death was literally an accepted offering in behalf of human kind is thus set forth in the words of the resurrected Christ, given through modern revelation:

"For behold, I, God, have suffered these things for all, that they might not suffer if they would repent, but if they would not repent, they must suffer even as I, which suffering caused myself, even God, the greatest of all, to tremble because of pain, and to bleed at every pore, and to suffer both body and spirit: and would that I might not drink the bitter cup and shrink—nevertheless, glory be to the Father, and I partook and finished my preparations unto the children of men."[35]

The vicarious effect of the atonement of Christ is twofold; it has wrought a universal redemption of all men from the mortal death incident to the transgression of Adam; and it has provided a means of propitiation for individual sin whereby the sinner may attain salvation through obedience. It is by His mortal life and sacrificial death in behalf of others,—and those others, all who have lived or shall live,—that Jesus the Christ earned His title, Savior and Redeemer of mankind. And as He by effort, sacrifice, and suffering, did for men what they never could accomplish for themselves, and so be-

---

[35]Doctrine and Covenants 19:16-19.

came in very truth the one and only Savior and Redeemer of the race, so may each of us by opening the way to our departed dead whereby they may be brought within the saving law of the Gospel, become in a small measure saviors unto those who would otherwise be left in darkness.[36]

In every instance of vicarious ministration, it is an indispensable requisite that the proxy be worthy and acceptable; and of necessity he must himself have obeyed the laws and ordinances of the Gospel before he can officiate in behalf of others. Further, the ministrations of the living representative must be in accordance with Divine appointment, and in no wise a merely human assumption. The acceptable sacrifices of ancient Israel were such as had been definitely specified and minutely prescribed; and the sacrificial rites could be solemnized only by authorized priests. The supreme sacrifice involved in the atoning death of Christ was as truly appointed and fore-ordained. Prophets, through the long centuries antedating the Christian era, predicted the birth, life, and death of our Lord as already provided for;[37] and these prophecies were confirmed by Jesus Himself.[38] Consider also the testimony of the apostles to the same effect. Peter specifically designates Christ as "a Lamb without blemish and without spot: who verily was foreordained before the foundation of the world."[39] The designation "Lamb" is indicative of a sacrificial victim. Paul in writing to the Romans characterizes our Lord as the one "Whom God hath set forth to be a propitiation through faith in his blood, to declare his righteousness for the remission of sins that are past."[40]

---

[36]See Obadiah 21; I Timothy 4:16; James 5:20.

[37]Deut. 18:15, 17-19; Job 19:25-27; Psalms 2:1-12; Zech. 9:9; 12:10; 13:6; Isa. 7:14; 9:6, 7; Micah 5:2.

[38]See Luke 24:27, 45, 46.

[39]I Peter 1:19, 20.

[40]Rom. 3:25. See further Rom. 16:25, 26; Eph. 3:9-11; Col. 1:24-26; II Tim, 1:8-10; Titus 1:2, 3; Rev. 13:8.

The Latter-day Saints affirm that their vicarious work in behalf of the dead is required of them by the call of the Lord through direct revelation; and that it becomes the duty and privilege of every individual who accepts the Gospel and enters the Church to labor for the salvation of his dead. He is expected and required by the obligations and responsibility he has assumed as a member of the Church of Jesus Christ, so to live as to be a worthy representative of his departed ancestors, in holy ordinance, and to be of clean life, that he may not forfeit his right to enter the sacred confines of the Lord's House, where alone he may officiate in that privileged capacity.

Let it not be assumed that this doctrine of vicarious labor for the dead implies even remotely, that the administration of ordinances in behalf of departed spirits operates in any manner to interfere with the right of choice and the exercise of free agency on their part. They are at liberty to accept or reject the ministrations in their behalf; and so they will accept or reject, in accordance with their converted or unregenerate state, even as is the case with mortals to whom the Gospel message may come. Though baptism be duly administered to a living man in behalf of a dead ancestor, that spirit will derive no immediate advancement nor any benefit therefrom if he has not yet attained faith in the Lord Jesus Christ or if he be still unrepentant. Even as Christ offered salvation to all, though few there be who accept in the flesh, so temple ordinances may be administered for many in the realm of the departed who are not yet prepared to profit thereby.

It is evident, therefore, that labor in behalf of the dead is two-fold; that performed on earth would remain incomplete and futile but for its supplement and counterpart beyond the veil. Missionary work is in progress there— work, compared with which the evangelistic labor of earth is but a small undertaking. There are preachers and teachers, ministers invested with the Holy Priesthood, all engaged in declaring the glad tidings of the Gospel to spirits who have not yet found the light. As has been shown, this great labor amongst the dead was inaugurated by Jesus the Christ, during the brief period of His dis-embodiment.[41] The saving ministry so begun was left to be continued by others duly authorized and commissioned; even as the work of preaching the Gospel and administer-ing therein amongst the living was committed to the apos-tles in the Church of old.

Authority to Labor in Behalf of the Dead

In the closing chapter of the compilation of scriptures known to us as the Old Testament, the prophet Malachi thus describes a condition incident to the last days, im-mediately preceding the second coming of Christ:

"For, behold, the day cometh, that shall burn as an oven; and all the proud, yea, and all that do wickedly, shall be stubble: and the day that cometh shall burn them up, saith the Lord of hosts, that it shall leave them neither root nor branch.

"But unto you that fear my name shall the Sun of righteousness arise with healing in his wings."

The fateful prophecy concludes with the following blessed and far-reaching promise:

"Behold, I will send you Elijah the prophet before the coming of the great and dreadful day of the Lord:

"And he shall turn the heart of the fathers to the children, and the heart of the children to their fathers, lest I come and smite the earth with a curse."[42]

It has been held by theologians and Bible commen-tators that this prediction had reference to the birth and ministry of John the Baptist,[43] upon whom rested the spirit and power of Elias.[44] However, we have no record of Elijah having ministered unto the Baptist, and further-

---

[41]See pages 57-59.
[42]See Malachi 4:1, 2, 5, 6.
[43]Compare Matt. 11:14; 17:11; Mark 9:11; Luke 1:17.
[44]Luke 1:17.

more, the latter's ministry, glorious though it was, jus-
tifies no conclusion that in him did the prophecy find its
full realization. In addition, it should be remembered,
that the Lord's declaration through Malachi, relative
to the day of burning in which the wicked would be
destroyed as stubble, yet awaits fulfilment. It is evident,
therefore, that the commonly accepted interpretation is
at fault, and that we must look to a later date than the
time of John for the fulfilment of Malachi's prediction.
The later occasion has come; it belongs to the present
dispensation, and marks the inauguration of a work
specially reserved for the Church in these latter days. In
the course of a glorious manifestation to Joseph Smith
and Oliver Cowdery, in the Temple at Kirtland, Ohio,
April 3rd, 1836, there appeared unto them Elijah, the
prophet of old, who had been taken from earth while
still in the body. He declared unto them:

"Behold, the time has fully come, which was spoken of by the mouth
of Malachi, testifying that he (Elijah) should be sent before the great and
dreadful day of the Lord come, to turn the hearts of the fathers to the
children, and the children to the fathers, lest the whole earth be smitten
with a curse. Therefore the keys of this dispensation are committed into
your hands, and by this ye may know that the great and dreadful day of the
Lord is near, even at the doors."[45]

One of the fundamental principles underlying the doctrine of salvation for the dead, is that of the mutual de-
pendance of the fathers and the children. Family lineage
and the sequence of generations in each particular line of
descent are facts, and cannot be changed by death; on the
other hand it is evident from the olden scriptures already
cited, and attested by the equally sure word of modern
revelation, that the family relationships of earth are recognized in the spirit world. Neither the children nor the
fathers, neither progenitors nor descendants, can alone
attain perfection; and the requisite co-operation is effected
through baptism and related ordinances, administered to
the living in behalf of the dead.

---

[45]Doctrine and Covenants 110:13-16.

In this way and through this work are the hearts of the fathers and those of the children turned toward each other. As the living children learn that without their ancestors they cannot attain a perfect status in the eternal world, their own faith will be strengthened and they will be willing to labor for the redemption and salvation of their dead. And the dead, learning through the preaching of the Gospel in their world, that they are dependent upon their descendants as vicarious saviors, will turn with loving faith and prayerful effort toward their children yet living.

This uniting of the interests of fathers and children is a part of the necessary preparation for the yet future advent of the Christ as ruling King and Lord of earth. Joseph Smith thus taught:

"The earth will be smitten with a curse, unless there is a welding link of some kind or other, between the fathers and the children, upon some subject or other, and behold what is that subject? It is the baptism for the dead. For we without them cannot be made perfect; neither can they without us be made perfect."[46]

The Church today cites as authority for its administration of ordinances in behalf of the dead, the special bestowal of this power and office through the ministry of Elijah; and furthermore, the Church holds that the giving of that power marked the fulfilment of Malachi's portentous prediction. There appears an element of particular fitness in the fact that the minister through whom this great work has been inaugurated in the present dispensation, is none other than Elijah,—who, not having passed the portals of death, held a peculiar and special relation to both the dead and the living. As to the fidelity with which the Church has served under this special commission, the temples it has reared with such sacrifice and self-denial on the part of its devoted adherents, and the

---

[46]Doctrine and Covenants 128:18.

ordinance work already performed therein, are sufficient proof.

The importance with which the Latter-day Saints regard their temple work in behalf of the dead naturally produces among this people a vital interest in the genealogical records of their respective families. Ordinance work in the temples, in behalf of any departed person, can be done only as that person may be described on the record, as to name, relationship, time and place of birth and death, etc., by which data he may be fully and certainly isolated and identified.[47] It is a matter of common knowledge that interest in genealogical research has greatly increased in the United States and in Europe during the last seven or eight decades. Genealogical societies have been formed, and individual investigators have devoted great treasures of time and money to the compilation of records showing numerous lines of family descent and the many ramifications of complicated relationship. In all this work the Latter-day Saints profess to see the operation of an over-ruling power, by which their service for the dead is facilitated.

Temples Required for Vicarious Service

While the ordinances of baptism, imposition of hands for the bestowal of the Holy Ghost, and others, such as ordination to the Priesthood, may be performed upon the living in any suitable and proper place, the corresponding ordinances for and in behalf of the dead are acceptable unto the Lord, and therefore valid, only when administered in places specially provided, set apart, and dedicated for these and kindred purposes; that is to say, such ordinances belong exclusively to the House of the Lord. For a very brief period only, and that the earliest in modern Church history, before the people had opportunity to erect temples, did the Lord graciously accept a temporary sanctuary, even as He accepted the Taber-

---

[47]See Doctrine and Covenants 128:5-8.

nacle of old as a temporary temple during the period of Israel's wanderings.

In a revelation given to Joseph Smith, the prophet, at Nauvoo, Illinois, January 19th, 1841, the Lord called upon His people to build a house to His name "for the Most High to dwell therein," and added by way of explanation and instruction:

"For there is not a place found on earth that he may come and restore again that which was lost unto you, or which he hath taken away, even the fulness of the Priesthood;

"For a baptismal font there is not upon the earth, that they, my saints, may be baptized for those who are dead;

"For this ordinance belongeth to my house, and cannot be acceptable to me, only in the days of your poverty, wherein ye are not able to build a house unto me.

"But I command you, all ye my saints, to build a house unto me; and I grant unto you a sufficient time to build a house unto me, and during this time your baptisms shall be acceptable unto me.

"But behold, at the end of this appointment, your baptisms for your dead shall not be acceptable unto me; and if you do not these things at the end of the appointment, ye shall be rejected as a church, with your dead, saith the Lord your God.

"For verily I say unto you, that after you have had sufficient time to build a house to me, wherein the ordinance of baptizing for the dead belongeth, and for which the same was instituted from before the foundation of the world, your baptisms for your dead cannot be acceptable unto me,

"For therein are the keys of the holy Priesthood, ordained that you may receive honor and glory.

"And after this time, your baptisms for the dead, by those who are scattered abroad, are not acceptable unto me, saith the Lord;

"For it is ordained that in Zion, and in her Stakes, and in Jerusalem, those places which I have appointed for refuge, shall be the places for your baptisms for your dead.

"And again, verily I say unto you, How shall your washings be acceptable unto me, except ye perform them in a house which you have built to my name?

"For, for this cause I commanded Moses that he should build a tabernacle, that they should bear it with them in the wilderness, and to build a house in the land of promise, that those ordinances might be revealed which had been hid from before the world was;

"Therefore, verily I say unto you, that your anointings, and your washings, and your baptisms for the dead, and your solemn assemblies, and your memorials for your sacrifices, by the sons of Levi, and for your oracles in your most holy places, wherein you receive conversations, and your statutes and judgments, for the beginning of the revelations and foundation of Zion, and for the glory, honor, and endowment of all her municipals, are ordained by the ordinance of my holy house which my people are always commanded to build unto my holy name.

"And verily I say unto you, Let this house be built unto my name, that I may reveal mine ordinances therein, unto my people;

"For I deign to reveal unto my church, things which have been kept hid from before the foundation of the world, things that pertain to the dispensation of the fulness of times."[48]

This then is sufficient answer to the question as to why the Latter-day Saints build and maintain temples. They have been instructed and required so to do by the Lord of Hosts. They have learned that many essential ordinances of the Church are acceptable only when performed in temples specially erected and reserved for the purpose. They know that within these precincts of sanctity the Lord has revealed many great and important things pertaining to the Kingdom of God; and that He has promised to reveal yet more to man in houses sacred to His name. They have learned that a great part of the mission and ministry of the restored Church is the administration of vicarious ordinances in behalf of the unnumbered dead who never heard the tidings of the Gospel, and that for such sacred and saving service

Temples are a necessity.

----

[48]Doctrine and Covenants 124:28-41. Read the entire section.

CHAPTER IV

Modern Temple Ordinances

A more detailed consideration of modern temple service now claims our attention. The ceremonial work comprises:

1. Baptism, specifically Baptism for the Dead.
2. Ordination and associated Endowments in the Priesthood.
3. Marriage Ceremonies.
4. Other Sealing Ordinances.

As will be understood from what has been already written, each of these ceremonies or ordinances may be performed either for the living, present in person, or for the dead who are represented each by an individual living proxy. The living are but few compared with the dead; and it follows of necessity that the ordinance-work for the departed exceeds by a great preponderance that done for the living. The temples of today are maintained largely for the benefit and salvation of the uncounted dead.

Baptism for the Dead

As demonstrated in the preceding pages, the law of baptism is of universal application; in short, baptism is required of all who have lived to the age of accountability. Only those who die in infancy are exempt. Children, having no sin to expiate, and being unable to comprehend the natural of the baptismal obligation, are not to be baptized while living, nor is the ordinance to be performed for them should they die before reaching a responsible age and state. As to the child's part in the heritage of mortality incident to the transgression of

Adam, the atonement of Christ is of full effect, and the redemption of the child is assured.[1] Regarding the general applicability of the law prescribing baptism as essential to salvation, the scriptures make no distinction between the living and the dead. The atoning sacrifice of Christ was offered, not only for the few who lived upon the earth while He was in the flesh, nor for those alone who were born in mortality after His death, but for all inhabitants of earth then past, present, and future. He was ordained of the Father to be a judge of both quick and dead;[2] He is Lord alike of living and dead,[3] as men speak of dead and living, though all live unto Him.[4]

Among the pernicious dogmas taught by a perverted and mis-called Christianity, is the heinous doctrine that never-ending punishment or interminable bliss, unchanging in kind or degree, shall be the destiny of every soul,—the award being made according to the condition of that soul at the time of bodily death; a life of sin being thus nullified by a death-bed repentance, and a life of honor, if unmarked by the ceremonies of established sects, being followed by the tortures of hell without a possibility of relief. Such a dogma is to be ranked with the dread heresy which proclaims the condemnation of innocent babes who have not been sprinkled by man's assumed authority. In the justice of God no soul shall be finally condemned under a law of which he has had no chance to learn. True, eternal punishment has been decreed as the lot of the wicked; but the real meaning of the punishment so decreed has been made known by the Lord Himself.[5] Eternal punishment is God's punishment; endless punishment is His; for "Endless" and "Eternal" are among His names, and the words are descriptive of His attributes.

---

[1]For a concise treatment of Infant Baptism, see the author's "The Articles of Faith," Lecture VI, 13-17; and for treatment of Baptism for the Dead, see Lecture VII, 18-33.

[2]Acts 10:42; II Tim. 4:1; I Peter 4:5.

[3]Rom. 14:9.

[4]Luke 20:36, 38.

[5]Doctrine and Covenants 19:10-12.

No soul will be punished for sin beyond the time requisite to work the needed reformation and to vindicate justice, for which ends alone punishment is imposed. And no one will be eligible to enter any kingdom of glory in the abode of the blessed to which he is not entitled through obedience to law.

It follows as a plain necessity that the Gospel must be proclaimed in the spirit world; and that such ministry is provided for, the scriptures abundantly prove. Peter, defining the mission of the Redeemer, thus declares this solemn truth: "For this cause was the gospel preached also to them that are dead, that they might be judged according to men in the flesh, but live according to God in the spirit."[6] As already shown, the inauguration of this work among the dead was wrought by Christ in the interval between His death and resurrection.

In his first epistle to the Saints in Corinth, Paul presents a brief yet comprehensive treatment of the doctrine of the resurrection,—a subject which at that time and among those to whom he wrote, had given rise to much contention and debate;[7] and, having shown that through Christ the resurrection of the dead had been made possible, and that in due course all mankind shall be redeemed from bodily death, the apostle asks, "Else what shall they do which are baptized for the dead, if the dead rise not at all? why then are they baptized for the dead?"[8] As

---

[6]I Peter 4:6.

[7]I Cor. chap. 15; see specifically verse 29.

[8]This passage has been the subject of much controversy. Dr. Adam Clarke, in his masterly Commentary of the Scriptures, says: "This is certainly the most difficult verse in the New Testament; for, notwithstanding the greatest and wisest men have labored to explain it, there are to this day nearly as many different interpretations of it as there are interpreters." Yet, notwithstanding its enigmatic meaning, this passage of scripture is part of the prescribed burial service in the Episcopal Church, and is duly spoken by the priest at every funeral. But wherein lies the difficulty of comprehension? The passage is of plain import, and only when we attempt to make it figurative do difficulties arise. It is plain that in Paul's day the ordinance of baptism for the dead was both understood and practised, and the apostle's argument in support of the doctrine of a literal resurrection is sound: If the dead rise not at all, why then are they baptized for the dead?

the question is put by way of finality and climax to the
preceding argument, it is evident that the subject so introduced was no new or strange doctrine, but on the contrary, one with which the people addressed must have
been familiar, and which to them required no argument.
Baptism for the dead was, therefore, both known as a
principle and practised as an ordinance in apostolic times.
That the practise was continued in some form for a century or more after the apostles had passed from the earth
is evidenced by numerous passages in the writings of the
early Christian Fathers, and by later authorities on ecclesiastical history.

The Church of Jesus Christ of Latter-day Saints proclaims the present as the dispensation of the fulness of
times, in which shall be gathered and re-established all
the saving principles and essential ordinances of earlier
dispensations, and during which the great plan of universal redemption shall be fully revealed. The Church,
therefore, provides for the actual work of baptism for the
dead, and in the temples of today this sacred labor is in
uninterrupted progress. As will be seen, each of the temples is provided with a baptismal font, with every necessary provision for the administration of this ordinance.[9]

The rite of water-baptism in behalf of the dead
is followed by that of the laying-on of hands for the
bestowal of the Holy Ghost; and in this as in the preceding, the dead person is represented by the living proxy.
The imposition of hands for the conferring of the gift
of the Holy Ghost constitutes the higher baptism of the
Spirit required alike of all, and includes the rite of confirmation by which the person becomes a member of the
Church of Christ. In all essentials the ordinances of baptism and confirmation are identical, whether administered
to the living for themselves or as proxy for the dead. As
these ordinances are administered in existing temples it is

---

[9]Read Doctrine and Covenants 128:12, 13.

uired that, beside the recorder and the officiating elder, two witnesses be present, and that they attest the ceremony as duly performed.

Ordination and Endowment

Water-baptism, and the higher baptism of the Spirit by the authorized imposition of hands for the conferring of the Holy Ghost, constitute the two fundamental ordinances of the Gospel. The repentant soul who has thus entered the Church of Christ may afterward attain to position and authority in the Holy Priesthood—not as an earthly honor, not as a title of personal aggrandizement, not as a symbol of power to rule and possibly to oppress, —but as an endowment bespeaking authority and the express responsibility to use that authority in the service of his fellows and to the glory of God. In the temple service, the man who appears as proxy for his dead relative must be ordained to the Priesthood before he can pass beyond the baptismal font.

It is a precept of the Church that women of the Church share the authority of the Priesthood with their husbands, actual or prospective; and therefore women, whether taking the endowment for themselves or for the dead, are not ordained to specific rank in the Priesthood. Nevertheless there is no grade, rank, or phase of the temple endowment to which women are not eligible on an equality with men. True, there are certain of the higher ordinances to which an unmarried woman cannot be admitted, but the rule is equally in force as to a bachelor. The married state is regarded as sacred, sanctified, and holy in all temple procedure; and within the House of the Lord the woman is the equal and the help-meet of the man. In the privileges and blessings of that holy place, the utterance of Paul is regarded as a scriptural decree in full force and effect: "Neither is the man without the woman, neither the woman without the man, in the Lord."[10]

---

[10] I Cor. 11:11.

Faith and sincere repentance, followed first by water-
baptism and then by the laying-on of hands for the bestowal of the Holy Ghost, are the prescribed means of
admission into the Church of Christ and prospective salvation in the Kingdom of God. But there is a distinction
between salvation and exaltation. At this point it may
be well to consider this distinction, and to set forth the
doctrines of the restored Church as to the graded degrees
of exaltation beyond the grave.[11]

Salvation and Exaltation:—Some degree of salvation
will come to all who have not forfeited their right to it;
exaltation is given to those only who by active labors
have won a claim to God's merciful liberality by which it
is bestowed. Of the saved, not all will be exalted to the
higher glories; rewards will not be bestowed in violation
of justice; punishments will not be meted out to the ignor-
ing of mercy's claims. No one can be admitted to any
order of glory, in short, no soul can be saved, until justice
has been satisfied for violated law. In the Kingdom of
God there are numerous degrees of exaltation provided
for those who are worthy of them. The old idea, that in
the hereafter there will be but two places for the souls
of mankind,—a heaven and a hell, with the same glory
in all parts of the one, and the same terrors throughout
the other,—is wholly untenable in the light of Divine
revelation.

Degrees of Glory:—That the privileges and glories of
heaven are graded to suit the various capacities of the
blessed, is indicated in Christ's teachings. To His apostles He said: "In my Father's house are many mansions:
if it were not so, I would have told you. I go to prepare a place for you. And if I go and prepare a place for
you, I will come again, and receive you unto myself; that
where I am, there ye may be also."[12] This declaration is

---

[11]See the author's "The Articles of Faith," Lectures IV and XII, portions of
which are included in the present treatment.

[12]John 14:1-3.

supplemented by that of Paul, who speaks of the graded glories of the resurrection as follows:

"There are also celestial bodies, and bodies terrestrial: but the glory of the celestial is one, and the glory of the terrestrial is another.

"There is one glory of the sun, and another glory of the moon, and another glory of the stars: for one star differeth from another star in glory.

"So also is the resurrection of the dead."[13]

A fuller knowledge of this subject has been imparted in the present dispensation. From a revelation given in 1832[14] we learn the following: Three great kingdoms or degrees of glory are established for the future habitation of the human race; these are known as the Celestial, the Terrestrial, and the Telestial. Far below the last and least of these, is the state of eternal punishment prepared for the sons of perdition.

The Celestial Glory is provided for those who merit the highest honors of heaven; in the revelation referred to, we read of them:

"They are they who received the testimony of Jesus, and believed on his name and were baptized after the manner of his burial, being buried in the water in his name, and this according to the commandment which he has given, that by keeping the commandments they might be washed and cleansed from all their sins, and receive the Holy Spirit by the laying on of the hands of him who is ordained and sealed unto this power, and who overcome by faith, and are sealed by the Holy Spirit of promise, which the Father sheds forth upon all those who are just and true. They are they who are the Church of the First-born. They are they into whose hands the Father has given all things—they are they who are Priests and Kings, who have received of his fulness, and of his glory, and are Priests of the Most High, after the order of Melchisedek, which was after the order of Enoch, which was after the order of the Only Begotten Son; wherefore, as it is written, they are gods, even the sons of God—wherefore all things are theirs, whether life or death, or things present, or things to come, all are theirs and they are Christ's and Christ is God's. * * * * These shall dwell in the presence of God and his Christ for ever and ever. These are they whom he shall bring with him, when he shall come in the clouds of heaven, to reign on the earth over his people. These are they who shall have a part in the first resurrection. These are they who shall come forth in the resurrection of the just. * * * These are they who are just men made perfect through Jesus the mediator of the new covenant, who

13I Cor. 15:40-42.
14Doctrine and Covenants, Sec. 76.

wrought out this perfect atonement through the shedding of his own blood. These are they whose bodies are celestial, whose glory is that of the sun, even the glory of God, the highest of all, whose glory the sun of the firmament is written of as being typical."[15]

The Terrestrial Glory:—This, the next lower degree, will be received by many whose works do not merit the highest reward. We read of them:

"These are they who are of the terrestrial, whose glory differs from that of the Church of the First-born who have received the fulness of the Father, even as that of the moon differs from the sun in the firmament. Behold, these are they who died without law, and also they who are the spirits of men kept in prison, whom the Son visited, and preached the Gospel unto them, that they might be judged according to men in the flesh, who received not the testimony of Jesus in the flesh, but afterwards received it. These are they who are honorable men of the earth, who were blinded by the craftiness of men. These are they who receive of his glory, but not of his fulness. These are they who receive of the presence of the Son, but not of the fulness of the Father; wherefore they are bodies terrestrial, and not bodies celestial, and differ in glory as the moon differs from the sun. These are they who are not valiant in the testimony of Jesus; wherefore they obtain not the crown over the kingdom of our God."[16]

The Telestial Glory:—The revelation continues:

"And again, we saw the glory of the telestial, which glory is that of the lesser, even as the glory of the stars differs from that of the glory of the moon in the firmament. These are they who received not the gospel of Christ, neither the testimony of Jesus. These are they who deny not the Holy Spirit. These are they who are thrust down to hell. These are they who shall not be redeemed from the devil, until the last resurrection, until the Lord, even Christ the Lamb shall have finished his work."[17]

We learn further that the inhabitants of this kingdom are to be graded among themselves, comprising as they do the unenlightened among the varied opposing sects and divisions of men, and sinners of many types, whose offenses are not those of utter perdition:

"For as one star differs from another star in glory, even so differs one from another in glory in the telestial world; for these are they who are of Paul, and of Apollos, and of Cephas. These are they who say they are some of one and some of another—some of Christ and some of John, and some

---
[15]Doctrine and Covenants 76:51-70.
[16]Doctrine and Covenants 76:71-79.
[17]Doctrine and Covenants 76:81-86.

of Moses, and some of Elias, and some of Esaias, and some of Isaiah, and some of Enoch; but received not the gospel, neither the testimony of Jesus, neither the prophets, neither the everlasting covenant."[18]

The three kingdoms of widely differing glories are organized on an orderly plan of gradation. We have seen that the telestial kingdom comprises several subdivisions; this also is the case, we are told, with the celestial;[19] and, by analogy, we conclude that a similar condition prevails in the terrestrial. Thus the innumerable degrees of merit amongst mankind are provided for in an infinity of graded glories. The celestial kingdom is supremely honored by the personal ministrations of the Father and the Son. The terrestrial kingdom will be administered through the higher, without a fulness of glory. The telestial is governed through the ministrations of the terrestrial, by "angels who are appointed to minister for them."[20]

Exaltation in the kingdom of God implies attainment to the graded orders of the Holy Priesthood, and with these the ceremonies of the endowment are directly associated.

The Temple Endowment, as administered in modern temples, comprises instruction relating to the significance and sequence of past dispensations, and the importance of the present as the greatest and grandest era in human history. This course of instruction includes a recital of the most prominent events of the creative period, the condition of our first parents in the Garden of Eden, their disobedience and consequent expulsion from that blissful abode, their condition in the lone and dreary world when doomed to live by labor and sweat, the plan of redemption by which the great transgression may be atoned, the period of the great apostasy, the restoration of the Gospel with all its ancient powers and privileges, the absolute and indispensable condition of personal pur-

---

[18]Doctrine and Covenants 76:98-101.
[19]Doctrine and Covenants 131:1; see also II Cor. 12:1-4.
[20]See Doctrine and Covenants 76:86-88.

ity and devotion to the right in present life, and a strict compliance with Gospel requirements.

As will be shown, the temples erected by the Latter-day Saints provide for the giving of these instructions in separate rooms, each devoted to a particular part of the course; and by this provision it is possible to have several classes under instruction at one time.

The ordinances of the endowment embody certain obligations on the part of the individual, such as covenant and promise to observe the law of strict virtue and chastity, to be charitable, benevolent, tolerant and pure; to devote both talent and material means to the spread of truth and the uplifting of the race; to maintain devotion to the cause of truth; and to seek in every way to contribute to the great preparation that the earth may be made ready to receive her King,—the Lord Jesus Christ. With the taking of each covenant and the assuming of each obligation a promised blessing is pronounced, contingent upon the faithful observance of the conditions.

No jot, iota, or tittle of the temple rites is otherwise than uplifting and sanctifying. In every detail the endowment ceremony contributes to covenants of morality of life, consecration of person to high ideals, devotion to truth, patriotism to nation, and allegiance to God. The blessings of the House of the Lord are restricted to no privileged class; every member of the Church may have admission to the temple with the right to participate in the ordinances thereof, if he comes duly accredited as of worthy life and conduct.

Sealing in Marriage

The Latter-day Saints regard the marriage ceremony performed exclusively within temple precincts, as the one and only perfect contract of matrimony.[21] They recognize the full legal validity and moral obligation of any mar-

---

[21]See the author's treatment of "Marriage" in "The Articles of Faith," Lecture XXIV, pp. 455-460.

riage entered into under the secular law; but civil marriages and indeed all marriages made without the binding authority of the Holy Priesthood they regard as contracts for this life only, and therefore lacking the higher and superior elements of a complete and perpetual union. They hold that the family relationships of earth may be made lasting and .binding beyond the veil of death. They say that under the perfect law operative in the celestial worlds, the earthly relation of husband and wife, parent and child, will endure in full force and effect, provided such relationship has been sealed on earth by the power and authority of the Holy Priesthood. The ordinary rite of matrimony as established by secular law, and as prescribed by sectarian rule, unites the man and the woman for this world only; the higher law of marriage as divinely revealed joins the parties for time and eternity.

"Celestial Marriage" is a term in current use among the Latter-day Saints, though it does not occur in any revelation contained in the standard works of the Church. The Church adopts and validates the scriptures of earlier dispensations with respect to marriage. It holds that marriage is honorable[22] and ordained of God.[23] Under the teachings of the Church, marriage is the duty of all who are not debarred by physical or other effective disability from assuming the responsibilities of the wedded state. The Latter-day Saints declare that part of the birthright of every worthy man is to stand at the head of a family as husband and father; and equally strong is the right of every worthy woman to be an honored wife and mother.

The Church denounces as false and pernicious the teachings of misled and morbid men who say that the union of the sexes is but a carnal necessity inherited by man as an incident of his degraded nature; and it repudiates the thought that celibacy is a superior condition

---

[22]Heb. 13:4.
[23]Gen. 2:18, 24; 1:27; 5:2; 9:1, 7; Lev. 26:9.

more pleasing to God. Concerning such false teachers the Lord has spoken in this day:

"Whoso forbiddeth to marry is not ordained of God, for marriage is ordained of God unto man * * * that the earth might answer the end of its creation, and that it might be filled with the measure of man, according to his creation before the world was made."[24]

The Latter-day Saints affirm that perfect marriage provides for the eternal relation of the sexes. With this people marriage is not merely a contract for time, effective only as long as the parties shall live on earth, but a solemn covenant of union which shall endure beyond the grave. In the complete ceremony of marriage as ordained by the Church and as administered only within the temple halls, the man and the woman are placed under covenant of mutual fidelity, not until death do them part, but for time and for all eternity.

A contract as far-reaching as this, a covenant declared to be effective not only throughout the period of mortal life, but in the realm of the hereafter, of necessity requires for its validation an authority superior to any that man may originate. It is admitted without argument that men have the right to form among themselves associations and communities, to organize sects, parties, companies, churches, clubs, or any other union they may choose to create, provided, of course, such bodies are not inimical to law and order. It is further admitted that any established association of men may enact laws and ordain rules for the government of its members, provided the rights of individual liberty are not infringed thereby. Both church and state, therefore, may enact, prescribe, and ordain, lawful regulations as to marriage or as to any other form of contract; and such regulations are acknowledged to be of full effect within the domain of actual jurisdiction. Thus, marriages may be legally and properly authorized by states and nations, and the con-

---

[24]Doctrine and Covenants, 49:15-17.

tracts of marriage so made are effective during the life of the parties thereto.

But, can it be said that any association of men may create and establish an authority that shall be effective after death? Can any power legislate beyond its lawful jurisdiction? Can a man sitting in his own home prescribe family rules for the household of his neighbor? Can our nation ordain laws that shall be valid in a foreign realm? Can man enact laws to regulate the affairs of the Kingdom of God?

Only as God delegates authority to man, with the assurance that administration under that authority shall be acknowledged in heaven, can any contract be made on earth and be of assured effect after the death of the parties concerned. Authority to act in the name of the Lord is the distinguishing characteristic of the Holy Priesthood. As the Lord hath said:

"All covenants, contracts, bonds, obligations, oaths, vows, performances, connections, associations, or expectations, that are not made, and entered into, and sealed, by the Holy Spirit of promise, of him who is anointed, both as well for time and for all eternity, and that too most holy, by revelation and commandment through the medium of mine anointed, whom I have appointed on the earth to hold this power, * * * are of no efficacy, virtue or force, in and after the resurrection from the dead; for all contracts that are not made unto this end, have an end when men are dead."[25]

In application of this principle to the covenants of matrimony, the revelation continues:

"Therefore, if a man marry him a wife in the world, and he marry her not by me, nor by my word; and he covenant with her so long as he is in the world, and she with him, their covenant and marriage are not of force when they are dead, and when they are out of the world; therefore, they are not bound by any law when they are out of the world.

"Therefore, when they are out of the world, they neither marry, nor are given in marriage; but are appointed angels in heaven, which angels are ministering servants, to minister for those who are worthy of a far more, and an exceeding, and an eternal weight of glory;

"For these angels did not abide my law, therefore they cannot be en-

---

[25]Doctrine and Covenants 132:7.

larged, but remain separately and singly, without exaltation, in their saved condition, to all eternity, and from henceforth are not gods, but are angels of God, for ever and ever."[26]

This system of holy matrimony, involving covenants for both time and eternity, is known distinctively as *Celestial Marriage,* and is understood to be the order of marriage that exists in the celestial worlds. This sacred ordinance is administered by the Church to those only who are adjudged to be of worthy life, fit to be admitted to the House of the Lord; for this holy rite, together with others of eternal validity, may be solemnized only within the temples reared and dedicated for such exalted service.[27] Children born to parents thus married under the celestial law are heirs to the Priesthood; "children of the covenant" they are called; no ordinance of adoption or sealing is required to give them place in the blessed posterity of promise.

The Church, however, sanctions and acknowledges legal marriages for time only, and indeed solemnizes such unions between parties who may not be admitted to the House of the Lord, or who voluntarily choose the lesser and temporal order of matrimony.

Within the temple and not elsewhere, are marriages solemnized for and in behalf of parties who are dead. Husbands and wives who have lived in mortality together and now are dead, may be sealed under the authority of the Priesthood, provided, of course, the preliminary temple ordinances have been administered in their behalf. In the marriage rite for the dead as in other ordinances, the parties are represented by their living descendants acting in the capacity of proxy.

The ordinance of celestial marriage, whereby the contracting parties, whether living or dead, are united under the authority of the Holy Priesthood for time and eternity, is known distinctively as the ceremony of *Sealing*

---

[26]Doctrine and Covenants 132:15-17.
[27]Doctrine and Covenants 124:30-34.

in Marriage. Husband and wife so united are said to be sealed, whereas if united under the lesser law for time only, either by secular or ecclesiastical authority, they are only married.

Husband and wife who have been married for time only, either by secular or ecclesiastical ceremony, may afterward be sealed for time and eternity, provided they have become members of the Church, and are adjudged worthy to enter the temple for this purpose; but no such confirmation of an existing union, nor any sealing of married persons is possible unless the parties furnish proof that they have been legally and lawfully married. No marriage of living persons is performed in any of the temples except under license duly issued as required by the laws of the state. The sealing ordinance extends to other associations than those of matrimony as will be shown.

The actuality of the sealing ordinance in marriage finds an illustration in the personal teachings of the Savior. On one occasion there came unto Him certain Sadducees,[28] and these, be it remembered, denied the possibility of the resurrection of the dead. They sought to entrap Him by a difficult question. They thus stated their case:

"Master, Moses said, If a man die, having no children, his brother shall marry his wife, and raise up seed unto his brother.

"Now there were with us seven brethren: and the first, when he had married a wife, deceased, and, having no issue, left his wife unto his brother:

"Likewise the second also, and the third, unto the seventh.

"And last of all the woman died also.

"Therefore in the resurrection whose wife shall she be of the seven? for they all had her."

Note the sequel:

"Jesus answered and said unto them, Ye do err, not knowing the scriptures, nor the power of God.

"For in the resurrection they neither marry, nor are given in marriage, but are as the angels of God in heaven."

---

[28]See Matt. 22:23-33; Mark 12:18-27; Luke 20:27-40.

It is evident that in the resurrected state there could be no contest among the seven brothers as to whose wife the woman was,—for after death there was to be no marrying nor giving in marriage. The question of marriage between individuals was and is to be settled before that time. The woman would and could be the wife of but one in the eternal world, and that one the man to whom she was given by the authority of the Holy Priesthood on earth, as a consort for time and eternity. In short, the woman would be the wife of the man with whom she entered into covenant for eternity under the seal of Divine authority; and no contract or agreement for time only would be effective in the resurrection.

This exposition seems to have been convincing; the multitude were astonished, and the Sadducees were silenced;[29] moreover some of the Scribes declared: "Master, thou hast well said."[30] Our Lord added what appears to have been a supplementary question, coupled with instruction of the greatest import:

"But as touching the resurrection of the dead, have ye not read that which was spoken unto you by God, saying,

"I am the God of Abraham, and the God of Isaac, and the God of Jacob? God is not the God of the dead, but of the living."[31]

Other Sealing Ordinances

Children born outside celestial marriage, yet within legally established wedlock, are the lawful and legitimate heirs of their parents in all affairs of earth. They are the offspring of an earthly union that is in every respect a legal, moral, and proper relation under the laws of man. That these children will belong to their parents in the hereafter is as uncertain as that the parents will belong to each other. The parents have been but temporally and temporarily married, and the offspring are theirs

---

[29]Matt. 22:33, 34.
[30]Luke 20:39.
[31]Matt. 22:31, 32.

for the period of their own contract only. Even as husband and wife though legally wedded under the secular law must be sealed by the authority of the Holy Priesthood if their union is to be valid in eternity, so must children who have been born to parents married for time only be sealed to their parents after father and mother have been sealed to each other in the order of celestial marriage.

The Church affirms the eternal perpetuity of all family relationships existing on earth under the seal and authority of the Priesthood; and declares that none other relationship will be binding after death. The offspring of parents not joined in celestial marriage are thus sealed to or adopted by their parents as members of the family organization which shall endure through eternity; thus, husbands and wives who are dead are married or sealed to each other by proxy ministration, and their children are similarly sealed to them in the family relationship.

It will be seen, therefore, that the vicarious labor of the living for the dead, as performed in the temples of the present day, comprises more than baptism and confirmation. The work is completed on earth only when the parties, in the persons of their living representatives, have been baptized, confirmed, endowed, and sealed both in the relationship of husband and wife as once existent and in the family union of parents and children.

CHAPTER V

Modern Day Temples—The Temples At Kirtland and Nauvoo

As to general design, and indeed as to details of plan and construction of the earlier sanctuaries, much has been preserved to us through the pages of sacred writ. From the Biblical record alone it would be possible to practically reproduce the Tabernacle of the Congregation and the later Temple of Solomon; though, had we no information to supplement the Biblical account, we would know but little as to procedure requisite to the administration of ordinances specifically pertaining to temples.

Regarding the plan of building and the structural design of temples, we find no close similarity, far less of aught approaching identity, in these holy houses as erected in different dispensations; on the contrary we may affirm that direct revelation of temple plans is required for each distinctive period of the Priesthood's administration, that is to say for every dispensation of Divine authority. While the general purpose of temples is the same in all times, the special suitability of these edifices is determined by the needs of the dispensation to which they severally belong.

There is a definite sequence of development in the dealings of God with man throughout the centuries; and it is this unity of order and purpose that constitutes the eternal unchangeableness of the Supreme Being. Today is no mere repetition of yesterday; on the contrary, every today is a sum of all precedent time, so that in each succeeding age the Divine plan is farther advanced, and the grand finale in the great drama of human salvation is brought nearer.

From the days of the ancient Tabernacle of the Congregation, and thence onward to the meridian of time, animal sacrifice was required as an ordained rite of propitiation and worship; and such was in prototype of the sacrificial death predicted as part of the mission of the Son of Man. The temples of the Hebrews who were living under the Mosaic law, provided, therefore, for the slaughter of animals, for the ceremonial dividing of the carcasses and for the due disposal of the blood, for the convenient immolation of the offerings, and for numerous other details of ceremony associated with worship under the law of Moses.

The Latter-day Saints are one with other Christian sects in the unreserved acceptance of the doctrine that the atoning death of Christ terminated the Mosaic rites of sacrifice involving the ceremonial shedding of blood, that, in truth, the prototype was consummated in the reality. The temples of today are provided with no altars of sacrifice, no courts of slaughter, no shambles red with the blood of beasts, no pyres on which carcasses are burned, no censers of incense to becloud the fumes from burning flesh.

Even among the temples of the present dispensation there is a graded variety in the details of construction. The first temple of modern times was in a measure incomplete as compared with the holy houses of later construction. The fact was doubtless known to the Lord, though wisely hidden from common knowledge, that the Kirtland Temple would serve but for the beginning of the re-establishment of those distinctive ordinances for which tem-

ples are essential. Even as the Tabernacle of old was but
an inferior type of what would follow, designed for temporary use under special conditions, so the earlier temples
of the latter-day dispensation, specifically those of Kirtland and Nauvoo, were but temporary Houses of the
Lord, destined to serve for short periods only as sanctuaries.

Scarcely had The Church of Jesus Christ of Latter-day
Saints been organized when the Lord indicated the necessity of a temple, in which He could reveal His mind and
will to man, and in which the sanctifying ordinances of
the Gospel could be administered. In a revelation given
as early as December, 1830, the Lord said: "I am Jesus
Christ the Son of God: wherefore gird up your loins and
I will suddenly come to my temple."[1] In February 1831,
the Lord further indicated His purpose thus: "That my
covenant people may be gathered in one in that day when
I shall come to my temple. And this I do for the salvation of my people."[2] More definite instructions as to the
practical labors incident to the procuring of a site and the
rearing of a temple soon followed.

Temple Site At Independence, Missouri

The principal seat of the Church had been temporarily
established at Kirtland, Ohio; nevertheless the prophet
had learned through early revelation that Zion would be
established far to the west. In June, 1831, a conference
of elders was held at Kirtland, on which occasion a revelation[3] was received directing certain of the elders to start
westward, traveling in pairs and preaching by the way.
In the month following, these elders reassembled at a
designated place in western Missouri, all rejoicing in their
ministry and eager to learn the further will of the Lord.
The burden of their prayer and song is thus expressed by

[1]Doctrine and Covenants 36:8; compare Malachi 3:1.
[2]Doctrine and Covenants 42:36.
[3]See Doctrine and Covenants sec. 52; see also sec. 54.

the prophet: "When will the wilderness blossom as the rose? When will Zion be built up in her glory, and where will thy temple stand, unto which all nations shall come in the last days?"[4] In answer to their supplications the Lord spake by the mouth of His prophet, designating the western part of Missouri as the land of Zion, and the site occupied by the town of Independence as the "center place," and specifying a spot as that upon which a temple should be built.[5]

On the third of August, 1831, the prophet Joseph Smith and seven other elders of the Church assembled on the temple lot and dedicated the same to its sacred purpose. Though the company was small, the occasion was one of great solemnity and impressiveness. The prophet himself offered the prayer of dedication.[6] The temple so projected is yet to be built. Though the Latter-day Saints acquired by purchase title to and possession of the temple lot, they were later by violence compelled to abandon their rightful possessions.

The Kirtland Temple

The building of a temple in Missouri was regarded, even by the prophet and those who assisted him in dedicating the site, as an event of the future, perhaps even of the far distant future. The center of activity, the seat of the Church for the time being, was in Ohio, and Kirtland was the place of temporary gathering. In Kirtland too was to be erected the first temple of modern times.

In a revelation given December 27, 1832, the Lord commanded the establishment of a holy house.[7] Perhaps because their eyes were directed too steadily toward the "center place," and because the people were prone to con-

---

[4]History of the Church of Jesus Christ of Latter-day Saints, Vol. I, p. 189.

[5]See Doctrine and Covenants 57:1-4.

[6]See "History of the Church of Jesus Christ of Latter-day Saints," Vol. I, p. 199; also the "Life of Joseph Smith" by George Q. Cannon, p. 119; see also "History of Utah" by Orson F. Whitney, Vol. I, p. 91.

[7]Doctrine and Covenants sec. 88:119, 120.

template too absorbedly the glory of the future to the neglect of then present duties, compliance with the requirement to proceed at once with the erection of a temple was not prompt; and the Lord rebuked the people for their tardiness and neglect, declaring again His will that a house be reared to His name and promising success on condition of faithful effort.[8]

The Saints were aroused to great activity in the matter of erecting a temple for immediate use. A building committee was organized, and a call issued to all branches of the Church.[9] On the second day of August, 1833, the voice of the Lord was heard again respecting the matter of temple building, and while the specific requirement appears to directly apply to the temple of the future in Jackson County, Missouri, nevertheless the revelation had immediate effect in inspiring greater effort in the building of a temple at Kirtland.[10]

The Kirtland Temple was built as projected and designed, though the work was marked by an unbroken course of supreme sacrifice on the part of a poverty-laden people. Consider the words of one who was present and saw, one who helped and suffered, one who spoke from personal knowledge and keen remembrance. Eliza R. Snow, a gifted poetess and historian of modern-day Israel, has written:

"It [the Temple] was commenced in June, 1833, under the immediate direction of the Almighty, through his servant, Joseph Smith, whom he had called in his boyhood, like Samuel of old, to introduce the fulness of the everlasting gospel.

"At that time the Saints were few in number, and most of them very poor; and had it not been for the assurance that God had spoken, and had commanded that a house should be built to His name, of which He not only revealed the form, but also designated the dimensions, an attempt towards building that Temple, under the then existing circumstances, would have been, by all concerned, pronounced preposterous.

        *   *   *   *   *   *

---

[8]See Doctrine and Covenants sec. 95.

[9]See "History of the Church of Jesus Christ of Latter-day Saints," Vol. I, pp. 349, 350.

[10]Doctrine and Covenants 97:10-17.

"Its dimensions are eighty by fifty-nine feet; the walls fifty feet high, and the tower one hundred and ten feet. The two main halls are fifty-five by sixty-five feet in the inner court. The building has four vestries in front, and five rooms in the attic, which were devoted to literature and for meetings of the various quorums of the Priesthood.

"There was a peculiarity in the arrangement of the inner court which made it more than ordinarily impressive—so much so that a sense of sacred awe seemed to rest upon all who entered. Not only the Saints, but strangers also, manifested a high degree of reverential feeling. Four pulpits stood, one above another, in the center of the building, from north to south, both on the east and west ends. * * * In front of each of these two rows of pulpits was a sacrament table, for the administration of that sacred ordinance. In each corner of the court was an elevated pew for the singers—the choir being distributed into four compartments. In addition to the pulpit-curtains were others, intersecting at right angles, which divided the main ground-floor hall into four equal sections, giving to each one half of one set of pulpits.

"From the day the ground was broken for laying the foundation of the Temple, until its dedication on the 27th of March, 1836, the work was vigorously prosecuted.

"With very little capital except brain, bone, and sinew, combined with unwavering trust in God, men, women, and even children, worked with their might. While the brethren labored in their departments, the sisters were actively engaged in boarding and clothing workmen not otherwise provided for—all living as abstemiously as possible, so that every cent might be appropriated to the grand object, while their energies were stimulated by the prospect of participating in the blessing of a house built by the direction of the Most High, and accepted by Him."[11]

The corner stones had been laid July 23, 1833—just when opposition and persecution were most rife in the western branches of the Church, the very day, in fact, on which a lawless mob served notice of expulsion on the Saints in Missouri.[12] Nevertheless work on the Kirtland Temple continued without interruption, though to the eager Saints progress was all too slow. On the 7th of March, 1835, a solemn convocation was held in Kirtland, —"called for the purpose of blessing in the name of the Lord, those who have heretofore assisted in building, by their labor and other means, the House of the Lord in this place." The record gives names of those who had con-

---

[11]See "Life of Joseph, the Prophet" by Edward W. Tullidge, pp. 187-189.

[12]See "History of the Church of Jesus Christ of Latter-day Saints," Vol. I, page 400.

secrated their time, effort and means to the work.[13] Long
before the Temple was completed, parts of the structure
were used for council meetings and other gatherings of
the Priesthood. In January, 1836, a code of rules was
adopted "to be observed in the House of the Lord in
Kirtland."[14] On the 21st of the month last named a gathering of the Priesthood was held in the unfinished Temple,
on which occasion the Presiding Patriarch and the three
High Priests who composed the First Presidency of the
Church, assembled in a room by themselves and engaged
in solemn prayer. The Patriarch, Father Joseph Smith,
was anointed and blessed by the members of the First
Presidency in turn, after which he, by virtue of his office,
anointed and blessed them. Of the glorious manifestation
that followed, the prophet thus writes:

"The heavens were opened upon us, and I beheld the celestial kingdom
of God, and the glory thereof, whether in the body or out I cannot tell. I
saw the transcendent beauty of the gate through which the heirs of that
kingdom will enter, which was like unto circling flames of fire; also the
blazing throne of God, whereon was seated the Father and the Son. I saw
the beautiful streets of that kingdom, which had the appearance of being
paved with gold. * * * I saw the Twelve Apostles of the Lamb, who are
now upon the earth, who hold the keys of this last ministry, in foreign lands,
standing together in a circle, much fatigued, with their clothes tattered and
feet swollen, with their eyes cast downward, and Jesus standing in their
midst, and they did not behold Him. The Savior looked upon them and
wept.

*   *   *   *   *   *   *

"Many of my brethren who received the ordinance with me saw glorious
visions also. Angels ministered unto them as well as to myself, and the
power of the Highest rested upon us; the house was filled with the glory of
God, and we shouted 'Hosanna to God and the Lamb.' My scribe also received his anointing with us, and saw, in a vision, the armies of heaven
protecting the Saints in their return to Zion, and many things which I saw.

"The Bishop of Kirtland with his counselors, and the Bishop of Zion
with his counselors, were present with us, and received their anointings
under the hands of Father Smith, and this was confirmed by the Presidency,
and the glories of heaven were unfolded to them also.

---

[13]See "History of the Church of Jesus Christ of Latter-day Saints, Vol. II, pp.
205, 206.

[14]"History of the Church of Jesus Christ of Latter-day Saints," Vol. II, pp. 368,
369.

"We then invited the High Councilors of Kirtland and Zion into our room. * * *

"The visions of heaven were opened to them also. Some of them saw the face of the Savior, and others were ministered unto by holy angels, and the spirit of prophecy and revelation was poured out in mighty power; and loud hosannas, and glory to God in the highest, saluted the heavens, for we all communed with the heavenly host."[15]

The dedication of the Kirtland Temple occurred on Sunday, March 27, 1836. The early hour of 8 a. m. had been set as the time for opening the doors; but so intense was the interest and so eager the expectation, that long before the time hundreds had gathered about the doors. Between nine hundred and a thousand people attended the services. The congregation was seated in solemn assembly, each of the organized bodies of Priesthood with its presiding officers being in its appointed place. Singing, scripture reading, and supplication for Divine grace, were followed by brief addresses; after which the authorities of the Church as then constituted were presented to the people for acceptance or rejection, and a rising vote pledged unanimous support in every instance. The authorities of the Priesthood so sustained comprised all presiding officers from the First Presidency down to the presidency of the deacons. The dedicatory prayer was then offered by Joseph Smith, who affirms that the prayer was given to him by revelation.[16]

The question as to whether the House of the Lord was accepted as duly dedicated was put to the quorums of the Priesthood separately and to the congregation as a whole; the vote in the affirmative was unanimous. The Lord's Supper was then administered, and many of the elders bore solemn testimony to the divinity of the Gospel as restored. The prophet's journal continues:

"President Frederick G. Williams arose and testified that while President Rigdon was making his first prayer, an angel entered the window and took his seat between Father Smith and himself, and remained there during the

---

[15]"History of the Church of Jesus Christ of Latter-day Saints," Vol. II, pp. 380-382.

[16]See Doctrine and Covenants, sec. 109, where the prayer appears in full.

prayer. President David Whitmer also saw angels in the house. President Hyrum Smith made some appropriate remarks congratulating those who had endured so many toils and privations to build the house. President Rigdon then made a few appropriate closing remarks, and a short prayer, at the close of which we sealed the proceedings of the day by shouting 'Hosanna, Hosanna, Hosanna to God and the Lamb,' three times, sealing it each time with 'Amen, Amen, and Amen.' "[17]

In the evening of the day of dedication another meeting was held; this, however, was attended by officers of the Church only. The record as written by the prophet reads:

"I met the quorums in the evening and instructed them respecting the ordinance of washing of feet, which they were to attend to on Wednesday following; and gave them instructions in relation to the spirit of prophecy.

* * *

"Brother George A. Smith arose and began to prophesy, when a noise was heard like the sound of a rushing, mighty wind, which filled the Temple, and all the congregation simultaneously arose, being moved upon by an invisible power; many began to speak in tongues and prophesy; others saw glorious visions; and I beheld the Temple was filled with angels, which fact I declared to the congregation. The people of the neighborhood came running together (hearing an unusual sound within, and seeing a bright light like a pillar of fire resting upon the Temple), and were astonished at what was taking place. This continued until the meeting closed at 11 p. m."[18]

On the Thursday following that eventful Sabbath, another solemn assembly convened in the Temple, including as before the general authorities of the Church, and in addition such members as had not been able to secure admission on the earlier day. The services were in a measure a repetition of the proceedings on the first occasion; the dedicatory prayer was read, appropriate music was rendered and addresses were delivered.

That the building was in truth a Temple, a holy structure accepted by Him to whose name it had been reared, that it was veritably a House of the Lord, had been attested by the visitation of heavenly beings, and by

---

[17]"History of the Church of Jesus Christ of Latter-day Saints," Vol. II, pp. 427, 428.

[18]"History of the Church of Jesus Christ of Latter-day Saints," Vol. II, p. 428.

Divine manifestations surpassing all expectation, as witnessed on the evening of the dedication day. On the next Sabbath, April 3, 1836, visitations and manifestations of yet greater import were received. At the afternoon service the Lord's Supper was administered, after which, the prophet and his counselor, Oliver Cowdery, retired to the stand reserved for the presiding officers of the Melchisedek Priesthood,—which was enclosed by the curtains or veils lowered for the occasion. They solemnly testify that then and there did the Lord Jesus Christ reveal Himself. Afterward, other heavenly personages ministered unto them, each delivering or bestowing the particular authority with which he was specially invested. The testimony of Joseph Smith and Oliver Cowdery is as follows:

"The veil was taken from our minds, and the eyes of our understanding were opened.

"We saw the Lord standing upon the breast-work of the pulpit, before us, and under his feet was a paved work of pure gold in color like amber.

"His eyes were as a flame of fire, the hair of his head was white like the pure snow, his countenance shone above the brightness of the sun, and his voice was as the sound of the rushing of great waters, even the voice of Jehovah, saying—

"I am the first and the last, I am he who liveth, I am he who was slain, I am your advocate with the Father.

"Behold, your sins are forgiven you, you are clean before me, therefore lift up your heads and rejoice,

"Let the hearts of your brethren rejoice, and let the hearts of all my people rejoice, who have, with their might, built this house to my name,

"For behold, I have accepted this house, and my name shall be here, and I will manifest myself to my people in mercy in this house,

"Yea, I will appear unto my servants, and speak unto them with mine own voice, if my people will keep my commandments, and do not pollute this holy house.

"Yea, the hearts of thousands and tens of thousands shall greatly rejoice in consequence of the blessings which shall be poured out, and the endowment with which my servants have been endowed in this house;

"And the fame of this house shall spread to foreign lands, and this is the beginning of the blessing which shall be poured out upon the heads of my people. Even so. Amen.

"After this vision closed, the heavens were again opened unto us, and Moses appeared before us, and committed unto us the keys of the gathering of Israel from the four parts of the earth, and the leading of the ten tribes from the land of the north.

"After this, Elias appeared, and committed the dispensation of the gospel of Abraham, saying, that in us, and our seed, all generations after us should be blessed.

"After this vision had closed, another great and glorious vision burst upon us, for Elijah the prophet, who was taken to heaven without tasting death, stood before us, and said—

"Behold, the time has fully come, which was spoken of by the mouth of Malachi, testifying that he (Elijah) should be sent before the great and dreadful day of the Lord come,

"To turn the hearts of the fathers to the children, and the children to the fathers, lest the whole earth be smitten with a curse.

"Therefore the keys of this dispensation are committed into your hands, and by this ye may know that the great and dreadful day of the Lord is near, even at the doors."[19]

The erection of the Temple at Kirtland seemed to increase the hostile opposition to which the Church had been subjected since its organization; and persecution soon became so violent that all of the Saints who could dispose of their property and leave did so and joined their fellow religionists in Missouri. Within two years following the dedication, a general exodus of the Saints had taken place, and the Temple soon fell into the hands of the persecutors. The building is yet standing, and serves the purposes of an ordinary meeting-house for an obscure sect that manifests no visible activity in temple building, nor apparent belief in the sacred ordinances for which temples are erected. The people whose sacrifice and suffering reared the structure no longer assert claims of ownership. What was once the Temple of God, in which the Lord Jesus appeared in person, has become but a house,—a building whose sole claim to distinction among the innumerable structures built by man, lies in its wondrous past.

Temple Site At Far West, Missouri

From Ohio the Church migrated westward, and gathering-centers were established in Missouri, principally in

---

[19]Doctrine and Covenants sec. 110. See also "History of the Church of Jesus Christ of Latter-day Saints, Vol. II, pp. 434-436.

Jackson, Clay, and Caldwell counties. No time was lost in useless grieving over the enforced abandonment of the Temple at Kirtland. Even at that early day, but seven years after the organization of the Church, the people had come to regard persecution as an inevitable incident of their religion, and spoliation as their heritage. Resolutely they went to work in preparation for another temple, and a site was chosen at Far West, Caldwell County, Missouri. On the 5th of August, 1837, "the Presidency, High Council, and all the authorities of the Church in Missouri, assembled in council at Far West, and unanimously resolved to go on moderately and build a house unto the name of the Lord in Far West, as they had means."[20] On the 26th of April, 1838, a revelation was received directing the time and manner of beginning the work:

"Let the city, Far West, be a holy and consecrated land unto me, and it shall be called most holy, for the ground upon which thou standest is holy; therefore I command you to build an house unto me, for the gathering together of my Saints, that they may worship me; and let there be a beginning of this work, and a foundation, and a preparatory work, this following summer; and let the beginning be made on the fourth day of July next, and from that time forth let my people labor diligently to build an house unto my name, and in one year from this day let them re-commence laying the foundation of my house."[21]

On the fourth day of July, 1838, the corner stones were laid to the accompaniment of military parade and solemn procession.[22] It is plain from the revelation of April 26, 1838, that even the laying of the foundation of this proposed temple would not proceed uninterruptedly. The corner stones were placed on July 4th as had been commanded, and on the 8th another mention of the site is made with a specific requirement respecting the future work of the apostles. "Let them take leave of my

---

[20]"History of the Church of Jesus Christ of Latter-day Saints," Vol. II, p. 505.
[21]Doctrine and Covenants sec. 115:7-11.
[22]See "History of the Church of Jesus Christ of Latter-day Saints," Vol. III, pp. 41, 42.

Saints in the city of Far West, on the 26th day of April next, on the building spot of my house, saith the Lord."[23] The months following were marked by persecution and violence; hostile opponents declared that the commission should never be fulfilled. History attests, however, that on the 26th day of April, 1839, the apostles, several other officers of the Church, and a number of the members, assembled in the early hours of the morning, sang their hymns, delivered their exhortations, and began the work of laying the foundation stones. On the occasion two vacancies in the Council of the Twelve were filled by the ordination of Wilford Woodruff and George A. Smith, whose nominations had previously been voted upon. The apostles then took leave of the others present and proceeded on their missions. Almost immediately after the events last recorded, the Saints were forced to abandon their homes in Missouri.

The Latter-day Saints regard the long delay in the erection of temples on the dedicated sites in Missouri as largely the result of their own defection, neglect, and disobedience to the word of the Lord, in consequence of which their enemies were permitted to prevail. When, in 1834, the Saints in Missouri were subject to cruel persecution, their fellow religionists in the eastern branches of the Church were directed to go to their aid, and to send men with money to purchase the lands adjacent to the chosen sites, and moreover to consecrate their possessions to the redemption of Zion. To these requirements there was unsatisfactory response; and even in Zion's Camp, as the body of between one hundred and fifty and two hundred men who set out from Ohio for Missouri as directed, was called, there was much disaffection, murmuring, and lack of faith. On June 22, 1834, the Lord said through Joseph, the prophet:

"Behold, I say unto you, were it not for the transgressions of my people,

---

[23]Doctrine and Covenants 118:5.

speaking concerning the Church and not individuals, they might have been redeemed even now."[24]

Thus, through their own transgressions the Saints were hindered in the work required at their hands, and the harvest of blessings predicated upon this specific labor, has not yet ripened.

The Nauvoo Temple

After their expulsion from Missouri, the "Mormon" refugees turned their faces toward the east, crossed the Mississippi and established themselves in and about the obscure village of Commerce, Hancock County, Illinois. The people demonstrated again their marvelous recuperative power, and without delay or hesitation set about establishing new homes and a temple. By the early part of June, 1839, dwellings were in course of construction, and soon the hamlet was transformed into a city. To this new abiding place the Saints gave the name Nauvoo,— which to them meant all that the name City Beautiful could convey. It was situated but a few miles from Quincy, in a bend of the majestic river, giving the town three water fronts. It seemed to nestle there as if the Father of Waters was encircling it with his mighty arm.[25]

The best and most suitable site within the limits of the city as planned was selected, purchased, and duly set apart as the temple ground. The corner stones were laid April 6, 1841—the day on which the Church entered upon the twelfth year of its troubled yet progressive career. In the ceremonial of the day the Nauvoo Legion—a body of militia organized under the laws of Illinois,—took a conspicuous part, and two volunteer companies from Iowa Territory participated.[26] The south-east corner-stone was placed in position under the immediate direction of the

---

[24]Doctrine and Covenants 105:2; see also 103:23, and compare 105:8, 9; the two sections should be read in full.

[25]See "The Story of Mormonism" by the author, p. 35.

[26]See Joseph Smith's Journal, April 6, 1841; see "History of the Church of Jesus Christ of Latter-day Saints," Vol. IV, pp. 327-329.

First Presidency, and over it the President pronounced the following benediction:

"This principal corner-stone in representation of the First Presidency, is now duly laid in honor of the Great God; and, may it there remain until the whole fabric is completed; and may the same be accomplished speedily; that the Saints may have a place to worship God, and the Son of Man have where to lay His head."

Sidney Rigdon of the First Presidency then pronounced the following:

"May the persons employed in the erection of this house be preserved from all harm while engaged in its contruction, till the whole is completed, in the name of the Father, and of the Son, and of the Holy Ghost. Even so. Amen."[27]

After a recess of one hour, the congregation re-assembled and the remaining corner stones were laid in the order indicated. The south-west corner-stone was laid under the direction of the High Priests' organization, and the president pronounced the following:

"The second corner-stone of the temple now building by The Church of Jesus Christ of Latter-day Saints, in honor of the Great God, is duly laid, and may the same unanimity that has been manifested on this occasion continue till the whole is completed; that peace may rest upon it to the laying of the top-stone thereof, and the turning of the key thereof; that the Saints may participate in the blessings of Israel's God, within its walls, and the glory of God rest upon the same. Amen."

The north-west corner-stone was then lowered to its place under the superintendency of the High Council, with a benediction by Elias Higbee, as follows:

"The third corner-stone is now duly laid; may this stone be a firm support to the building that the whole may be completed as before proposed."

The stone at the north-east corner was laid by the Bishops, and Bishop Whitney pronounced the following:

"The fourth and last corner-stone, expressive of the Lesser Priesthood, is now duly laid, and may the blessings before pronounced, with all others desirable, rest upon the same forever. Amen."[28]

---

[27]"History of the Church of Jesus Christ of Latter-day Saints," Vol. IV, p. 329.
[28]See "History of the Church of Jesus Christ of Latter-day Saints," Vol. IV, p. 330.

Regarding the proper order of procedure in temple building, the prophet Joseph Smith wrote as follows in connection with the laying of the corner-stones at Nauvoo:

"If the strict order of the Priesthood were carried out in the building of temples, the first stone would be laid at the south-east corner, by the First Presidency of the Church. The south-west corner should be laid next; the third, or north-west corner next; and the fourth, or north-east corner last. The First Presidency should lay the south-east corner stone and dictate who are the proper persons to lay the other corner stones.

"If a temple is built at a distance, and the First Presidency are not present, then the Quorum of the Twelve Apostles are the persons to dictate the order for that temple; and in the absence of the Twelve Apostles, then the Presidency of the Stake will lay the south-east corner stone; the Melchisedek Priesthood laying the corner stones on the east side of the temple, and the Lesser Priesthood those on the west side."[29]

The Nauvoo Temple was erected by the people, who contributed liberally both through tithes and freewill offerings of money and labor. Most of the work was done by men who tithed themselves as to time, and devoted their energies in the proportion of at least one day in ten to labor on the Temple.[30]

The work progressed slowly but without marked interruption; and this fact becomes surprising when the many unfavorable conditions are considered. The Saints had found but temporary respite from persecution; and as the Temple rose opposition increased.[31]

Interest had been aroused and energy stimulated in temple matters, through a revelation by which the Lord made known His will and the provisions of heavenly law concerning the sacred ordinance of baptism for the dead. It will be remembered that no provision for this rite had been made in the Kirtland Temple, for at the time of the erection of that structure nothing thereto pertaining had

---

[29]"History of the Church of Jesus Christ of Latter-day Saints," Vol. IV, p. 331.

[30]See "History of the Church of Jesus Christ of Latter-day Saints," Vol. IV, p. 517.

[31]In the "Times and Seasons" of May 2, 1842, appeared an editorial dealing with the progress of work on the Temple, and this writing has been incorporated in the prophet's journal. See "History of the Church of Jesus Christ of Latter-day Saints," Vol. V, pp. 608-610.

been revealed in modern times. On January 19, 1841, the Lord had spoken through the prophet, explaining the need of a holy house with its baptistry, largely and specifically for the benefit of the dead.[32] So eager were the Saints to render vicarious service in behalf of their dead, that before the temple walls were much above the basement level, the construction of a font was in progress. On November 8, 1841, the font was ready for dedication, and the ceremony was performed by the prophet himself. Thus, long before the Temple was finished, ordinance work was in progress within its precincts, the font being enclosed by temporary walls. A description written by Joseph Smith follows:

"The baptismal font is situated in the center of the basement room, under the main hall of the Temple; it is constructed of pine timber, and put together of staves tongued and grooved, oval shaped, sixteen feet long east and west, and twelve feet wide, seven feet high from the foundation, the basin four feet deep; the moulding of the cap and base are formed of beautiful carved work in antique style. The sides are finished with panel work. A flight of stairs in the north and south sides lead up and down into the basin, guarded by side railing.

"The font stands upon twelve oxen, four on each side, and two at each end, their heads, shoulders, and fore-legs projecting out from under the font; they are carved out of pine plank, glued together, and copied after the most beautiful five-year-old steer that could be found in the country, and they are an excellent striking likeness of the original; the horns were formed after the most perfect horn that could be procured.

"The oxen and ornamental mouldings of the font were carved by Elder Elijah Fordham, from the city of New York, which occupied eight months of time. The font was enclosed by a temporary frame building sided up with split oak clapboards, with a roof of the same material, and was so low that the timbers of the first story [of the Temple] were laid above it. The water was supplied from a well thirty feet deep in the east end of the basement."[33]

Beside the baptistry, other parts of the Temple were prepared for temporary occupancy while yet work on the walls was in progress, and on Sunday, October 30, 1842, a general assembly was convened therein. This is recorded

---

[32]See Doctrine and Covenants 124:28-31. For an extended extract see pages 73-74 of this book.

[33]"History of the Church of Jesus Christ of Latter-day Saints," Vol. IV, pp. 446, 447.

as the first meeting held in the Temple.[34] At later dates other meetings were held within the unfinished structure; and notwithstanding the violent opposition of foes without, and yet more effective hindrances caused by the apostate spirit manifested by a few within the Church, the work was vigorously prosecuted.

It was not permitted that Joseph Smith the prophet, nor Hyrum Smith, one-time counselor in the First Presidency and later Patriarch of the Church, should live to see the completion of the building. On the 27th of June, 1844, these men of God fell victims of the bullets of assassins, at Carthage, Illinois.[35] Though heavy the blow and cruel the affliction suffered by the Saints in the martyrdom of their leaders, the work of the Church showed scarcely perceptible hindrance. Within two weeks after the dread event, construction on the Temple was resumed, and from that time till the completion the work was prosecuted with increased vigor and determination. A few months prior to his martyrdom, Patriarch Hyrum Smith, acting as one of the Temple Committee, had made a call on the women of the Church, asking from them a weekly subscription of one cent apiece, the money to be used in purchasing material, particularly glass and nails, for the Temple. It is recorded that "there was soon a great anxiety manifest among the sisters to pay their portion, and nearly all paid a year's subscription in advance."[36]

The Church archives for 1844 and 1845 contain numerous references to the progress of the work. On the 24th of May, 1845, the capstone was laid, with impressive ceremony, under the direction of President Brigham Young and other members of the Council of the Twelve Apostles, beside whom there were in attendance many general and local authorities of the Church. After the top-stone had been duly laid, the President said:

[34]"History of the Church of Jesus Christ of Latter-day Saints," Vol. V, p. 182.

[35]See "History of the Church of Jesus Christ of Latter-day Saints," Vol. VI, pp. 612-631; also Doctrine and Covenants, sec. 135.

[36]"Historical Record," Salt Lake City, June, 1889, Vol. VIII, pp. 865, 866.

"The last stone is laid upon the Temple, and I pray the Almighty in the name of Jesus to defend us in this place, and sustain us until the Temple is finished and we have all got our endowments."[37]

Then followed the solemn and sacred shout: "Hosanna! Hosanna! Hosanna! To God and the Lamb! Amen! Amen! and Amen!" This was repeated a second and a third time; and in conclusion the President said: "So let it be, thou Lord Almighty."[38]

The somber clouds of persecution were gathering and thickening about the devoted people. Under counsel from their leaders the people prepared once again to leave their homes; and this time they resolved to go beyond the boundaries of civilization. A general exodus was imminent; and as early as February, 1846, this had begun. Most of the Saints, however, remained for a short time; and with these the completion of the Temple was the main purpose and object of life. Though they knew the sacred edifice would soon be abandoned, they labored diligently to complete it, even to the smallest detail.

By October, 1845, the building was so well advanced that large assemblies therein were possible. The general autumnal conference of the Church for that year was held within the walls; and the congregation present on October 5th numbered fully five thousand souls. During December, 1845, and the early months of 1846, many of the Saints received their blessings and endowments in the Temple, for which purpose parts of the structure had been duly consecrated; but not until the end of April was the building as a whole ready for dedication.

The Nauvoo Temple was constructed for the most part of a close-grained, light-gray limestone, a material at once hard and durable, yet easily tooled, and therefore readily adapted to ornamental finish. The entire building was one hundred and twenty-eight feet by eighty-eight feet, and sixty-five feet high in the clear. The top of the

---

[37]See "Historical Record," Salt Lake City, June, 1889, Vol. VII, p. 870.
[38]"Historical Record," Vol. VII, p. 870.

spire was one hundred and sixty-five feet above the ground and bore the figure of a flying herald sounding a trumpet. The plan of construction was that of a solid and stable four-walled building, two and a half stories high, with a hexagonal tower at the front rising in four terraces and a dome. Over the front center door, and immediately beneath the base of the tower, appeared an inscription:

THE HOUSE OF THE LORD

Built by the Church of Jesus Christ of Latter-day Saints
Holiness to the Lord

On the outside were thirty pilasters, nine on each side and six at each end. At its base each pilaster presented in hewn relief the crescent moon, and ended above in a capital of cut stone depicting the face of the sun allegorically featured, with a pair of hands holding horns. Above the capitals was a frieze or cornice in which appeared thirty star-stones. In the late hours of April 30, 1846, the Temple was privately, yet officially, dedicated, in the presence of such general authorities of the Church as could be convened. President Joseph Young of the First Council of Seventy offered the dedicatory prayer. The semi-private character of the dedication was due to the thought that possibly there would be interference in a public ceremony, so active was the spirit of intolerance and persecution. On the day following, that is to say May 1, 1846, services of a general and public nature were held in the Temple, under the direction of Elders Orson Hyde and Wilford Woodruff of the Council of the Twelve Apostles.

The Saints had met the requirement made of them by the Lord in the building of another House to His name. Ordinance work continued a few months more, even though the exodus of the people was in progress. In

September, 1846, the Nauvoo Temple was in possession
of the mob; and the people whose energy and substance,
whose sweat and blood had been spent in its rearing,
were driven into the wilderness or slain. For two years
the once hallowed structure stood as an abandoned building; then on November 19, 1848, it fell a prey to the
wanton act of an incendiary. After the conflagration,
only blackened walls remained where once had stood so
stately a sanctuary. Strange to say, an attempt was
made by the Icarians, a local organization, to rebuild on
the ruins, the professed intent being to provide for a
school; but while the work was in its early stages a tornado demolished the greater part of the walls. This
occurred on May 27, 1850. What remained of the Temple has been taken away as souvenirs or used as building
material for other structures. Stones of the Temple have
been carried into most of the states of the Union and
beyond the seas, but upon the site where once stood the
House of the Lord not one stone is left upon another.
Before the demolition of the Nauvoo Temple was complete, the Latter-day Saints had established themselves
in the vales of Utah, and were already preparing to build
another and a greater sanctuary to the name and service
of their God.

CHAPTER VI

The Great Temple at Salt Lake City, Utah Historical

Where in 1847 nought but a wilderness of sagebrush and sunflowers stretched from the Wasatch barrier westward toward the shores of the great salt sea, now appears a stately city, even as was then foreseen in prophetic vision. On the site selected but four days after the advent of the pioneer band of "Mormon" colonizers, stands a massive structure, dedicated to the name of the Most High. It is at once an object of wonder and admiration to the visitor, and a subject of sanctifying joy and righteous pride to the people whose sacrifice and effort have given it being.

On the east center tower appears an inscription, the letters deep-cut in stone and lined with gold:

Holiness to the Lord

THE HOUSE OF THE LORD

Built by the Church of Jesus Christ of Latter-day Saints

Commenced April 6, 1853

Completed April 6, 1893

In one of the upper rooms a splendid art window presents an excellent view of the completed building, with side inscriptions as follows:

Corner stone laid April 6, 1853, by
President Brigham Young

Assisted by his Counselors
Heber C. Kimball, Willard Richards

Dedicated April 6, 1893, by
President Wilford Woodruff
Assisted by his Counselors
George Q. Cannon, Joseph F. Smith

These memorial tablets in stone and jeweled glass give the essentials as to dates in the history of the great Temple; some further data, however, may be of interest to the reader.

The Temple Block, a square of ten acres, was laid off in 1847, and is today one of the choicest sites within the city. At the General Conference of the Church held in April, 1851, an official vote was taken whereby the erection of the Temple was authorized. Be it remembered that this action was that of a people despoiled and in poverty, struggling with the unsubdued desert, the while menaced by hostile savages; and that at the time the entire population of Utah did not exceed thirty thousand souls, of whom fewer than five thousand were living within the area of the prospective city. A general epistle issued by the First Presidency of the Church, April 7, 1851, is instructive in this connection:

"A railroad has been chartered to extend from the Temple Block in this city to the stone quarry and mountain on the east, for the conveyance of building materials; the construction to commence immediately. * * * We contemplate laying a wall around the Temple Block this season, preparatory to laying the foundation of a Temple the year following; and this we will be sure to do, if all the Saints shall prove themselves as ready to pay their tithing, and sacrifice and consecrate of their substance, as freely as we will; and if the Saints do not pay their tithing, we can neither build nor prepare for building; and if there shall be no Temple built, the Saints can have no endowments, and if they do not receive their endowments, they can never attain unto that salvation they are anxiously looking for."[1]

It had been decided to surround the entire block by a

---

[1]See Contributor, Vol. XIV: No. 6; April, 1893; p. 248.

substantial wall. The beginning of work on this enclosure was deferred through lack of material and men until August 3, 1852; but from that date it progressed with fair rapidity, and on May 23, 1857, the wall was finished, practically as it now stands. It extends a full city block, —one eighth of a mile in each of its four directions; and, it is interesting to note, these dimensions are practically the same as those which, according to Josephus, enclosed the grounds on which stood the Temple of Herod.[2] The wall has a base of cut stone,—a red sandstone from the mountains on the east; the base is four feet in height, and supports courses of adobes which extend ten feet higher; then follows a coping of red sandstone one foot in thickness, giving the wall a total height of fifteen feet. The adobes are hidden by a durable dressing of cement. Passage to and from the square is provided for by large gates in the center of each of the four sides. When this wall was built, City Creek ran through Temple Block; the stream is now confined to a straight channel north of the block; and the arches under which the stream once passed may be seen in the base of the wall both on the east and west sides.

The construction of the wall, in itself a great and costly undertaking for people situated as were its builders, was but an incident to the greater labor of erecting the Temple. Interest in the work was never allowed to flag; it was the theme of both poet and preacher, and the ever-pressing duty was kept in public view. The people were given to understand that the commission to build the Lord's House was theirs, and not that of their leaders alone.

The site was dedicated and ground first broken for the foundation February 14, 1853. The occasion was a notable one, and was observed by the Saints as a day of general rejoicing. Between the date of breaking ground

---

[2]See Josephus, Antiquities of the Jews, Book XV, 11:3.

and the time of the next succeeding conference of the Church, preparations for the laying of the corner-stones were carried on with determination and vigor. The glad event occurred on the 6th of April, 1853,—the twenty-third anniversary of the organization of the Church,—and was celebrated by the people with such evidences of thanksgiving and genuine joy as assured their devotion to the work so auspiciously begun. Civic and military bodies took part; there were processions with bands of music, and solemn services with prayer. The mayor of the city was marshal of the day; the city police served as a guard of honor, and the territorial militia marched with the congregation of the Saints. The placing of the corner-stones was celebrated as an accomplished triumph, though but a beginning.

Let it not be imagined that the work was carried through without hindrance or set-back. The foundation was commenced at the south-east corner June 16, 1853, and was completed July 23, 1855. A course of rubble was laid on the actual foundation and this was succeeded by courses of flagstone. The work had gone forward but slowly, when, in 1857, a serious interruption occurred. At that time the people prepared to abandon their homes, temporarily at least, and seek an abiding place elsewhere in the desert. The cause of the portending exodus was the approach of an armed force sent by the United States government to subdue an alleged rebellion in Utah. This military movement had been ordered through an utter misunderstanding of facts, based on vicious misrepresentation. The coming of the soldiery had been heralded with dire threats of violence; and while the people knew themselves innocent of any act of disloyalty toward the government or its officers, they had not forgotten the harrowing scenes of organized persecution in Missouri and Illinois, due to misapprehension, and they preferred the uncertainties of the desert to the dread alternative of a possible repetition of the past. In the saddening preparations for departure, the people carefully covered the foundation work on the site of the Temple; excavations were re-filled, and every vestige of masonry was obscured. At that time no part of the foundation had been carried above ground-level. When the covering-up process was complete, the site showed nothing more attractive than a remote resemblance to the barren stretch of a roughly plowed field.

It is pleasing to note that a peaceable adjustment between the army and the people was effected. The Saints returned to their homes; and the soldiers established a camp,—afterward to become a post,—at a distance of forty miles from the city.[3]

The interruption in building operations thus occasioned was followed by a short period of comparative inactivity, after the return of the people. The foundations were uncovered; but, before the resumption of stone-laying, it was found that the rubble overlying the foundation proper and immediately under the flagstone layers seemed to have less stability than was required; and straightway both flagging and rubble were removed. Stone of best quality was substituted, and the work of actual construction was continued with renewed energy. The reconstruction was a work of years.

The temple enclosure was for a brief period the communal center of mechanical industry,—the one great work-shop of the intermountain commonwealth. The Church had established there its public works, comprising a power plant in which the energy of City Creek was harnessed to the wheel, air-blast equipment, iron foundry, and machine shops for the working of both wood and metal.[4] Much of the work here done had no connection

---

[3]See the author's "The Story of Mormonism," pp. 63-81.

[4]For description of this feature of early enterprise, see an admirable article, "The Salt Lake Temple," by James H. Anderson, in "The Contributor," Vol. XIV, No. 6, April, 1893. The article gives much detailed information concerning the work of erecting the Great Temple.

with the extensive building operations on Temple Block.

Beside the interruptions and delays already noted, other hindrances were inevitable, and, under the best of conditions progress could be but slow. Not until years after the "move" incident to the entrance of the federal soldiery, had the material of the main structure been decided upon. As far back as the October conference of 1852 the question of material had been considered. Oolite from the quarries in Sanpete County, red sandstone from the hills near-by, adobes with intermixed pebbles,—each had been suggested; and the matter was brought to vote, though it must be admitted, the question presented was somewhat indefinite in form. At the forenoon session of the conference on October 9, 1852, President Heber C. Kimball submitted the question: "Shall we have the Temple built of stone from Red Butte, adobes, rock, or the best stone the mountains afford?" In reply a resolution was adopted by unanimous vote to the effect "that we build a Temple of the best materials that can be obtained in the mountains of North America, and that the Presidency dictate where the stone and other materials shall be obtained." The action is significant as showing the faith, reliance, and determination of the people. The Temple they were about to rear should be in every particular the best the people could produce. This modern House of the Lord was to be no temporary structure, nor of small proportions, nor of poor material, nor of mean or inadequate design. It was known at the outset that the building could not be finished for many a long year, for decades, perhaps, and by that time this colony would have become a commonwealth, the few would have grown to a multitude of souls. The Temple was to be worthy of the great future. Sandstone, oolite, adobe blocks, each and all were considered, and in turn rejected. The decision was to this effect,—the walls should be of solid granite. An enormous deposit of this durable stone had been discovered in the Cottonwood canyons, twenty miles to the south-east, and to those faith-impelled people it was enough to know that suitable material was available. At whatever cost of toil and sacrifice, at whatever toll of self-denial and suffering, it should be procured.

The so-called "temple granite" is in reality a syenite, and occurs as an immense laccolith in the Cottonwood section of the Wasatch. The erosion of long ages had cut deep canyons through the eruptive mass; and glaciers, descending with irresistible force, had dislodged and transported countless boulders, many of them of colossal size. These isolated blocks, known as erratics, furnished the supply of building stone; it was not found necessary to quarry into the granite mountain-mass in place. In the canyon the boulders were divided mostly by the use of hand-drills and wedges, though low power explosives were used to a small extent. The rough blocks were conveyed at first by ox-teams; four yoke were required for each block, and every trip was a labored journey of three or four days. A canal for the conveyance of the rock by water was projected, and, indeed, work thereon was begun, but the plan was abandoned as the prospect of railroad transportation became more certain.

The plan of the building was given by Brigham Young, President of the Church, and the structural details were worked out under his direction by the Church architect—Truman O. Angell. A description by the latter was published as early as 1854, both in Utah[5] and abroad[6] For convenience of comparison with the details of actual construction as now appear, this early announcement of what was then to be is here reproduced:

"The Temple Block is forty rods square, the lines running north and south, east and west, and contains ten acres. The center of the Temple is

[5]See "Deseret News," Salt Lake City, August 17, 1854.

[6]See "Millennial Star," Liverpool, Vol. 16, p. 753. "The Illustrated London News" of June 13, 1857, contains an article, "Mormon Temple in Salt Lake City," in which are given many specifications of construction. In connection with the text appears a large woodcut of the great building in perspective; and this picture is a true representation of the finished structure except as to details of spires and finials.

one hundred and fifty-six feet six inches due west from the center of the east line of the block. The length of said House, east and west, is one hundred and eighty-six and a half feet, including towers, and the width ninety-nine feet. On the east end there are three towers, as also on the west. Draw a line north and south one hundred and eighteen and a half feet through the center of the towers, and you have the north and south extent of ground plan, including pedestal.

"We depress into the earth, at the east end, to the depth of sixteen feet, and enlarge all around beyond the lines of wall three feet for a footing.

"The north and south walls are eight feet thick, clear of pedestal; they stand upon a footing of sixteen feet wall, on its bearing, which slopes three feet on each side to the height of seven and a half feet. The footing of the towers rises to the same height as the side, and is one solid piece of masonry of rough ashlars, laid in good lime mortar.

"The basement of the main building is divided into many rooms by walls, all having footings. The line of the basement floor is six inches above the top of the footing. From the tower on the east to the tower on the west, the face of the earth slopes six feet; four inches above the earth on the east line, begins a promenade walk, from eleven to twenty-two feet wide, around the entire building, and approached by stone steps on all sides.

"There are four towers on the four corners of the building, each starting from their footing, of twenty-six feet square; these continue sixteen and a half feet and come to the line of the base string course, which is eight feet above the promenade walk. At this point the towers are reduced to twenty-five feet square; they then continue to the height of thirty-eight feet, or the height of the second string course. At this point they are reduced to twenty-three feet square; they then continue thirty-eight feet high, to the third string course. The string courses continue all around the building, except when separated by buttresses. These string courses are massive mouldings from solid blocks of stone.

"The two east towers then rise twenty-five feet to a string course, or cornice. The two west towers rise nineteen feet and come to their string course or cornice. The four towers then rise nine feet to the top of battlements. These towers are cylindrical, having seventeen feet diameter inside, within which stairs ascend around a solid column four feet in diameter, allowing landings at the various sections of the building. These towers have each five ornamental windows on two sides, above the basement. The two center towers occupy the center of the east and west ends of the building, starting from their footings thirty-one feet square, and break off in sections in line with the corner towers to the height of the third string course. The east center tower then rises forty feet to the top of battlements; the west center tower rises thirty-four feet to the top of battlements. All the towers have spires, the details of which are not decided on.

"All these towers, at their corners, have octagon turrets, terminated by octagon pinnacles five feet diameter at base, four feet at first story, and three feet from there up. There are also on each side of these towers two buttresses, except when they come in contact with the body of the main building. The top of these buttresses show forty-eight in number, and

The St. George Temple

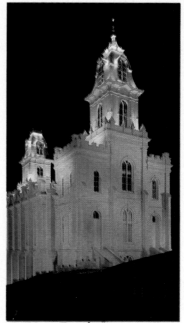

The Logan Temple

The Manti Temple

The Salt Lake Temple

The Hawaii Temple

The Alberta Temple

The Arizona Temple

The Idaho Falls Temple

The Los Angeles Temple

The Swiss Temple

The New Zealand Temple

The London Temple

The Oakland Temple

The Ogden Temple

The Provo Temple

The Washington D.C. Temple

Architect's rendering of the
Sao Paulo Temple

Architect's rendering of the Tokyo Temple

Baptismal Font, Salt Lake Temple

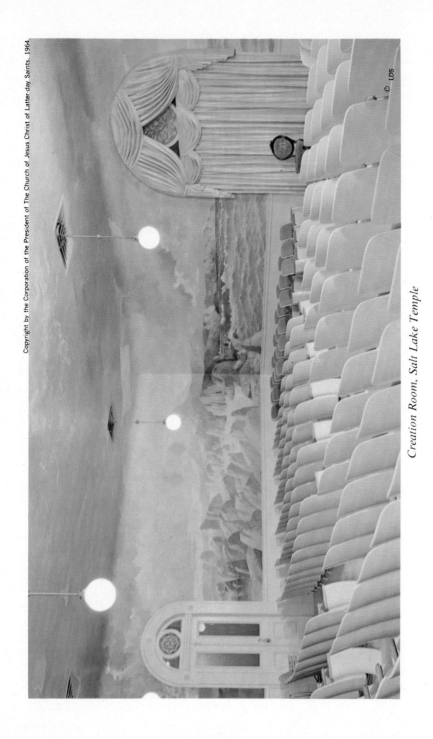

© LDS

Creation Room, Salt Lake Temple

Garden Room, St. George Temple

Scene from the Garden Room, Los Angeles Temple

World Room, Salt Lake Temple

Terrestrial Room, Salt Lake Temple

Celestial Room, Salt Lake Temple

Sealing Room in the Manti Temple

Council Room in the Salt Lake Temple, where the First Presidency and the Council of the Twelve meet each week

Assembly Room in the Salt Lake Temple, where special meetings are held

stand upon pedestals. The space between the buttresses and turrets is two feet at first story. On the front of two center towers are two large windows, each thirty-two feet high, one above the other, neatly prepared for that place.

"On the two west corner towers, and on the west end, a few feet below the top of battlements, may be seen in bold or alto relievo, the great dipper, or Ursa Major, with the pointers ranging nearly towards the North Star. (Moral, the lost may find themselves by the Priesthood.)

"I will now glance at the main body of the House. I have before stated that the basement was divided into many rooms. The center one is arranged for a baptismal font, and is fifty-seven feet long by thirty-five feet wide, separated from the main wall by four rooms, two on each side, nineteen feet long by twelve wide. On the east and west sides of these rooms are four passages twelve feet wide; these lead to and from by outside doors, two on the north and two on the south. Further east and west from these passages are four more rooms, two at each end, twenty-eight feet wide by thirty-eight and one-half long. These and their walls occupy the basement. All the walls start off their footings, and rise sixteen and one-half feet, and there stop with ground ceiling.

"We are now up to the line of the base string course, eight feet above the promenade, or steps rising to the Temple, which terminates the cope of pedestal, and to the first floor of said House. This room is joined to the outer courts, these courts being the width between towers, sixteen feet by nine in the clear. We ascend to the floors of these courts (they being on a line with first floor of main house) by four flights of stone steps nine and one-half feet wide, arranged in the basement work; the first step ranging to the outer line of towers. From these courts doors admit to any part of the building.

"The size of the first large room is one hundred and twenty feet long by eighty feet wide; the height reaches nearly to the second string course. The room is arched over in the center with an elliptical arch which drops at its flank ten feet, and has thirty-eight feet span. The side ceilings have one-fourth elliptical arches which start from the side walls of the main building, sixteen feet high, and terminate at the capitals of the columns or foot of center arch, at the height of twenty-four feet. The columns obtain their bearings direct from the footings of said house; these columns extend up to support the floor above.

"The outside walls of this story are seven feet thick. The space from the termination of the foot of the center arch to the outer wall, is divided into sixteen compartments, eight on each side, making rooms fourteen feet by fourteen, clear of partitions, and ten feet high, leaving a passage six feet wide next to each flank of center arch, which is approached from the ends, These rooms are each lighted by an elliptical or oval window, whose major axis is vertical.

"The second large room is one foot wider than the room below; this is in consequence of the wall being but six feet thick, falling off six inches on the inner, and six on the outer side. The second string course provides for this on the outside. The rooms of this story are similar to those below. The side walls have nine buttresses on a side, and have eight tiers of windows, five on each tier.

"The foot of the basement windows are eight inches above the promenade, rise three feet perpendicular, and terminate with a semi-circular
head. The first story windows have twelve feet length of sash, to top of semi-
circular head. The oval windows have six and one-half feet length of sash.
The windows of the second story are the same as those below. All these
frames have four and one-half feet width of sash.

"The pedestals under all the buttresses project at their base two feet;
above their base, which is fifteen inches by four and a half feet wide, on
each front, is a figure of a globe three feet eleven inches across, whose
axis corresponds with the axis of the earth.

"The base string course forms a cope for those pedestals. Above this
cope the buttresses are three and a half feet, and continue to the height of
one hundred feet. Above the promenade, close under the second string
course, on each of the buttresses, is the moon, represented in its different
phases. Close under the third string course, or cornice, is the face of the
sun. Immediately above is Saturn with her rings. The buttresses terminate
with a projected cope.

"The only difference between the tower buttresses, and the one just
described is, instead of Saturn being on them, we have clouds and rays of
light descending downwards.

"All of these symbols are to be chiseled in bas-relief on solid stone.
The side walls continue above the string course, or cornice, eight and a
half feet, making the walls ninety-six feet high, and are formed in battlements, interspersed with stars.

"The roof is quite flat, rising only eight feet, and is to be covered
with galvanized iron, or some other metal. The building is to be otherwise
ornamented in many places. The whole structure is designed to symbolize
some of the great architectural work above.

"The basement windows recede in, from the face of outer wall to
sash frame, eighteen inches, and are relieved by a large caveto. Those
windows above the base recede from face of wall to sash frame, three
feet, and are surrounded by stone jambs formed in mouldings, and surmounted by labels over each, which terminate at their horizon, excepting
the oval windows, whose labels terminate on columns which extend from
an enriched string course, at the foot of each window, to the center of
major axis.

"My chief object in the last paragraph is to show to the judgment of
any who may be baffled, how those windows can be come at, etc. All the
windows in the towers are moulded, and have stone jambs; each being
crowned with label mouldings.

"For further particulars, wait till the House is done, then come and
see it.

"The whole House covers an area of twenty-one thousand eight hundred and fifty feet."

The entrance of the Union Pacific Railway into Utah,
in 1868, served temporarily to retard work on the Temple, as the call for laborers on the great trans-continental

line was deemed imperative. Eventually, however, the activity in railroad construction operated as a great assistance in the undertaking; for, to the main line, branches succeeded; and, by 1873, a side line had reached the granite quarries. From the city station a track was constructed up South Temple Street, and into Temple Block.

The work of construction proceeded so slowly as to arouse a feeling akin to impatience in the hearts of over-anxious Saints, and mild restraint was called for. At other times gentle urging was necessary. The work was apportioned to the people of the Territory, which, for convenience, was divided into temple districts. Stakes and wards and quorums of the Priesthood were assigned their parts, and an effective system of divided labor and responsibility was developed.[7]

President Brigham Young died in 1877, at which time the granite walls of the Temple had reached a height of about twenty feet above ground. During the administration of his successor, President John Taylor, the work was continued without important interruption for another decade, and thereafter was urged with even greater vigor under the direction of Wilford Woodruff, the next President of the Church. As the concluding laps of a race are generally marked by increased energy incident to the final spurt—the supreme effort to reach, the end in glory and triumph, as in a powerful drama, interest becomes more intense, and action more concentrated with the approach of the finale, so, in this great undertaking, the fact that the end was looming above the horizon of sight called forth redoubled energies on the part of the people. When the granite had risen to the square, and when the spires began to appear in place, a feeling of almost feverish anxiety was manifest throughout the Church.

---

[7]As an instance of these separate assignments, and as an example of direct appeal to the various organizations within the Church, see the circular letter, issued in 1876 by the authority of the First Presidency and the Council of the Twelve Apostles, addressed to Elders, Seventies, and High Priests; this appears in "Contributor," Vol. XIV, pp. 267-8.

Laying of the Capstone

The sixth day of April, 1892, was determined upon as the date for placing in position the capstone of the Temple, and the announcement was hailed with joy in every ward and branch of the Church, and in every household of the Saints.

The day marked the close of the annual Conference, and was hallowed by all the observances of solemn assembly. As a preliminary to the principal ceremony, a vast congregation had assembled in the Tabernacle at an early hour, and in this the several organizations of the Priesthood occupied distinctive places on the main floor while the galleries were reserved for the accommodation of the general public. At the close of an impressive service, the multitude proceeded in formal procession to the open space on the south side of the Temple, where a temporary platform had been erected with the flag of the nation waving above. An adjoining stand accommodated the choir, which numbered over two hundred singers. There was band music of the highest order, and every essential element of fervent worship combined with joyous celebration had been provided.

Over forty thousand people were gathered within the confines of Temple Block; and other thousands, unable to find a place in the great square, stood in the streets or looked down from roofs and windows of adjoining buildings. It is of record unchallenged that this assembly was the largest ever known in Utah. At high noon the special service was begun. The music of both band and choir, the marches, and anthems, and hymns, had been specially composed for the joyous occasion. The prayer was offered by President Joseph F. Smith, of the First Presidency, and the great "Amen" was echoed by two score thousand throats. A hymn followed; and then the venerable President of the Church, Wilford Woodruff, stepped to the front and announced that the auspicious moment, so long awaited, had arrived. These were his ringing words:

"Attention all ye house of Israel, and all ye nations of the earth! We will now lay the top-stone of the Temple of our God, the foundation of which was laid and dedicated by the Prophet, Seer, and Revelator, Brigham Young."

At this juncture the president closed an electric circuit on the stand, and the granite hemisphere, forming the highest block of the great Temple, slowly descended into position. Then followed a scene the like of which is never enacted by this people except on occasions of extraordinary solemnity, namely, the rendering of the sacred Hosanna shout. Led by Lorenzo Snow, President of the Council of the Twelve Apostles, the forty thousand Saints shouted as with the voice of one:

"Hosanna! Hosanna! Hosanna! to God and the Lamb! Amen! Amen! Amen!"

This was repeated thrice, each shout accompanied by the waving of white kerchiefs.

From the roof of the building came the voice of the architect-in-charge, J. Don Carlos Young, declaring that the capstone was duly laid, and choir and congregation broke forth in triumphant song:

"The Spirit of God like a fire is burning!
The latter-day glory begins to come forth;
The visions and blessings of old are returning,
And angels are coming to visit the earth.
We'll sing and we'll shout with the armies of heaven,
Hosanna, hosanna to God and the Lamb!
Let glory to them in the highest be given,
Henceforth and forever; Amen and Amen!"

Elder Francis M. Lyman of the Council of the Twelve then proposed the adoption of the resolution presented below:

"Believing that the instruction of President Woodruff, respecting the early completion of the Salt Lake Temple, is the word of the Lord unto us, I propose that this assemblage pledge themselves, collectively and individually, to furnish, as fast as it may be needed, all the money that may be required to complete the Temple at the earliest time possible, so that the dedication may take place on April 6th, 1893."

The adoption was manifested by a deafening shout from the assembled multitude, accompanied by the raising of hands. The final anthem was the glorious "Song of the Redeemed"—particularly appropriate to the hour; and the benediction was pronounced by President George Q. Cannon.

The topstone and the granite block upon which it immediately rests form a sphere. Within the lower half a cavity had been prepared; and in this were placed certain books and other articles, so that, as the capstone was laid, it formed a secure and massive lid to this stone receptacle. The stone contains a copy of the Holy Bible, Book of Mormon, Doctrine and Covenants, Voice of Warning, Spencer's Letters, Key to Theology, Hymn Book, Compendium, Pearl of Great Price, and some other books; also photographs of Joseph and Hyrum Smith, Brigham Young, John Taylor, Wilford Woodruff, George Q. Cannon, and Joseph F. Smith, a photograph of the Temple as it appeared at the time; and, in addition, an engraved tablet of copper setting forth the principal dates in the history of the building and bearing the names of the general authorities of the Church as they stood April 6, 1853, and as constituted at the time of the capstone ceremony, April 6, 1892.

Later in the day, the top-stone was surmounted by the great statue—a figure intended to represent Moroni, the heavenly messenger who ministered to the youthful prophet, Joseph Smith, in 1823. The figure, over twelve feet in height, is of copper heavily gilded. It is in the form of a herald with a trumpet at his lips.[8]

Completion of the Building and its Dedication

The adoption of a plan or the formal passing of a resolution by vote is an easy matter, compared with which the working out of that plan, the achieving of what was

---

[8]See Revelation 14:6, 7; also Pearl of Great Price, Writings of Joseph Smith II, 30-48.

provided for by the vote, may be a gigantic task. Such was the contrast between the action of the assembled multitude on the 6th of April, 1892, and the work accomplished in the year that followed.

When the capstone of the Temple was laid, the scene inside the walls was that of chaos and confusion. To finish the interior within a year appeared a practical impossibility. The task the people had taken upon themselves was almost superhuman. Nevertheless, they considered the instruction to complete the building within the specified time to be verily the word of the Lord unto them, and they remembered the utterance of the ancient prophet, "I know that the Lord giveth no commandments unto the children of men, save he shall prepare a way for them that they may accomplish the thing which he commandeth them."[9] The Saints regarded their act of voting to be equivalent to the affixing of their individual signatures to a note of promise. As to how well they met their obligation and kept their promise, let the achievement of the year speak.

The people had pledged themselves "collectively and individually to furnish as fast as it may be needed, all the money that may be required to complete the Temple at as early a time as possible, so that the dedication may take place on April 6, 1893." The pledge was met in full. Under date of April 21, 1892, the First Presidency issued a general epistle addressed to the Latter-day Saints in Zion and throughout the world, directing that the people gather in their places of worship on Sunday, the first day of May, and devote the day to solemn fasting and prayer. To this call the people responded faithfully. Mingled with their thanksgiving for the manifold blessings of the past, were fervent supplications for success in the work of completing the Lord's House within the time prescribed.[10]

---

[9]See Book of Mormon, I Nephi 3:7.
[10]For the epistle in full, see "Contributor," Vol. XIV, pp. 280-281.

In the work of finishing the Temple, it was all-important that there be a competent, responsible man in charge, who should be invested with executive authority in every department of the labor. While the First Presidency and the Council of the Twelve retained in their hands the directing power, they needed an agent who could be trusted to act with promptness, decision, and authority on every question that should arise. The choice of the presiding authorities for a man to fill this responsible position fell upon John R. Winder, who was at that time Second Counselor in the Presiding Bishopric, and who afterward became First Counselor in the First Presidency of the Church. At the time of his appointment to the responsible position of General Superintendent of Temple Work, April 16, 1892, President Winder was in his seventy-second year, yet he possessed the energy and activity of youth, combined with the wisdom and discretion that age alone can give. Under his efficient supervision, work on the interior of the Temple progressed at a rate that surprised even the workers. Laborers of all classes, mechanics, masons, plasterers, carpenters, glaziers, plumbers, painters, decorators, artisans and artificers of every kind, were put to work. The people verily believed that a power above that of man was operating to assist them in their great undertaking. Material, much of which was of special manufacture, came in from the east and the west, with few of the usual delays of transit.

Heating and lighting systems were installed; and this installation necessitated the erection of a boiler house, with all accessories of equipment. Moreover, the Annex had to be built. At this point it may be well to explain that each of the Temples in Utah is connected with a separate structure, known as the Annex,—in the nature of an ante-building,—in which preliminary services are held, and wherein record is made of the ordinance work to be done by the parties present, before they are permitted to enter the Temple on the day of service. The Annex to the Temple in Salt Lake City stands about one hundred feet north from the main structure.

Even as late as one month prior to the date set for the dedication, there was so much yet to be done, as to make many feel that for once at least, the people had been mistaken in their belief that the Lord had spoken, and that the completion of the work by the time set, was a physical impossibility. On the 18th of March, 1893, the First Presidency issued the following epistle:

"To the Officers and Members of the Church of Jesus Christ of Latter-day Saints:

"The near approach of the date for the dedication of the Temple of our God moves us to express with some degree of fulness our feelings to our brethren, the officers of the Church, who with us bear the Priesthood of the Son of God, and to the Latter-day Saints generally; to the end that in entering that holy building we may all be found acceptable ourselves, with our households, and that the building which we shall dedicate may also be acceptable unto the Lord.

"The Latter-day Saints have used their means freely to erect other Temples in these valleys, and our Father has blessed us in our efforts. Today we enjoy the great happiness of having three of these sacred structures completed, dedicated to and accepted of the Lord, wherein the Saints can enter and attend to those ordinances which He, in His infinite goodness and kindness, has revealed. But for forty years the hopes, desires, and anticipations of the entire Church have been centered upon the completion of this edifice in the principal city of Zion. Its foundation was laid in the early days of our settlement in these mountains; and from that day until the present, the eyes of the members of the Church in every land have been lovingly directed toward it. Looking upon it as the Temple of temples, the people during all these years have labored with unceasing toil, undiminished patience, and ungrudging expenditure of means to bring it to its present condition of completion; and now that the toils and the sacrifices of forty years are crowned so successfully and happily, now that the great building is at last finished and ready to be used for divine purposes, need we say that we draw near an event whose consummation is to us as a people momentous in the highest degree? Far-reaching in its consequence, as that occasion is certain to be, what remains for us to say in order to impress the entire Church with a sense of its tremendous importance?

"On this point, surely nothing; yet may we offer a few words upon a phase that directly touches it. No member of the Church who would be deemed worthy to enter that sacred house can be considered ignorant of the principles of the Gospel. It is not too much to presume that every one knows what his duty is to God and to his fellowman. None is so forgetful as to have lost sight of the admonition that we must be filled with love for and charity toward our brethren. And hence none can for a moment doubt the supreme importance of every member of the congregation being at peace with all his or her brethren and sisters, and at peace with God. How else can we hope to gain the blessings He has promised save by complying with the requirements for which those blessings are the reward?

"Can men and women who are violating a law of God, or those who are derelict in yielding obedience to His commands, expect that the mere going into His holy house and taking part in its dedication will render them worthy to receive, and cause them to receive, His blessing?

"Do they think that repentance and turning away from sin may be so lightly dispensed with?

"Do they dare, even in thought, thus to accuse our Father of injustice and partiality, and attribute to Him carelessness in the fulfilment of His own words?

"Assuredly no one claiming to belong to His people would be guilty of such a thing.

"Then must those who are unworthy cease to expect a blessing from their attendance at the Temple while sin unrepented of still casts its odor about them, and while bitterness or even an unforgiving coolness exists in their hearts against their brethren and sisters.

"On this latter subject we feel that much might be said. In the striving after compliance with the apparently weightier matters of the law, there is a possibility that the importance of this spirit of love and kindness and charity may be underestimated. For ourselves, we cannot think of any precept that at present requires more earnest inculcation.

"During the past eighteen months there has been a division of the Latter-day Saints upon national party lines. Political campaigns have been conducted, elections have been held, and feelings, more or less intense, have been engendered in the minds of brethren and sisters upon one side and the other.

"We have been cognizant of conduct and have heard of many expressions that have been very painful to us and have grieved our spirits.

"We know they have been an offense unto the God of peace and love, and a stumbling block unto many of the Saints.

"We feel now that a time for reconciliation has come; that before entering into the Temple to present ourselves before the Lord in solemn assembly, we shall divest ourselves of every harsh and unkind feeling against each other; that not only our bickerings shall cease, but that the cause of them shall be removed, and every sentiment that prompted and has maintained them shall be dispelled; that we shall confess our sins one to another, and ask forgiveness one of another; that we shall plead with the Lord for the spirit of repentance, and, having obtained it, follow its promptings; so that in humbling ourselves before Him and seeking forgiveness from each other, we shall yield that charity and generosity to those who crave our forgiveness that we ask for and expect from heaven.

"Thus may we come up into the holy place with our hearts free from guile and our souls prepared for the edification that is promised! Thus shall our supplications, undisturbed by a thought of discord, unitedly mount into the ears of Jehovah and draw down the choice blessings of the God of Heaven!

"As your brethren, sustained by your vote and in your faith as the First Presidency of the Church, we have this to say to the Latter-day Saints, in our individual as well as our official capacity: If there is a single member of the Church who has feelings against us, we do not wish to cross the threshold of the Temple until we have satisfied him and have removed from him all cause of feeling, either by explanation or by making proper amends and atonement; neither would we wish to enter the sacred portals of that edifice until we have sought an explanation, or amends, or atonement, from any against whom we may have either a real or fancied grievance.

"In now announcing this course for ourselves, we say to all the other officers of the Church that we desire them to follow our example. We wish them from the highest to the lowest and throughout all the stakes and wards of Zion to take heed of this counsel. Let them invite all who may have feelings against them to come forward and make them known; let them then endeavor to correct any misapprehensions or misunderstandings which may exist, or give redress for any wrong or injury that may have been done.

"We say the same—and when the officers have taken the course indicated we wish them to say the same—to the individual members of the Church. We call upon them to seek to have the fellowship of their brethren and their sisters, and their entire confidence and love; above all to seek to have the fellowship and union of the Holy Ghost. Let this spirit be sought and cherished as diligently within the smallest and humblest family circle, as within the membership of the highest organization and quorum. Let it permeate the hearts of the brothers and sisters, the parents and children of the household, as well as the hearts of the First Presidency and Twelve. Let it mellow and soften all differences between members of the Stake Presidencies and the High Councils, as well as between neighbors living in the same ward. Let it unite young and old, male and female, flock and shepherd, people and Priesthood, in the bounds of gratitude and forgiveness and love, so that Israel may feel approved of the Lord, and that we may all come before Him with a conscience void of offense before all men. Then there will be no disappointment as to the blessings promised those who sincerely worship Him. The sweet whisperings of the Holy Spirit will be given to them and the treasures of heaven, the communion of angels, will be added from time to time, for His promise has gone forth and it cannot fail!

"Asking God's blessing upon you all in your endeavor to carry out this counsel, and desirous of seeing it take the form of a united effort on the part of the whole people, we suggest that Saturday, March 25, 1893, be set apart as a day of fasting and prayer. On that occasion we advise that the Presidencies of Stakes, the High Councils, the Bishops and their Counselors, meet together with the Saints in their several meeting houses, confess their sins one to another, and draw out from the people all feelings of anger, of distrust, or of unfriendliness that may have found a lodgment; so that entire confidence may then and there be restored and love from this time prevail through all the congregations of the Saints."

It was evident that the authorities of the Church realized the importance of preparing for the great event of the dedication in other ways than by material construction and costly furnishings. The hearts of the people had to be made ready; it was necessary that Israel be sanctified. Throughout the length and breadth of Zion there was a general cleansing of mind and soul; enmity was buried; bickering ceased; differences between brethren were adjusted; offenses were atoned and forgiven; a veritable jubilee was celebrated.

The finishing touches to the interior of the building were made late in the afternoon of April 5th, and in the evening of that day, the Temple was thrown open to general inspection. Not only were members of the Church admitted; many honorable men and women who had never affiliated with the Church were invited to the number of over one thousand, and they passed through the Temple from basement to top. In view of the current belief that the Temples of the Latter-day Saints are never open to the gaze of non-members, this fact is of significant importance.

On the morning of the 6th of April, 1893, Wilford Woodruff, President of the Church, led the way through the south-west door into the sacred precincts. The event has been not inaptly likened to that of Joshua leading Israel into the promised land. The venerable President was followed by the rest of the general authorities of the Church, and these in turn by other Church officials and such members as had been specially designated to take part in the first dedication service. Of the tens of thousands of Saints who desired to be present, whose rightful privilege it was to attend, and who had contributed of their substance to the building of the greatest Temple of modern times, but few could be accommodated on the day of dedication. The assembly room, which with its vestries occupies the entire upper floor, had been furnished with seating accommodations for two thousand two hundred and fifty-two persons. It was arranged, therefore, that services be repeated twice daily, to continue from April 6th until all who were entitled to admission had had opportunity to be present.

On the first day, the following were admitted to take part in what will always be remembered as the official dedicatory session: The First Presidency, the Council of the Twelve Apostles, the Presiding Patriarch, the First Council of the Seventy, the Presiding Bishopric, and all other general authorities of the Church, and in addition, Presidents of Stakes and their Counselors, members of Stake High Councils, Patriarchs, Presidents of High Priests' Quorums and their Counselors, Presidents of Quorums of Seventies, Bishops of Wards and their Counselors. Admission was extended to the wives and immediate families of all the Church officials named. To the later sessions, admission was regulated so that particular wards and stakes had each a special assignment as to time.

No one was admitted without a formal certificate, conventionally known as a "recommend," signed by the Bishop of his ward and the President of his stake. In a circular of instruction relating to the dedication the following appears: "It will be necessary for each applicant to show his or her recommend to the gate-keeper, in order to pass. The recommend will then be taken up by a ticket-man inside the gate. No person will be admitted without a recommend, on any occasion." Services were held daily from April 6th, to April 18th, inclusive, and again on the 23rd and 24th. Usually two sessions were held each day, but on the 7th of April, an evening session was added. While children under eight years of age, and therefore unbaptized, were not admitted to the general sessions, special days were set apart for their accommodation; thus April 21st and 22nd,—Friday and Saturday,— were reserved for Sunday School children, under the prescribed age for baptism.

At the first service,—the official dedication,—the prayer was offered by President Wilford Woodruff, and at each succeeding session the prayer was read. The prayer itself is at once a sermon and a supplication; it is expressive of the inmost thoughts of the people; it is an epitome of the history of the Saints and the condition of the Church at that time.

The prayer follows in full:

"Our Father in heaven, thou who hast created the heavens and the earth, and all things that are therein; thou most glorious One, perfect in mercy, love, and truth, we, thy children, come this day before thee, and in this house which we have built to thy most holy name, humbly plead the atoning blood of thine Only Begotten Son, that our sins may be remembered no more against us forever, but that our prayers may ascend unto thee and have free access to thy throne, that we may be heard in thy holy habitation. And may it graciously please thee to hearken unto our petitions, answer them according to thine infinite wisdom and love, and grant that the blessings which we seek may be bestowed upon us, even a hundred fold, inasmuch as we seek with purity of heart and fulness of purpose to do thy will and glorify thy name.

"We thank thee, O thou Great Elohim, that thou didst raise up thy servant, Joseph Smith, through the loins of Abraham, Isaac, and Jacob, and made him a Prophet, Seer, and Revelator, and through the assistance and administrations of angels from heaven, thou didst enable him to bring forth the Book of Mormon,—the stick of Joseph, in the hand of Ephraim,—in fulfilment of the prophecies of Isaiah and other prophets, which record has been translated and published in many languages. We also thank thee, our Father in heaven, that thou didst inspire thy servant and give him power on the earth to organize thy Church in this goodly land, in all its fulness, power and glory, with Apostles, Prophets, Pastors, and Teachers, with all the gifts and graces belonging thereto, and all this by the power of the Aaronic and Melchisedek Priesthood, which thou didst bestow upon him by the administration of holy angels, who held that Priesthood in the days of the Savior. We thank thee, our God, that thou didst enable thy servant Joseph to build two temples, in which ordinances were administered for the living and the dead; that he also lived to send the Gospel to the nations of the earth and to the islands of the sea, and labored exceedingly until he was martyred for the word of God and the testimony of Jesus Christ.

"We also thank thee, O our Father in heaven, that thou didst raise up thy servant Brigham Young, who held the keys of thy Priesthood on the earth for many years, and who led thy people to these valleys of the mountains, and laid the corner-stone of this great Temple and dedicated it unto thee, and who did direct the building of three other temples in these Rocky Mountains which have been dedicated unto thy holy name, in which temples many thousands of the living have been blessed and the dead redeemed.

"Our Father in heaven, we are also thankful to thee for thy servant John Taylor, who followed in the footsteps of thy servant Brigham, until he laid down his life in exile.

"Thou hast called thy servants Wilford Woodruff, George Q. Cannon, and Joseph F. Smith, to hold the keys of the Presidency and Priesthood this day, and for these shepherds of thy flock we feel to give thee thanksgiving and praise. Thy servant Wilford is bound to acknowledge thy hand, O Father, in the preservation of his life from the hour of his birth to the present day. Nothing but thy power could have preserved him through that which he has passed during the eighty-six years that thou hast granted him life on the earth.

"For the raising up of the Twelve Apostles, we also thank thee, our God, and for the perfect union which exists among us.

"We thank thee, O Lord, for the perfect organizations of thy Church as they exist at the present time.

"O Lord, we regard with intense and indescribable feelings the completion of this sacred house. Deign to accept this the fourth temple which thy covenant children have been assisted by thee in erecting in these mountains. In past ages thou didst inspire with thy Holy Spirit thy servants, the prophets, to speak of a time in the latter days when the mountain of the Lord's house should be established in the top of the mountains, and should be exalted above the hills. We thank thee that we have had the glorious opportunity of contributing to the fulfilment of these visions of thine ancient seers, and that thou hast condescended to permit us to take part in the great work. And as this portion of thy servants' words has thus so marvelously been brought to pass, we pray thee, with increased faith and renewed hope, that all their words with regard to thy great work in gathering thine Israel and building up thy kingdom on earth in the last days may be as amply fulfilled, and that, O Lord, speedily.

"We come before thee with joy and thanksgiving, with spirits jubilant and hearts filled with praise, that thou hast permitted us to see this day for which, during these forty years, we have hoped, and toiled, and prayed, when we can dedicate unto thee this house which we have built to thy most glorious name. One year ago we set the capstone with shouts of Hosanna to God and the Lamb. And today we dedicate the whole unto thee, with all that pertains unto it, that it may be holy in thy sight; that it may be a house of prayer, a house of praise and of worship; that thy glory may rest upon it; that thy holy presence may be continually in it; that it may be the abode of thy Well-Beloved Son, our Savior; that the angels who stand before thy face may be the hallowed messengers who shall visit it, bearing to us thy wishes and thy will, that it may be sanctified and consecrated in all its parts holy unto thee, the God of Israel, the Almighty Ruler of mankind. And we pray thee that all people who may enter upon the threshold of this, thine house, may feel thy power and be constrained to acknowledge that thou hast sanctified it, that it is thy house, a place of thy holiness.

"We pray thee, Heavenly Father, to accept this building in all its parts from foundation to capstone, with the statue that is on the latter placed, and all the finials and other ornaments that adorn its exterior. We pray thee to bless, that they decay not, all the walls, partitions, floors, ceilings, roofs, and bridging, the elevators, stairways, railings and steps, the frames, doors, windows, and other openings, all things connected with the lighting, heating, and sanitary apparatus, the boilers, engines, and dynamos, the connecting pipes and wires, the lamps and burners, and all utensils, furniture and articles used in or connected with the holy ordinances administered in this house, the veils and the altars, the baptismal font and the oxen on which it rests, and all that pertains thereto, the baths, washstands and basins. Also the safes and vaults in which the records are preserved, with the records themselves, and all books, documents, and papers appertaining to the office of the recorder, likewise the library with all the books, maps, instruments, etc., that may belong thereto. We also present before thee, for thine acceptance, all the additions and buildings not forming a part of the main edifice but being appendages thereto; and we pray thee to bless all the furniture, seats, cushions, curtains, hangings, locks and fastenings, and multitudinous other appliances and appurtenances found in and belonging to this Temple and its annexes, with all the work of ornamentation thereon, the painting and plastering, the gilding and bronzing, the fine work in wood and metal of every kind, the embroidery and needlework, the pictures and statuary, the carved work and canopies. Also the materials of which the buildings and their contents are made or composed—the rock, lime, mortar and plaster, the timbers and lath, the wood of various trees, the gold and silver, the brass and iron, and all other metals, the silk, wool, and cotton, the skins and furs, the glass, china, and precious stones, all these and all else herein we humbly present for thine acceptance and sanctifying blessing.

"Our Father in heaven, we present before thee the altars which we have prepared for thy servants and handmaidens to receive their sealing blessings. We dedicate them in the name of the Lord Jesus Christ, unto thy most holy name, and we ask thee to sanctify these altars, that those who come unto them may feel the power of the Holy Ghost resting upon them, and realize the sacredness of the covenants they enter into. And we pray that our covenants and contracts which we make with thee and with each other may be directed by thy Holy Spirit, be sacredly kept by us, and accepted by thee, and that all the blessings pronounced may be realized by all thy Saints who come to these altars, in the morning of the resurrection of the just.

"O Lord, we pray thee to bless and sanctify the whole of this block or piece of ground on which these buildings stand, with the surrounding walls and fences, the walks, paths, and ornamental beds, also the trees, plants, flowers and shrubbery that grow in its soil; may they bloom and blossom and become exceedingly beautiful and fragrant; and may thy Spirit dwell in the midst thereof, that this plot of ground may be a place of rest and peace, for holy meditation and inspired thought.

"Preserve these buildings, we beseech thee, from injury or destruction by flood or fire; from the rage of the elements, the shafts of the vivid lightning, the overwhelming blasts of the hurricane, the flames of consuming fire, and the upheavals of the earthquake, O Lord, protect them.

"Bless, we pray thee, heavenly Father, all who may be workers in this house. Remember continually thy servant who shall be appointed to preside within its walls; endow him richly with the wisdom of the Holy One, with the spirit of his calling, with the power of his Priesthood, and with the gift of discernment. Bless, according to their calling, his assistants and all who are associated with him in the performance of the ordinances,— baptisms, confirmations, washings, anointings, sealings, endowments, and ordinations which are performed herein, that all that is done may be holy and acceptable unto thee, thou God of our salvation. Bless the recorders and copyists, that the records of the Temple may be kept perfect, and without omissions and errors, and that they may also be accepted of thee. Bless, in their several positions, the engineers, watchmen, guards, and all others who have duties to perform in connection with the house, that they may perform them unto thee with an eye single to thy glory.

"Remember also in thy mercy all those who have labored in the erection of this house, or who have, in any way, by their means or influence aided in its completion; may they in no wise lose their reward.

"O thou God of our fathers, Abraham, Isaac, and Jacob, whose God thou delightest to be called, we thank thee with all the fervor of overflowing gratitude that thou hast revealed the powers by which the hearts of the children are being turned to their fathers and the hearts of the fathers to the children, that the sons of men, in all their generations can be made partakers of the glories and joys of the kingdom of heaven. Confirm upon us the spirit of Elijah, we pray thee, that we may thus redeem our dead and also connect ourselves with our fathers who have passed behind the veil, and furthermore seal up our dead to come forth in the first resurrection, that we who dwell on earth may be bound to those who dwell in heaven. We thank thee for their sake who have finished their work in mortality, as well as for our own, that the prison doors have been opened that deliverance has been proclaimed to the captive, and the bonds have been loosened from those who were bound. We praise thee that our fathers, from last to first, from now, back to the beginning, can be united with us in indissoluble links, welded by the holy Priesthood, and that as one great family united in thee and cemented by thy power we shall together stand before thee, and by the power of the atoning blood of thy Son be delivered from all evil, be saved and sanctified, exalted and glorified. Wilt thou also permit holy messengers to visit us within these sacred walls and make known unto us with regard to the work we should perform in behalf of our dead. And, as thou hast inclined the hearts of many who have not yet entered into covenant with thee to search out their progenitors, and in so doing they have traced the ancestry of many of thy Saints, we pray thee that thou wilt increase this desire in their bosoms, that they may in this way aid in the accomplishment of their work. Bless them, we pray thee, in their labors, that they may not fall into errors in preparing their genealogies; and furthermore, we ask thee to open before them new avenues of information, and place in their hands the records of the past that their work may not only be correct but complete also.

"O thou Great Father of the spirits of all flesh, graciously bless and fully qualify those upon whom thou hast placed a portion of thine authority, and who bear the responsibilities and powers of the Priesthood which is after the order of thy Son. Bless them all from first to last, from thy servant who represents thee in all the world to the latest who has been ordained to the Deacon's office. Upon each and all confer the spirit of their calling, with a comprehension of its duties and a loving zeal to fulfil them. Endow them with faith, patience and understanding. May their lives be strong in virtue and adorned with humility; may their ministrations be effectual, their prayers be availing, and their teachings the path of salvation. May they be united by the Spirit and power of God in all their labors, and in every thought, word and act may they glorify thy name and vindicate the wisdom that has made them kings and priests unto thee.

"For thy servants of the First Presidency of the Church we first of all pray. Reveal, in great clearness, thy mind and will unto them in all things essential for the welfare of thy people; give them heavenly wisdom, abounding faith, and the power and gifts necessary to enable them to preside acceptably unto thee over the officers and members of thy Church. Remember in love thy servant whom thou hast called to be a Prophet, Seer, and Revelator to all mankind, whose days have been many upon the earth; yet lengthen out his span of mortal life, we pray thee, and grant unto him all the powers and gifts, in their completeness, of the office thou hast conferred upon him; and in like manner bless his associates in the Presidency of thy Church.

"Confer upon thy servants, the Twelve Apostles, a rich endowment of thy Spirit. Under their guidance may the Gospel of the kingdom go forth into all the world, to be preached to all nations, kindreds, tongues, and people, that the honest in heart in every land may hear the glad tidings of joy and salvation. Overrule, we pray thee, in the midst of the governments of the earth, that the barriers that now stand in the way of the spread of thy truths may be removed, and liberty of conscience be accorded to all peoples.

"Remember in loving kindness thy servants, the Patriarchs. May they be full of blessings for thy people Israel. May they bear with them the seeds of comfort and consolation, of encouragement and blessing. Fill them with the Holy Spirit of promise, and be graciously pleased to fulfil their words of prophecy, that thy name may be extolled in the people of thy Church and their faith in thee and in the promises of thy ministering servants be increasingly strengthened.

"With thy servants of the Twelve bless their associates, the Seventies; may they be powerful in the preaching of thy word and in bearing it to the four quarters of the earth. May an ever-widening way be opened before them until they shall have raised the Gospel standard in every land and proclaimed its saving truths in every tongue, that all the islands and the continents may rejoice in the testimony of the great work thou art in these latter days performing on the earth.

"Bless abundantly, O Lord, the High Priests in all the varied duties and positions to which thou hast called them. As standing ministers of thy word in the multiplying Stakes of Zion wilt thou endow them richly with the spirit of their exalted callings. As Presidents, Counselors, Bishops, members of High Councils, and in every other office which their Priesthood gives them the right to fill, may they be righteous ministers of thy holy law, loving fathers of the people, and as judges in the midst of the Saints may they deal out just and impartial judgment tempered with mercy and love.

"So also, in their various callings, confer precious gifts of wisdom, faith and knowledge upon thy servants, the Elders, Priests, Teachers, and Deacons, that all may diligently perform their part in the glorious labors thou hast called thy Priesthood to bear.

"Forget not, we beseech thee, thy servants the missionaries, who are proclaiming the saving truths that thou hast revealed for man's redemption to the millions who are now overshadowed by deep spiritual darkness. Preserve them from all evil, deliver them from mob violence, may they want no good thing, but be greatly blessed with the gifts and powers of their ministry. Remember also their families, that they may be sustained and comforted by thee and be cherished and cared for by thy Saints.

"We pray thee for the members of thy Holy Church throughout all the world, that thy people may be so guided and governed of thee, that all who profess to be and call themselves Saints may be preserved in the unity of the faith, in the way of truth, in the bonds of peace, and in holiness of life. Strengthen the weak, we pray thee, and impart thy Spirit unto all.

"Our Father, may peace abide in all the homes of thy Saints; may holy angels guard them; may they be encompassed by thine arms of love; may prosperity shine upon them, and may the tempter and the destroyer be removed far from them. May the days of thy covenant people be lengthened out in righteousness, and sickness and disease be rebuked from their midst. May the land they inhabit be made fruitful by thy grace, may its waters be increased and the climate be tempered to the comfort and need of thy people; may drought, devastating storms, cyclones, and hurricanes be kept afar off, and earthquakes never disturb the land which thou hast given us. May locusts, caterpillars and other insects not destroy our gardens and desolate our fields; but may we be a people blessed of thee in our bodies and spirits, in our homes and habitations, in our flocks and herds, in ourselves and our posterity, and in all that thou hast made us stewards over.

"Now pray we for the youth of Zion—the children of thy people; endow them richly with the spirit of faith and righteousness and with increasing love for thee and for thy law. Prosper all the institutions that thou hast established in our midst for their well-being. Give to our Church Schools an ever-increasing power for good. May thy Holy Spirit dominate the teachings given therein and also control the hearts and illumine the minds of the students. Bless marvelously thy servants, the General Superintendent, and all the principals, teachers and other officers, and also those who form the General Board of Education of thy Church. Remember likewise in thy loving kindness the Sunday Schools, with all who, either as teachers or scholars, belong thereto; may the influence of the instruction given therein broaden and deepen, to thy glory and the salvation of thy children, until the perfect day. Bless the members of the General Board of the Deseret Sunday School Union with the wisdom necessary for the proper fulfilment of their duties, and for the accomplishment of the purposes for which this Board was created.

"We also uphold before thee the Young Men's and Young Ladies' Mutual Improvement Associations, with all their officers, general and local, and the members. May they be prospered of thee, their membership be enlarged, and the good that they accomplish increase with every succeeding year. For the Primaries and Religion Classes we also seek thy constant blessing and guiding care; may the spirit of instruction be poured out upon the presidents and associate officers and teachers. May they keep pace with the rest of the educational establishments in thy Church; so that from their earliest years our children may be diligently brought up in the ways of the Lord, and thy name be magnified in their growth in virtue and intelligence.

"Nor would we forget, O Lord, the normal training classes among the people, whether these classes be connected with the Church Schools, the Improvement Associations, or the Sunday Schools. Grant that these classes may be the means of spreading true education throughout all the borders of the Saints by the creation of a body of teachers who will not only be possessed of rare intelligence but be filled also with the spirit of the Gospel, and be powerful in the testimony of thy truth and in implanting a love for thee and for thy works in the hearts of all whom they instruct.

"We would hold up before thee, O Lord, the Relief Societies, with all their members; and all those who preside in their midst according to their callings and appointments, general or local. Bless the Teachers in their labors of mercy and charity, who, as ministering angels, visit the homes of the sick and the needy, bearing succor, consolation and comfort to the unfortunate and sorrowful. And bless, we beseech thee, most merciful Father, the poor of thy people, that the cry of want and suffering may not ascend unto thee from the midst of thy Saints whom thou hast blessed so abundantly with the comforts of this world. Open up new avenues by which the needy can obtain a livelihood by honest industry, and also incline the hearts of those blessed more abundantly, to give generously of their substance to their, in this respect, less favored brethren and sisters, that thou mayest not have reason to chide us for the neglect of even the least among thy covenant children.

"O God of Israel, turn thy face, we pray thee, in loving kindness toward thy stricken people of the house of Judah. Oh, deliver them from those that oppress them. Heal up their wounds, comfort their hearts, strengthen their feet, and give them ministers after thine own heart who shall lead them as of old, in thy way. May the days of their tribulation soon cease, and they be planted by thee in the valleys and plains of their ancient home; and may Jerusalem rejoice and Judea be glad for the multitude of her sons and daughters, for the sweet voices of children in her streets, and the rich outpouring of thy saving mercies upon them. May Israel no more bow the head, nor bend the neck to the oppressor, but may his feet be made strong on the everlasting hills, never more, by violence, to be banished therefrom, and the praise and the glory shall be thine.

"Remember in like pity the dwindling remnants of the house of Israel, descendants of thy servant Lehi. Restore them, we pray thee, to thine ancient favor, fulfil in their completeness the promises given to their fathers, and make of them a white and delightsome race, a loved and holy people as in former days. May the time also be nigh at hand when thou wilt gather the dispersed of Israel from the islands of the sea and from every land in which thou hast scattered them, and the ten tribes of Jacob from their hiding place in the north, and restore them to communion and fellowship with their kinsmen of the seed of Abraham.

"We thank thee, O God of Israel, that thou didst raise up patriotic men to lay the foundation of this great American government. Thou didst inspire them to frame a good Constitution and laws which guarantee to all of the inhabitants of the land equal rights and privileges to worship thee according to the dictates of their own consciences. Bless the officers, both judicial and executive. Confer abundant favors upon the President, his Cabinet, and Congress. Enlightened and guided by thy Spirit may they maintain and uphold the glorious principles of human liberty. Our hearts are filled with gratitude to thee, our Father in heaven, for thy kindness unto us in softening the hearts of our fellow citizens, the people of this nation, towards us. That which thou hast done has been marvelous in our eyes. We thank thee that thou didst move upon the heart of the President of our nation to issue a general amnesty; that thou hast removed prejudice and misunderstanding from the minds of many of the people concerning us and our purposes, and they are disposed to treat us as fellow citizens, and not as enemies. In this holy house we feel to give thee glory therefor, and we humbly ask thee to increase this feeling in their hearts. Enable them to see us in our true light. Show unto them that we are their friends, that we love liberty, that we will join with them in upholding the rights of the people, the Constitution and laws of our country; and give unto us and our children an increased disposition to always be loyal, and to do everything in our power to maintain constitutional rights and the freedom of all within the confines of this great Republic.

"Remember in mercy, O Lord, the kings, and princes, the nobles, the rulers and governors, and the great ones of the earth, and likewise all the poor, the afflicted and the oppressed, and indeed, all people, that their hearts may be softened when thy servants go forth to bear testimony of thy name, that their prejudices may give way before the truth, and thy people find favor in their eyes. So control the affairs of the nations of the earth, that the way may be prepared for the ushering in of a reign of righteousness and truth. We desire to see liberty spread throughout the earth, to see oppression cease, the yoke of the tyrant broken, and every despotic form of government overthrown by which thy children are degraded and crushed, and prevented from enjoying their share of the blessings of the earth, which thou hast created for their habitation.

"O God, the Eternal Father, thou knowest all things. Thou seest the course thy people have been led to take in political matters. They have, in many instances, joined the two great national parties. Campaigns have been entered upon, elections have been held, and much party feeling has been engendered. Many things have been said and done which have wounded the feelings of the humble and the meek, and which have been a cause of offense. We beseech thee, in thine infinite mercy and goodness, to forgive thy people wherein they have sinned in this direction. Show them, O Father, their faults and their errors, that they may see the same in the light of the Holy Spirit, and repent truly and sincerely, and cultivate that spirit of affection and love which thou art desirous that all the children of men should entertain one for another, and which thy Saints, above all others, should cherish. Enable thy people hereafter to avoid bitterness and strife, and to refrain from words and acts in political discussions that shall create feeling and grieve thy Holy Spirit.

"Heavenly Father, when thy people shall not have the opportunity of entering this holy house to offer their supplications unto thee, and they are oppressed and in trouble, surrounded by difficulties or assailed by temptation, and shall turn their faces towards this thy holy house and ask thee for deliverance, for help, for thy power to be extended in their behalf, we beseech thee to look down from thy holy habitation in mercy and tender compassion upon them, and listen to their cries. Or when the children of thy people, in years to come, shall be separated, through any cause, from this place, and their hearts shall turn in remembrance of thy promises to this holy Temple, and they shall cry unto thee from the depths of their affliction and sorrow to extend relief and deliverance to them, we humbly entreat thee to turn thine ear in mercy to them; hearken to their cries, and grant unto them the blessings for which they ask.

"Almighty Father, increase within us the powers of that faith delivered to and possessed by thy Saints. Strengthen us by the memories of the glorious deliverances of the past, by the remembrance of the sacred covenants that thou hast made with us, so that, when evil overshadows us, when trouble encompasses us, when we pass through the valley of humiliation, we may not falter, may not doubt, but in the strength of thy holy name may accomplish all thy righteous purposes with regard to us, fill the measure of our creation, and triumph gloriously, by thy grace, over every besetting sin, be redeemed from every evil, and be numbered in the kingdom of heaven amongst those who shall dwell in thy presence forever.

"And now, our Father, we bless thee, we praise thee, we glorify thee, we worship thee, day by day we magnify thee, and give thee thanks for thy great goodness towards us, thy children, and we pray thee, in the name of thy Son Jesus Christ, our Savior, to hear these our humble petitions, and answer us from heaven, thy holy dwelling place, where thou sittest enthroned in glory, might, majesty, and dominion, and with an infinitude of power which we, thy mortal creatures, cannot imagine, much less comprehend. Amen and Amen."

All who attended the dedicatory services on the morning of the 6th of April, 1893, remember the impressiveness of the day. The sky was overcast and lowering, and shortly before the hour of beginning, a strong wind set in from the north-west. This wind increased to a veritable hurricane and throughout the morning session it seemed indeed, that the prince of the air was in full control; but the peace and serenity of the assembly was rendered the more impressive by contrast with the turmoil and storm without.

A large pipe-organ had been set up in the assembly room, and served as an accompaniment to the choir of selected voices, by whom the anthems and hymns, specially composed for the occasion, were rendered. The essential and characteristic feature of the service was, of course, the offering of the dedicatory prayer; and to this were added brief addresses by officials of the Church. At the first session, each of the First Presidency delivered an address, replete with promise and prophecy. Throughout the service, ran the solemn refrain, which was voiced in anthem, sermon, and prayer:

"The House of the Lord is completed."

CHAPTER VII

The Great Temple at Salt Lake City— Exterior

Before us stands the completed structure, the visible result of four decades of devoted toil,—a period marked in the beginning by poverty and penury followed by relative prosperity and plenty. The impression produced by a first view of the exterior is that of massiveness coupled with a sense of assured stability. Closer examination and more intimate acquaintance serve to intensify this early impression, while revealing numerous details of uniqueness in plan and of excellence in construction. As to architectural design the Temple belongs to a class of its own. Originality rather than novelty characterizes every prominent feature. And yet there is nothing apparent that speaks of strained effect nor of conscious effort for departure from more conventional lines. The Temple is no oddity in architecture; on the contrary it is strictly in place both as to material environment and spiritual atmosphere.

The building is of composite style, presenting features of both the Gothic and the Roman. By architects of experience it has been described as a modification of the Round Gothic, while others have called it Romanesque, in that it follows in part the castellated style so highly developed in England. But, even if this description be true as to the exterior, it is wholly inapplicable within. There are no high-vaulted Gothic ceilings, nor massive beams after the style Romanesque; on the contrary the interior partakes rather of the nature of Renaissance design.[1]

The Temple was constructed for specific use; it was intended for service widely different from that of cathedral, tabernacle, mosque, or synagogue; and the building was planned and patterned to suit its distinctive purpose. Such was and is the reason for its being, the explanation of its design, both vindication and justification of its plan.

As has been shown, the plans of the building were made known, and a fairly detailed description thereof was published in 1854.[2] A careful examination of the structure as it now appears shows that in every essential particular the original plan of the exterior has been followed almost to exactness. Details of spires, turrets, and finials, had not been determined when the design was first announced; and in these as in certain other particulars the original plan has been added to; but no essential alteration has been introduced.

As it stands, the building is one hundred eighty-six feet six inches long, and one hundred eighteen feet six inches wide including ground-level extensions of the corner towers, or ninety-nine feet wide in the main body. The side walls are one hundred sixty-seven feet six inches high; the west center tower has a height of two hundred and four feet, and the corresponding tower at the east rises six feet higher. The entire area covered by the building is twenty-one thousand eight hundred and fifty square feet.

The walls are set upon a massive footing, which extends sixteen feet below ground, is sixteen feet wide at

---

[1] Joseph D. C. Young, the architect-in-charge during the later period of construction, wrote as follows in answer to an inquiry of the author in January, 1912; "Questions as to the style of architecture embodied in the great Temple have been asked time and time again. Some prominent architects have classed it as Round Gothic; others have said that it is practically unclassifiable, it being 'all material and not at all design.' In my judgment it might be called the Romanesque modified by the Castellated style."

[2] See pages 119-122.

the base, and narrows to nine feet at the top. From the ground-level to the globes surmounting the spires the walls are of granite, every block accurately cut as to dimension and pattern, and fitted with equal nicety outside and inside. The windows, both arched and oval, all deeply set in their granite recesses, are framed with oolite. Throughout the first story the walls are eight feet thick; in the upper structure the thickness is reduced by stages to a minimum of six feet. The buttresses are uniformly one foot thicker than the walls proper.

The building consists of three towers at each end—east and west, and between these extends the main body, suggesting, to the observer at a distance, a vast intermediate nave. In ground-plan the Temple is strikingly symmetrical, each of the central axes being an axis of symmetry. The westerly half is a repetition of the easterly, and the southerly half duplicates the northerly. Lines running north and south through the centre of the three towers at either end are also lines of symmetry, dividing the towers into corresponding parts.

Repetition of parts appears also in vertical section. Thus, above the first belt or string course, that is to say, immediately above the basement or first floor, is the second story, indicated without by a series of high arched windows between the buttresses; above these is a series of elliptical or oval windows. The belt course immediately above these oval openings marks the centre of construction as seen in the vertical section of the main body. The upper half, up to the level of the top belt-course, is in general a repetition of the lower. The roof has so little pitch as to be practically flat, there being a rise of but eight feet from edge to centre. Between the end towers, that is to say in the main body of the building, the walls carry nine buttresses or pilasters on both north and south sides. Each of these pilasters rises above the parapets and battlement walls, and is capped by a granite block three and a half feet square at its base and two and a half feet high. Of these pilaster caps, four on either wall are open and constitute the tops of ventilator shafts which extend to the basement.

Above the roof level rise the upper sections of the towers with their spires and finials. Octagonal turrets occupy the corners of the towers, and each turret is surmounted by a pyramidal monolith, six feet high and three feet in diameter at the base; the apex of this pyramid is cut to represent an acanthus cluster. Each of the six towers is surmounted by a pyramidal spire, which terminates in a spherical capstone. The cut blocks forming the spires are two feet in thickness; the capstones of the four corner towers are three feet in diameter, while those of the two center towers measure eight inches more.

The spherical termination of the east center tower, which is the highest stone in the building, and therefore the capstone proper, supports a statue, the crown of which marks the point of greatest altitude in the entire structure. The figure, which stands twelve and a half feet high, is that of a man in the character of a herald or messenger, blowing a trumpet. In pose and proportion the figure is graceful and gentle, yet virile and strong; the drapings are simple, and leave only feet, arms, neck, and head bare. Around the head is a slender circlet supporting high-power incandescent lamps. The statue is of hammered copper thickly overlaid with gold-leaf. It is the work of C. E. Dallin, Utah-born, and now of more than national fame as a sculptor. The figure is intended to represent Moroni, the Nephite prophet, who died about 421 A. D., and who, as a resurrected being, came in 1823 to the boy-prophet Joseph Smith, and delivered to him the message of the restored Gospel, in accordance with the prediction of the ancient Seer:

"And I saw another angel fly in the midst of heaven, having the everlasting Gospel to preach unto them that dwell on the earth, and to every nation, and kindred, and tongue, and people, saying with a loud voice, Fear God, and give glory to him; for the hour of his judgment is come:

and worship him that made heaven, and earth, and the sea, and the fountains of water."[3]

As has been described in connection with the ceremonies of the capstone-laying, April 6, 1892, the stone upon which rests the statue is one of the record stones of the Temple.[4] Another record stone is to be noted. This lies at the south-east corner of the building immediately beneath the first layer of granite. It is a quartzite block three feet in length and twenty inches in both width and depth. A cavity one square foot in cross-section holds printed books, periodicals, and manuscript records, which were placed therein at the time of laying the first granite course. A slab of quartzite closes the cavity and is cemented in place with due provision against the entrance of moisture.

There are in the walls several series of stones of emblematical design and significance, such as those representing the earth, moon, sun, and stars, and in addition are cloud stones, and stones bearing inscriptions.

The earth-stones are thirty-four in number, eleven on each side and six on each end of the building. They are set on the pedestal course, or first granite course, extending twenty-eight inches above ground. There is one of these stones in each buttress, excepting only the buttresses at the junction of the towers with the main body. These earth-stones constitute the largest cuboidal blocks in the building; each of them measures five feet six inches in height, four feet six inches in width, and one foot eight inches in thickness, and weighs little less than three and one-half tons. Each of these massive blocks is cut to show part of the surface of a sphere, the segment having a diameter of over three feet.

Blocks cut to represent the moon in its several phases, and known as moon-stones, occupy conspicuous places in the buttresses immediately below the second string-course

---

[3]Rev. 14:6, 7.
[4]See page 126.

or water-table; they are therefore on a level with the top of the first or lower line of oval windows corresponding to the ceiling of the Mezzanine story. There are fifty such moon-stones; each four feet seven inches high, three feet six inches wide, and one foot thick.

Sun-stones are set in the buttresses directly under the third belt-course or water-table, which is practically the level of the roof. There are fifty of these, each cut to represent the body of the sun, with a serrated edge of fifty-two points illustrative of the sun's rays. These stones are each four feet seven inches high, three feet six inches wide, and ten inches thick.

Star-stones are numerous; each bears in relief the figure of a five-pointed star. On the east center-tower immediately below the battlements are sixteen of these, four of each face; and on each of the east corner-towers are twelve such stones, making forty on these towers alone. The keystones of the doorways and those of the window arches belong to this class, each bearing a single star.

Star-stones of another kind appear on the face of the center tower at the west. Here, above the highest window and extending to the base of the battlement course, are seen the seven stars of the northern constellation Ursa Major or Great Bear, otherwise known as the Dipper. The group is so placed that the two stars called pointers are practically in line with the North Star itself.

Cloud-stones, two in number, are seen on the upper face of the east center tower, immediately under the cappings of the main buttresses. These show a cluster of cumulus clouds through which the sun's rays are breaking. The face so carved is five feet by three and a half feet in area.

Reference has been made to inscription-stones which form part of the exterior walls. The principal stone of this class is seen on the east centre tower, above the windows, corresponding in position to the starry constellation on the center tower at the west. The main inscription, which occupies a surface a little over twenty by six feet, consists of letters deeply cut and heavily gilded.[5] In the arches over the great windows of the central towers appear inscriptions which are alike at both ends of the building. The keystone of the lower window bears on a carven scroll *"I am Alpha and Omega."*[6] This inscription, a figurative epitome of both time and eternity, and a proclamation of Him who is without beginning and without end, has a peculiar appropriateness over the central casements of this, the House of the Lord; and he who pauses to read may well consider the text and its context in full: "I am Alpha and Omega, the beginning and the ending, saith the Lord, which is, and which was, and which is to come, the Almighty."[7]

Immediately beneath this inscription in the lower window arch of the centre tower appears in relief the emblem of the clasped hands, betokening the bond of brotherhood and the free offering of the right hand of fellowship. On the corresponding stones above the upper windows in each of the center towers is a carven emblem of the All-seeing Eye.

Entrance to the Temple directly from without is afforded by four great doorways, two at either end; each of these portals occupies a court between the center tower and the adjoining corner tower. The four doorways are of like construction. A flight of sixteen granits steps leads up the court; the lowest of these steps is approximately sixteen feet in length, the top step about nine feet, and each of the steps between about ten feet long. On the uppermost granite slab rests the threshold or door-step proper, which is of cast bronze. The doorway is eight feet wide, and sixteen feet six inches in extreme height. This is closed by double doors with

[5]See page 113.
[6]See Rev. 1:8, 11; 21:6; 22:13
[7]Rev. 1:8.

arched transom. The doors proper are twelve feet high, and each single door is four feet wide. In each door the bottom panel is of oak, while the middle and upper panels are occupied by beveled plate glass protected by bronze grills of intricate pattern carrying a bee-hive medallion in the center. The hardware attachments are all of cast bronze, and are of special design. The door-knob bears in relief the bee-hive, above which, in a curved line, appear the words, "Holiness to the Lord." The escutcheon presents in relief the clasped hands within a wreath of olive twigs, an arch with keystone, and the dates "1853-1893"—the years in which the great building was commenced and completed.

On the side of each of the doorways flanking the center tower is a canopied niche in the granite, large enough to receive a statue of heroic proportions.[8]

Such is the great Temple as seen from without. The massive pile impresses even the casual observer as a type of permanency, and the embodiment of the stable and the durable. It stands as an isolated mass of the everlasting hills. As nearly as any work of man may so do, it suggests duration.

---

[8]For a number of years the niches at the east end of the Temple were occupied by bronze figures of Joseph Smith the prophet and Hyrum Smith the patriarch. These figures have since been removed to the open grounds within the Temple Block enclosure.

CHAPTER VIII

The Great Temple at Salt Lake City—Interior

The Temple Annex: While there are four doorways leading into the Temple directly from the outside, the usual entrance is through the detached building known as the Annex. Under ordinary conditions only Church authorities who assemble in council meetings enter by the outer doors, though on the rare occasions of special convocations of the Priesthood many pass those portals.

The Annex is entered on the ground-level through a spacious vestibule, eighteen by twenty-one feet, with wave-glass on three of its sides. The floor is of mosaic tiling, bordered with marble blocks. This ante-room is supplied with steam heat and serves the incidental purposes of a cloak room. At the Annex door stand two large columns of marble mosaic, and in contact with the adjoining walls are two other columns, of the same material and of corresponding design. Within the Annex on this floor there are well-equipped office rooms, with desk facilities for the extensive routine work of registration and record.

The main apartment, however, is the Annex Assembly Room. This occupies the central part of the building, and has seating capacity for three hundred persons. The room consists of a central area thirty-six feet square, with a semi-circular alcove of nine feet radius at both north and south sides. The north alcove is occupied by a platform or stand, raised ten inches above the floor, and is furnished with a small lectern. The central body of the room has an imposing column of Corinthian design in each of its four corners; these columns rest upon massive pedestals and extend to the ceiling. Small columns of similar design support the arches which divide the alcoves from the main auditorium. Over the arches at the north end appear portraits of the living First Presidency; and around the walls are portraits of the present Council of the Twelve Apostles, arranged in the order of seniority of ordination. Within the alcoves hang the portraits of the dead,—at the north those of past members of the First Presidency, and in the south recess, those of Apostles now deceased. On the west wall is a full-size reproduction of Munkacsy's famous canvas, "Christ before Pilate"; this copy is the work of Dan Weggeland, one of Utah's veteran artists. The ceiling is formed by the intersection of four arches, producing a quadruple groin structure. Each of the four lunettes is occupied by triple series of arched windows consisting of colored glass in simple design.

On the west side of the building is a small refectory where a noon-day lunch is served to recorders and other officials on duty for the day. A stairway leads to the basement, which is occupied by storage rooms and lavatories.

The Annex Passage: The foot of the stairway marks the beginning of a semi-subterranean passage, which runs south ninety feet to the Temple wall. This passage receives air and natural light through side windows in three large ventilator cupolas which rise six feet above the ground. Artificial illumination is supplied by three electroliers, each holding twelve globes. Near the south end is the entrance to a side corridor leading to machine rooms in which is installed a very efficient apparatus for vacuum cleaning; this is connected with every room in the Temple.[1] The passage terminates at the foot of a short flight of granite steps—at the centre of the north wall of the main structure. The top of these steps marks the threshold of the Temple. Heavy doors divide the Annex from the Temple.

The Lower Corridor: The doorway from the annex passage opens directly into the lower corridor of the Temple. This extends entirely across the building, from north to south, and is a little over twelve feet in width. The floor is richly carpeted, the walls are finely finished, and the corridor as a whole presents an imposing contrast with the exceedingly plain passage without. The walls are embellished with large paintings, the chief of which is a canvas fifteen by thirteen feet, showing Joseph Smith preaching to the Indian tribes of the east. At the north end is a drinking fountain of Utah onyx—one of many of this unique design distributed throughout the building.

The Baptistry: West from the lower corridor, and occupying the central third of the entire floor on that side, is the baptismal room, in which stands the great font. This apartment is thirty-two by forty-five feet, and is floored with white marble. A ten-inch wainscot of the same material extends along each wall, with grained wood-work above. The walls are virtually a succession of double door, of which the lower half is of paneled wood, and the upper of pebbled glass. Each doorway is arched, and carries a large semi-circular transom with a central aperture occupied by an open grill of metal. Of these doors there are six pairs on both north and south sides, and two pairs on both east and west. There are twenty-six fluted pilasters around the walls, each extending from floor to ceiling. The only natural light the room receives is borrowed from windows with-

---

[1]Prior to 1911 the Temple was supplied with heat and light from its own boilers and dynamos; and during that period electric generators were operated in these rooms. Steam and electricity are now furnished from a central plant situated immediately west of the Temple Block. See chapter IX.

out; but abundant artificial light is supplied by a large central electrolier and numerous side lamps.

The baptismal font is, of course, the most prominent feature of the room. To provide for the font, a depression or well has been excavated to a depth of three feet below the floor level. This well, tiled with marble, is circular, twenty-one feet in diameter, and is surrounded by an ornamental iron railing two feet high. In this depression stand twelve, life-sized oxen, of cast iron, with bronzed bodies and silvered horns. The oxen face outward in groups of three and support the massive font.[2] The font is of cast iron enameled in white, elliptical in form, of ten and six feet in its longer and shorter axes respectively, and four feet deep; its capacity is over four hundred gallons. The rim is reached by a flight of seven steps at either end, with balustrade and top-rail of iron; five inside steps at either end provide for descent into the font. Facilities for quickly replenishing and renewing hot and cold water in the font are adequate and efficient, and due attention has been given to ventilation and sanitary requirements throughout.

The landing at the top of the steps on the west end of the font expands into two small platforms, one at either side; these are enclosed by extensions of the balustrades. On the south side is a small table for the use of the recorder, and on the north are seats for the witnesses whose presence is essential at every baptism performed in behalf of the dead [3]

The placing of the baptistry on the lower or basement floor was not a matter of mere convenience. Most of the baptisms performed within the Temple are in behalf of the dead, and the symbolism of the font location is set forth by authority:

---

[2]Compare with the "molten sea" in the Temple of Solomon, I Kings 7:23-26; II Chron. 4:3-5.

[3]See Doctrine and Covenants, section 128.

"The baptismal font was instituted as a simile of the grave, and was commanded to be in a place underneath where the living are wont to assemble, to show forth the living and the dead."[4]

On the north side of the baptistry is a large room divided into a number of apartments used as dressing rooms and in which are performed certain ordinances of anointing, for men. A similar arrangement for women exists on the south side. In these ceremonies only women administer to women, and men to men.

The Lower Lecture Room: On the east of the lower corridor are two assembly rooms. The first of these is about forty by forty-five feet, and is finished and furnished in great plainness. Its walls are without ornament; and, except for the six electroliers, the only approach to decorative embellishment is a drinking fountain of variegated marble and onyx on the south side. The room is comfortably carpeted but in marked simplicity,— without a suggestion of bright color. The seats are folding lecture chairs, of plain design, and provision is made for two hundred and fifty persons. This room is used for preliminary instruction purposes, and may be called for convenience the Lower Lecture Room.

The Garden Room: In striking contrast with the room last described is the apartment on the south, entered from the lecture room by an arched doorway hung with portieres. While of about the same size as the room described, and seated to accommodate the same number of persons, in all its appointments it is of more elaborate design. Ceiling and walls are embellished with oil paintings—the former to represent clouds and sky, with sun and moon and stars; the latter showing landscape scenes of rare beauty. There are sylvan grottoes and mossy dells, lakelets and brooks, waterfalls and rivulets, trees, vines and flowers, insects, birds and beasts, in short, the earth beautiful,—as it was before the Fall. It may be called the Garden of Eden Room, for in every part and

---

[4]Doctrine and Covenants. 128:13.

appurtenance it speaks of sweet content and blessed repose. There is no suggestion of disturbance, enmity or hostility; the beasts are at peace and the birds live in amity. In the centre of the south wall, is a platform and an altar of prayer, reached by three steps. The altar is upholstered in velvet, and on it rests the Holy Bible. On the sides ‘of the altar are large doorways opening directly into a conservatory of living plants.

The Grand Stairway starts near the south end of the lower corridor already described. It is provided with a stately newel post and a massive balustrade, both of solid cherry. This stairway comprises thirty-five steps with three landings, and at its top is the upper corridor, running forty feet north and south. A large canvas depicting the resurrected Christ instructing the Nephites on the western continent occupies twenty feet of wall space on the east of this corridor; and smaller paintings adorn the other walls.

The World Room: Leading off to the west from the first landing below the top of the grand stairway is a side corridor nine feet wide and fifteen feet long. This contains an art window in rich colors, elliptical in form, about ten feet in height, depicting the expulsion from Eden. It is of special significance in the journey from the Garden Room below to the symbolical apartment into which this side passage leads. At either end the corridor terminates in an arch way; between these the ceiling is of fine panel work. The room is of equal size with those below, forty-five by forty feet. It is carpeted in rich brown, and is seated in the usual way. At the west end is an upholstered prayer altar, on which are placed in readiness for use the Holy Scriptures. Near the altar is a stairway leading to a small waiting room adjoining the elevator landing.

The walls are entirely covered with scenic paintings and the ceiling is pictured to represent sky and cloud. The earth scenes are in strong contrast with those in the

Garden Room below. Here the rocks are rent and riven; the earth-story is that of mountain uplift and seismic disruption. Beasts are contending in deadly strife, or engaged in murderous attack, or already rending their prey. The more timorous creatures are fleeing from their ravenous foes or cowering in half-concealed retreats. There are lions in combat, a tiger gloating over a fallen deer, wolves and foxes in hungry search. Birds of prey are slaying or being slain. On the summit of a rugged cliff is an eagle's eyrie, the mother and her brood watching the approach of the male bird holding a lambkin in his claws. All the forest folk and the wild things of the mountain are living under the ever-present menace of death, and it is by death they live. The trees are gnarled, misshapen, and blasted; shrubs maintain a precarious root-hold in rocky clefts; thorns, thistles, cacti, and noxious weeds abound; and in one quarter a destructive storm is raging.

The scenes are typical of the world's condition under the curse of God. Nevertheless there is a certain weird attractiveness in the scenes and in their suggestiveness. The story is that of struggle and strife; of victory and triumph or of defeat and death. From Eden man has been driven out to meet contention, to struggle with difficulties, to live by strife and sweat. This chamber may well be known as the room of the fallen world, or more briefly, the World Room.

The Terrestrial Room: From the north-west corner of the room last described is a large door-way leading into another apartment, lofty, spacious, and beautiful. Its general effect is that of combined richness and simplicity. Following the elaborate decoration of the World Room, this is restful in its soft coloring and air of comfort. The carpet is of lavender velvet woven with simple figures. The walls are of pale blue, the ceiling and woodwork of white with trimmings in gold. At the west end is a large mirror framed in white and gold. The chairs are upholstered to harmonize with the floor-covering. From the paneled ceiling hang three electroliers, massive, yet simple, holding opaline globes. Two sets of conical shades enclosing incandescent bulbs occupy circular recesses in the ceiling, and torch-shaped brackets supporting additional lamps are affixed to the wall pilasters. A few framed canvases hang from the walls, the largest of which is the original painting by Girard—Joseph interpreting the dreams of the butler and baker. Other pictures are delineations of incidents in the life of Christ and scenes in Bible lands.

An upholstered altar stands near the east end of the room, with copies of sacred writ in place. In this room, lectures are given pertaining to the endowments and emphasizing the practical duties of a religious life. It is therefore commonly known as the upper lecture room, but in view of its relation to the room that follows, we may for convenience designate it the Terrestrial Room. At the east end is a raised floor reached by three steps, across which springs an arch of thirty feet span. The arch is supported by five columns between which hangs a silken portiere in four sections. This is the Veil of the Temple.

The Celestial Room: From the room last described to the one now under consideration the passage leads through the Veil. This is a large and lofty apartment about sixty by forty-five feet in area and thirty-four feet in height, occupying the northeast section of the building on this floor. In finish and furnishings it is the grandest of all the large rooms within the walls. If the last room described could be considered typical of the terrestrial state, this is suggestive of conditions yet more exalted; and it may appropriately be called the Celestial Room. The west end is occupied wholly by the Veil. The east wall is in part taken up by two triple mirrors, thirteen feet high; the central section of each is three feet eight inches wide, and the side sections each three feet in width. Along the walls are twenty-two columns in pairs, with Corinthian caps; these support entablatures from which spring ten arches, four on either side and one at each end. Within the recesses formed by these arches and suspended from the wall-columns, are paintings and busts of past and living leaders of the Church, and canvases depicting scenes in Bible lands and incidents of interest in Church history. Prominent among these are paintings by Lambourne, showing the Hill Cumorah[5] and Adam-ondi-Ahman.[6] Choice canvases illustrative of scenes in the life of Christ and small statuary are disposed with excellent effect about the room. The ceiling is a combination of vault and panel construction elaborately finished. Massive cornices and beams separating the ceiling panels are richly embellished with clusters of fruit and flowers. The color scheme of the walls is soft brown relieved by the light blue of the fluted columns and by abundant trimmings in gold. Eight electroliers with shades of richly finished glass depend from the ceiling, and each of the twenty-two columns holds a bracket of lights in corresponding design. A newel-post at the east bears a flower-cluster of colored globes with an artistic support in bronze. The floor is covered by a heavy carpet and the movable furniture is all of rich yet appropriate design. Palms and other living plants are held in shapely jardinieres of finest ware. At the east is a short flight of stairs leading into an office reserved for the president of the Temple.

Each of the four arched-window recesses in the north is framed by draped curtains of silk, which in material and design match the Veil. On the south side are four pairs of double doors in position and size symmetrically corresponding with the windows on the north. The portal at the south-west, which is fitted with swinging doors, opens directly into the upper corridor at the head of the grand

---

[5]See "The Articles of Faith," XIV:1-3.
[6]See Doctrine and Covenants, section 116.

stairway already described; each of the three other portals is fitted with sliding doors, and opens into a
separate apartment slightly raised above the floor of the
large room, and reserved for special ceremonial work,
more specifically described beyond.

Sealing Room for the Dead: The first of these three
small rooms is about ten by thirteen feet in the square
with a semi-circular recess five feet deep on the south
side. This room is raised two steps above the main floor.
In the wall of this recess is a bay art window of stained
glass, representing with effective and impressing detail
the resurrected prophet Moroni delivering the plates of
the Book of Mormon to the youthful seer, Joseph Smith.
It is a fitting symbol of the actuality of communication
between the dead and the living; and it is to ordinances
pertaining to this relationship the room is devoted; this
is the Sealing Room for the Dead. The west wall is occupied by a large mirror. In the center stands a richly
upholstered altar finished in old-rose velvet and gold.
The altar is six by three feet six inches at its base and
two feet six inches in height. Here kneel in humble service the living proxies representing deceased husbands
and wives, parents and children. The only other furniture consists of chairs for the officiating elder, the witnesses, and persons awaiting the ordinances at the altar.

Sealing Room for the Living: The easterly room of
the three is in size and shape a counterpart of the last
described. Its finishing, however, is in brighter tone;
the altar and chairs are upholstered in crimson velvet, and
the walls are of light tint. A mirror extends from floor
to ceiling on the east wall. This is the Sealing Room for
the Living. Here is solemnized the sacred ordinance of
marriage between parties who come to plight their vows
of marital fidelity for time and eternity, and to receive
the seal of the eternal Priesthood upon their union. Here
also are performed the ordinances of sealing or adoption
of living children by their parents who were not at first

united in the order of celestial marriage.[7] On the south side of this room is a door with transom and side panels of jeweled glass in floral design, leading into a reception room which is provided for the accommodation of parties awaiting the sealing ordinance. This room connects on the west by a short passage with a smaller apartment,— another waiting room, and this in turn opens upon the upper corridor at the head of the grand stairway.

The Holy of Holies: The central of the three small apartments connected with the Celestial Room,—situated therefore between the Sealing Room for the Living and Sealing Room for the Dead,—is of all the smaller apartments within the Temple walls by far the most beautiful. Yet its excellence is that of splendid simplicity rather than of sumptuous splendor. It is raised above the other two rooms and is reached by an additional flight of six steps inside the sliding doors. The short staircase is bordered by hand-carved balustrades, which terminate in a pair of newel-posts bearing bronze figures symbolical of inno-cent childhood; these support flower clusters, each jeweled blossom enclosing an electric bulb. On the landing at the head of the steps is another archway, beneath which are sliding doors; these doors mark the threshold of the inner room or Holy of Holies of the Temple, and corres-pond to the inner curtain or veil that shielded from public view the most sacred precincts of Tabernacle and Temple in the earlier dispensations.

The floor is of native hard-wood blocks, each an inch in cross-section. The room is of circular outline, eighteen feet in diameter, with paneled walls, the panels separated by carved pillars supporting arches; it is decorated in blue and gold. The entrance doorway and the panels are framed in red velvet with an outer border finished in gold. Four wall niches, bordered in crimson and gold, have a deep blue background, and within these are tall vases holding flowers. The room is practically without

---

[7]See page 88.

natural light, but it is brilliantly illumined by a large electrolier and eight side clusters of lamps. The ceiling is a dome in which are set circular and semicircular windows of jeweled glass, and on the outer side of these, therefore above the ceiling, are electric globes whose light penetrates into the room in countless hues of subdued intensity.

On the south side of this room, opposite the entrance doorway, and corresponding in size therewith, is a window of colored glass depicting the appearance of the Eternal Father and His Son Jesus Christ to the boy Joseph Smith. The event here delineated marked the ushering-in of the dispensation of the fulness of times. The scene is laid in a grove; the celestial Personages are clothed in white, and appear in the attitude of instructing the boy prophet, who kneels with uplifted face and outstretched arms. Beneath is inscribed the scriptures through which Joseph was led to seek Divine instruction:

"If any of you lack wisdom, let him ask of God, that giveth to all men liberally, and upbraideth not; and it shall be given him."

And Below:

"This is my beloved Son, hear Him."

This room is reserved for the higher ordinances in the Priesthood relating to the exaltation of both living and dead.

Dome Room: Near the landing of the granite stairway in the southeast tower on the third floor, is the entrance to the large Dome Room, thirty-nine by forty-four feet. On the south side are three oval windows, and opposite these on the north are semi-discs of pebbled glass looking down into the Celestial Room and set in the arches thereof. In the center appears a large dome, fifty-one feet in circumference at its base and seven feet high. This is set with seventeen jeweled windows and may be readily recognized as the ceiling of the Holy of Holies already described as a prominent feature of the second floor. In each of these windows electric bulbs are placed, and it is from these the room below derives its beauty of ceiling illumination and coloring. The walls are hung with portraits of Church authorities. No specific ordinance work belongs to this apartment. At the northwest corner this room opens into a hall or corridor seventy-five feet long, eight feet wide throughout the first fifteen feet of its extent, and ten feet wide for the rest of its course. From the corridor rooms open on either side.

The Elders' Room is the first apartment on the south side of the corridor, west from the Dome Room. It is thirty-one by thirteen feet and is lighted by one oval window. The furniture consists of an altar for prayer, chairs and a table. The room is reserved for council and prayer by the several quorums of elders within the Salt Lake City stakes, each body having the right of occupancy within specified times.

The Council Room of the Twelve Apostles lies to the west from the last, on the south side of the corridor. This is twenty-eight by twenty-nine feet, and has two oval windows on the south. It is furnished with twelve chairs of oak upholstered in leather, other chairs for recorders or clerks, desks, table, and altar. On the walls are seen portraits of latter-day Apostles now living. Adjoining this chamber is an ante-room fourteen by twenty-one feet.

The Council Room of the Seventy is entered from the corridor near its westerly termination. The room is twenty-eight by fourteen feet, and has one oval window on the south side. This chamber is reserved for the use of the First Seven Presidents of the Seventies, or more accurately stated, the First Council of the Seventy. It is furnished for its purpose with seven chairs of a kind, an extra chair for the recorder or clerk, a table and a prayer altar.

The Council Room of the First Presidency and the

Twelve Apostles is situated on the north side of the corridor, and with its ante-room occupies the greater part of that side. The main apartment is forty by twenty-eight feet. In the center is a prayer altar of white wood upholstered in crimson velvet. Twelve large upholstered chairs of oak are arranged in three quadrants of a circle around the altar. The other quadrant is occupied by a table, behind which are three chairs of a kind for the three presiding high priests who constitute the First Presidency of the Church, and another chair for the Presiding Patriarch. These pieces, with desk, table, and chair for the use of the recorder, constitute the essential furniture of the room; all additional pieces are decorative. The walls support several fine paintings, among which are two canvases depicting the descent from the cross, one of the burial of the crucified Christ, and others of scenes in the life of the Savior. Beside these there are original canvases showing landscape scenes of interest in the history of the restored Church.

The ante-room to this chamber is sixteen by fourteen feet. On the north side is seen a commemorative window of colored glass, presenting in the central panel a splendid picture of the finished Temple, above which appears the sacred inscription, "Holiness to the Lord." Each of the side panels presents an escutcheon with scroll and inscriptions.[8]

The High Council Room: Immediately north from the ante-room to the chamber reserved for the First Presidency and the Twelve Apostles, is a room twenty-five by sixteen feet, allotted to the use of the Presidency and High Council of each of the stakes of Zion included within this district. The occupancy of this room is regulated by rule, and the presiding bodies of each of the stakes concerned have access thereto at appointed times, specifically for devotional service. In business session these

[8]See page 113.

organizations meet elsewhere, not in the Temple. The room is furnished with the requisite number of chairs, a table, a desk, and an altar.

The Main Assembly Room, which with its vestries and the end corridors occupies the whole of the fourth floor, is one hundred and twenty by eighty feet in area, and thirty-six feet in height. A commodious gallery extends along both sides, and but for the space occupied by the stands, includes the ends. At either end of this great auditorium is a spacious stand,—a terraced platform, —a multiple series of pulpits. The two are alike as to finish and furniture; a description of one will serve for both.

The stand comprises four terraces, the lowest of which is one foot above the floor, while each of the other three has a rise of two feet. On each of the lower three terraces is a settee or dais eighteen feet long; the upper terrace is furnished with a settee eight feet long for the seating of the president and his two counselors. On each terrace is a central lectern, with a smaller desk of corresponding design on either side. All the woodwork on these terraced platforms is hand carved, and is finished in white and gold.

The upper stand at either end of the room is covered by a canopy, supported by columns, and bearing on its front the designation of the order of Priesthood to which the end is devoted. The stand at the west end is inscribed "Aaronic Priesthood," and the one at the east, "Melchisedek Priesthood." It will be remembered in connection with the description of the Temple exterior that the towers at the east rise to a greater height than do those at the west. It is now seen that this difference is in accordance with the graded orders of Priesthood, stationed within, the Higher at the east and the Lesser at the west.

Flanking the official stands at either end of this auditorium are seats for officials in the Priesthood not directly called to officiate in the services of the day. The gallery and the wings of the stands are furnished with folding chairs; the seats belonging to the body of the auditorium are of reversible construction, so that the auditors may face the stand in which the Priesthood officiating on the occasion belongs.

This great room is finished in white and gold. From the paneled ceiling large electroliers depend, and these with the cornice lights present a total of three hundred and four electric globes. In the rear of each stand are commodious vestries with entrances on either side. In each corner of this imposing auditorium, is a spiral stairway leading to the gallery; the stairway is of graceful design with hand-carved embellishments.

The Upper floors: Above the level of the main assembly room with its accessories, there are no rooms. The next floor has an elevator landing at the west and a cross-corridor connecting the two corner towers at both the east and west ends of the Temple, but these are all. The next landing is on a level with the roof of the Temple, above which are only spires and finials.

The Four Granite Stairways: In each of the four corner towers is a stairway leading from basement to roof, each and every step of solid granite. The stairs are attached to a central column of granite four feet in diameter, and every step is set and anchored to withstand for ages any and all ordinary loosening by time. In each of these four corner stairways there are one hundred and seventy-seven steps, a total of seven hundred and eight in all. Each step is six feet long with an insert of three inches at either end; at the narrow end each step is five inches wide, and at the other end twenty inches; the steps present a projecting tread of one inch and a half. There are broad landings at convenient intervals in the long spiral. Each complete step weighs over seventeen hundred pounds, and the aggregate weight of the granite in the four stairways is over one and a quarter million pounds. On each floor is a cross corridor ten feet in width, running north and south, connecting the tower

stairways. At the west end of the structure are two commodious elevators running in separate shafts of granite
from basement to roof. At first hydraulic elevators were
installed, but these have been replaced by automatic
electric lifts.

Be it remembered that the Temple has been built not
for the present alone. In structure it is stable and of the
best construction skill and devotion could achieve. In the
interior its appearance is strictly in keeping with the stability of the walls and in harmony with the impressive and
imposing appearance presented without. In no part is
there evidence of hurried plan or careless execution. Even
the attic rooms and muniments—but seldom used—are
well and fully furnished.

However, the Temple is not beautified throughout
with equal elaboration. There has been no lavish nor unnecessary expenditure in embellishment. The predominating intent has been that of appropriateness. There are
many rooms of plain design, furnished in but simple style;
there are others in which no effort has been spared nor
cost considered to secure the essentials of grandeur and
sublimity. In no part is there a hint of incompleteness;
nowhere is there a suggestion of the excessively ornate.
Every room has been planned and constructed for a definite purpose, and both finished and furnished in strict
accordance therewith. Within this, the greatest Temple of
the present dispensation, there is no mere display, no
wasting of material, no over-ornamentation. The Temple
has been planned and built as was believed to be most
appropriate to

The House of the Lord.

Chapter IX

Temple Block

Marvelous as was the achievement of the people in rearing the great Temple, and particularly so in the commencement of the work under conditions that appeared so generally unfavorable, the undertaking becomes even more remarkable when we take into consideration other building-work carried on while the Temple was in course of erection. Not only were three other Temples begun and completed during this period, but meeting-houses were reared all in the various wards and stakes, and other structures of yet greater capacity were erected for assemblies of the Church in general. The buildings constructed on Temple Block in Salt Lake City represent in and of themselves great undertakings when considered in the light of circumstances prevailing at the time. Among such buildings are the existing Tabernacle; the structure long since removed and now referred to as the Old Tabernacle, and the Assembly Hall.

It is interesting to know that the first shelters erected for public gatherings within what is now Salt Lake City were boweries; among these the Old Bowery is distinctively named and known. On the 31st of July, 1847— but one week after the arrival of the pioneers in the valley of the Great Salt Lake, a detachment of the Mormon

Battalion,[1] which had just reached the settlement, or as it was even then called, the city, built for the accommodation of worshipping assemblies a bowery of poles and brush. This in time was superseded by a yet larger structure of the kind, one hundred feet by sixty feet, which came to be known in local history as the Old Bowery. It consisted of posts set up at convenient intervals around the sides of a quadrangle, the tops of the posts being joined by poles held in place by wooden pegs or lashed in position by rawhide thongs, and upon this skeleton-roof, willows, evergreens, sagebrush, and other shrubs were piled, resulting in a covering which was a partial protection from the sun, though but a poor barrier against wind and rain.

The old Taberancle: At first this building was known as the Tabernacle; since the erection of the present building bearing that name, the earlier structure has come to be known as the Old Tabernacle. It was one hundred and twenty-six feet in length by sixty-four feet in width, and occupied the site of the present Assembly Hall in the south-west corner of Temple Block. For its day and time it was a large and pretentious building. As to its seating capacity, we read that at the time of its dedication during the April conference of 1852, there were twenty-five hundred persons present at one session. Its ceiling was arched and was supported without pillars. Many of the posts and poles of the Old Bowery entered into the construction of the Old Tabernacle.[2]

---

[1] The Mormon Battalion was a body of five hundred men furnished by the migrating people on demand of the general government to assist in the war between the United States and Mexico. The Battalion was mustered into service in July, 1846, and formed part of the forces commanded by General Stephen F. Kearney. The main part of the Battalion marched from Fort Leavenworth to Santa Fe, and arrived in southern California during January, 1847. A detachment from this band, comprising those who had become disabled while on the march, had wintered at Pueblo; this body reached Salt Lake Valley in July, 1847, but a few days after the entrance of the Pioneers.

[2] Descriptions of the Old Tabernacle and accounts of the proceedings incident to its dedication and opening for public use appear in the "Deseret News" of that time, April, 1852. Reprints in part appear in the "Latter-day Saints' Millennial Star," Vol. XIV, Nos. 22 and 23, July 24th and 31st, 1852. These accounts comprise also synopses of the minutes of the general conference of the Church for that year and include the dedicatory prayer.

The Tabernacle: The building now so known was distinctively designated the New Tabernacle at the time of its construction. It was begun in July, 1864, and was so far advanced as to permit the holding of the general conference beneath its roof in October, 1867. This remarkable structure was planned and erected under the direction of President Brigham Young. For it no claim of architectural beauty is asserted; the general appearance is that of a huge inverted bowl resting on pillars. It is in truth a vast elliptical dome supported at the edge by massive sandstone walls and buttresses. The buttresses measure nine feet in width or depth and three feet in thickness. The space between the buttresses is occupied by doors, windows, and walls; the doors open outward, thus affording ready means of exit. The building measures two hundred and fifty feet in length and one hundred and fifty feet in width at the center. The ceiling is seventy feet from the floor in the middle; and from the ceiling to roof the distance is ten feet. A capacious gallery, thirty feet wide, extends along the inner walls and is broken at the west end only, where it gives place to the grand organ and the seats reserved for the great choir. In contrast with the usual methods of construction this enormous gallery is not continuous with the walls. At intervals of twelve to fifteen feet great beams connect the gallery with the wall buttresses, but between these beams the gallery is set forward two and one-half feet from the inside of the walls and the open spaces are guarded by a high railing. It is believed that the surprising acoustic properties of the building are due in part to this feature of construction; the great dome is, in fact, a colossal whispering gallery, as the hundreds of thousands of visitors who have inspected the building know. When it is emptied save for the few, the fall of a pin dropped at the focal point of the ellipse near one end of the building may be heard at the corresponding point near the other end. The convenient seating capacity of the building, including that of the gallery, is nearly nine thousand, though under conditions of crowding, congregations much larger than this have assembled.

At the west end are the stands including the pulpits. There are really three pulpits rising in tiers or terraces; these afford accommodations for the Church officers of different grades in authority. On either side of the pulpit-terraces are extended platforms for other bodies of Priesthood. Behind the stands and pulpits, rising on either side to the level of the gallery and occupying the space in front of the great organ, is the choir space, seated to accommodate approximately three hundred singers, with extra provision in the gallery for nearly as many more.

At the west end of the building is the great organ, generally admitted to be one of the best instruments of its class ever built. At the time of its construction it was the largest organ in this country and the second or third largest in the world. One of the many surprising features connected with the instrument lies in the fact of its having been constructed by local artisans; the woodwork, including pipe and mechanical equipment, is wholly of native material. The organ occupies a floor-space of thirty-three by thirty feet, and rises to a height of forty feet for the body of the organ itself, while the towers in front reach a height of forty-eight feet. Its stops and regulators number one hundred and ten; it contains over three thousand six hundred pipes, which range from half an inch to thirty-two feet in speaking length. There are four complete finger key-boards and one pedal system, making in all five individual organs. In size and proportions the organ comports with the great building in which it is installed; while in tonal quality and mechanical equipment it is of an order of excellence corresponding to the other appointments of this splendid auditorium.

The domed roof is constructed on the principle of lattice-work support, and is self-sustaining throughout its entire extent, there being no pillars between ceiling and floor. The roof-work is of wood, and at the time of its construction the beams and trusses were held together by wooden pegs and rawhide thongs. These materials were used instead of nails from necessity rather than from choice; nails were obtainable only as new supplies were brought in by prairie wagons, and the cost of the long haul precluded their use. While at present there are many larger roof-spans in the great buildings of the country, most of the more recent structures are of steel; and it is doubtful if ever there has been made a more stable structure of its kind consisting wholly of wood.

The Assembly Hall: In the south-west corner of Temple Block stands the Assembly Hall, a substantial structure designed for congregations of smaller size than those requiring the great Tabernacle auditorium. During the summer of 1877 the Old Tabernacle, about which so many pleasant memories had clustered, was removed to make room for the new building. The Assembly Hall was begun in the year named, and, though meetings were held in the unfinished structure, it was not until 1882 that the building was ready for dedication. The edifice is one hundred and twenty by sixty-eight feet, including the extreme recesses. The walls are of granite from the quarries in Cottonwood canyon.

General Service Plant: All the buildings at present occupying Temple Block, together with many others on adjoining squares, are supplied with steam, hot-water, and electric current for light, heat, and power, from an independent plant situated near the middle of the city square immediately west from Temple Block. From this plant great subterranean tunnels lead to the several buildings connected therewith. The main tunnel is six feet six inches in height, by five feet six inches in width; through this run all pipes for steam and water, ammonia pipes for cooling purposes, and, in addition, a full equipment of electric conductors. The diverging branch-tunnels are each six feet six inches by four feet. The buildings supplied from this plant with electric light, heat, and power, and with steam and hot water, are the following:

1. All the buildings on Temple Block, comprising the great Temple and its accessories, viz., the Annex, the conservatory, the gate house or porter's cottage, the Tabernacle, the Assembly Hall, and the Bureau of Information.

2. All the buildings belonging to the Latter-day Saints' University, comprising the Business College, Barratt Hall, the Brigham Young Memorial Building, and the Lion House.

3. The Bishop's Building, and the old Tithing Office or Bishop's Store House, now used for work in connection with the Latter-day Saints' University.

4. The Deseret Gymnasium.

5. The offices of the First Presidency of the Church, together with the official residence of the President, known as the Bee Hive House. These buildings are situated at a distance of two and one-half city squares from the main plant.

6. The large and famous hostelry, the Hotel Utah.

7. The Deseret News Building and the Deseret News Annex.

8. The Vermont Building.

9. The Sharon Building, and several other smaller structures.

The entire length of the tunnel system is over fourteen hundred feet, and the tunnels are constructed of reinforced concrete with walls six inches thick. From this brief and partial description, it will be seen that the equipment of buildings occupying or adjoining Temple Block, is commensurate and adequate.

Chapter X

Other Utah Temples

Of the sanctuaries reared by the Latter-day Saints, the great Temple at Salt Lake City has been the first to be considered specifically and in detail in these pages. This course has been followed because of the fact that among modern Temples the one at Salt Lake City is the largest, the costliest, and by far the most generally known; and moreover, as already stated, of the four Temples thus far erected in Utah this was the first begun and the last finished. While it was in course of construction three other Temples were proposed, planned, built, dedicated, and opened to sacred ordinance service. These are known from their locations as the St. George Temple, the Logan Temple, and the Manti Temple. The sequence in which they are named is the order in which they were completed and opened; it will be convenient to follow this order in further considering them.

Each of the three is constructed on the same general plan, and for similar specific purposes. While they are of varying richness, and each is smaller and less elaborate than the great Temple at Salt Lake City, their appointments and equipment are essentially the same. No detailed description of internal arrangements or furnishings will be attempted, as such would be little more than a reiteration in part of what has been said.

The St. George Temple

The city of St. George, the county seat of Washington county, Utah, is situated near the southwesterly corner of the State, about two hundred and seventy miles from Salt Lake City in a direct line, and three hundred and thirty as the road runs. Before the walls of the Temple at Salt Lake City had been carried above the basement story, the erection of a Temple in the southern part of the Territory of Utah had been fully determined. The site for the St. George Temple when selected by President Brigham Young lay in the suburbs of the city. The grounds comprise an entire city block of six acres.

On Thursday, November 9th, 1871, President Brigham Young and his First Counselor, George A. Smith, together with Erastus Snow, then President of the Southern Mission, Joseph W. Young, then President of the St. George Stake of Zion, a goodly number of other bearers of the Priesthood, and the general public, dedicated the site and broke ground preparatory to laying the foundation of the building. After the prayer, which was offered by Elder George A. Smith, President Brigham Young addressed the people. From the report of his remarks the following excerpts are taken, as they furnish an illustration of the earnestness with which the commission to build Temples was regarded, and of the practical nature of what the people considered to be their duties as members of the Church. The President urged a concentration of effort on the part of the people in the work, and continued:

"The idea may arise that this is a hard land in which to get a living. Now I am very thankful for the land just as it is. I am glad that it is just as it is. It is a splendid country to rear Saints in. Among our other duties we have to build a temple here. I advise that the Bishop of this city, the Bishop of Santa Clara, and the Bishop of Washington, apportion labor among the members of their respective wards to excavate the ground for the foundation of the temple, and to haul rock, sand, clay and other material. If the brethren undertake to do this work with one heart and mind, we shall be blessed exceedingly, and prospered of the Lord in our earthly substance. Now, if the people present are one with the First Presidency in this work, and will unite with them to prosecute the labor of building this temple, by faith, prayers and good works, let all, brethren and sisters, manifest it by the uplifted hand."

The people with one accord raised their hands. The official record continues as follows:

"President Young took a shovel in his hand and said, pointing to the stake which had previously been driven in the south-east corner of the building site: 'Immediately under this stake and in the foundation will be placed a stone containing sacred records, and immediately over this stake, when the building is completed, will be placed another stone containing records of the temple' He then said, suiting the action to the word: 'I now commence by moving this dirt in the name of Israel's God.' All the people said 'Amen.'"

An address was delivered by Elder Erastus Snow in which he called to mind the promises and prophecies made ten years before, relative to the prosperity that would attend the people in the southern region, and furthermore he pointed out the fulfilment of many of the predictions. Then followed the solemn Hosanna shout.

Work on the excavation began immediately; on the afternoon of the very day of dedication, plows and scrapers were put in action. As announced at the time of the dedication of the site, the following specifications as to dimensions and construction had been decided upon:

"Outside measurement, 142 feet long by 96 feet wide, including the buttresses, and 80 feet high to the top of the parapet. It will be built of stone, plastered outside and inside. There will be a tower in the center of the east end, and on the extreme corners of the same end, right and left of the tower, are cylindrical staircases; one side of the stairs rests in the cylinder, the other side in a newel in the center of the cylinder. The roof will be flat, and covered with roofing similar to that on the New Tabernacle in Salt Lake City. The building will consist of two stories and a basement. The two main rooms or halls, one over the other, will each be 100 feet by 80 feet. The ceiling of these will be arched, resting upon columns, and so constructed as to admit of sixteen rooms for council and other purposes in each of those two main stories. The height of the main ceiling in the centre is 27 feet; the height of the other ceilings about 9 feet. The basement will contain the font, and will be used for ceremonial purposes."[1]

---

[1]See "Dedication of St. George Temple Site," by James G. Bleak, Historian of Southern Mission, published in the "Latter-day Saints' Millennial Star," Liverpool, England, Volume XXXVI, No. 16, April 21, 1874. See also an earlier publication, in the "Star," Volume XXXIII, No. 51, Dec. 19, 1871.

A record-stone was placed at the south-east corner of the building, and therein were deposited, on March 31, 1873, a metallic box containing copies of the scriptures and other publications of the Church, together with a silver plate bearing the following inscription:

"Holiness to the Lord.

"The Church of Jesus Christ of Latter-day Saints was organized and established agreeable to the laws of our country, by the will and commandments of God, on the sixth of April, 1830. Which commandments were given to Joseph Smith, Jr., who was called of God, and ordained an Apostle of Jesus Christ, to be the first Elder in the Church.

"Joseph Smith, Jr., President, with his brother Hyrum, Patriarch of the whole Church, suffered martyrdom in Carthage, Illinois, June 27th, 1844, and the Church was driven into the wilderness in 1846."

Then followed the names of all the general authorities of the Church as at that time constituted.[2]

To the specifications given in the foregoing it is necessary to add only the following to make the description fairly complete. The tower is thirty-one feet square; the vane on the tower is one hundred and seventy-five feet from the ground. The foundation of the entire basement story consists of a black basaltic lava, a rock occurring abundantly in the region and well adapted to the purpose. The soil of the place is sandy and heavily impregnated with alkaline mineral salts; and no rock that readily undergoes disintegration, either through abrasion or as the result of a solution of cementing material, is suitable for foundation work in this soil. The foundation of the building extends below the ground-level ten feet. About two-thirds of the east end and a portion of the northerly side rest on bed-rock in place; throughout the rest of its extent the foundation is laid on a thick layer of broken volcanic rock firmly compacted under the blows of a nine-hundred-pound pile driver. A capacious drain encircles the building and connects with a yet larger drain fifty feet easterly from the square tower. The foundation is twelve

---

[2]See "Deseret News," Vol. XXIII, p. 152. See also an interesting article based on information furnished by George Kirkham, Jr., "Deseret News," Vol. XXV, p. 193.

feet wide at the bottom, and the walls are gradually diminished in width so that at the level of the basement window sills they have a thickness of three feet eight inches. Above the basement story the building is constructed of the fine red sandstone of the region, from quarries specifically located and opened for this work. Timber and lumber had to be hauled by team from distances of from seventy to ninety miles.

The Temple stands in the open plain on but a slight elevation, practically devoid of all the prominence that belongs to a commanding position of altitude. The ground on which the building rests, as well as the region for miles round about, is of a prevailing dark-red color; and this, too, is the color of the sandstone of which the Temple is built. Naturally, the building as a whole would blend with its surroundings, so as to be practically invisible from even a moderate distance. A contrast has been afforded by whitening the walls; and as a result the structure has become a striking feature of the landscape.

As to the interior it may be sufficient to say that all the ordinance work connected with baptism, ordination, endowment, and sealing, as performed in the Temple at Salt Lake City, is administered in a similar manner in this Temple, and provision therefor is made. For all the sacred ordinances there is ample equipment of rooms and furnishings. The basement floor is divided into fourteen rooms of which the baptistry or font-room, thirty-five by forty feet, is one of the largest and most important. As is usual, the baptistry is situated below the general level of the assembly rooms. Also as in the other temples, the baptismal font rests upon twelve oxen of cast iron, which occupy a depression slightly below the floor. The font, oxen, iron stairs, and all accessories, weighing in all over eighteen thousand pounds, were cast in Salt Lake City and were hauled by team thence to St. George. The entire baptistry equipment was the personal gift of President Brigham Young.

Above the basement there are two stories. In each of these there is one main room ninety-nine by seventy-eight feet inside measurement, with an arched or elliptical ceiling twenty-seven feet from the floor in the center. Flanking this main apartment on either side are a number of smaller rooms used for ordinance work and as assembly rooms for councils of the Priesthood. The large room on the middle floor corresponds in use to the splendid Celestial Room already described as a prominent feature of the Temple at Salt Lake City. In the same way the large room on the upper floor corresponds to the main assembly room on the fourth floor of the Salt Lake City Temple, and is provided with pulpits at both east and west ends, the former devoted to the use of the Higher or Melchisedek Priesthood, the latter reserved for the officials of the Lesser or Aaronic order of Priesthood.

Adjoining the main building is an accessory structure known as the Annex; this is seventy-four feet long by twenty-four feet wide, exclusive of a "lean-to" on the east side, which is forty-three feet by nine feet. The Annex was built in 1882. It contains boiler and engine rooms, apartments for the guard, a refectory for the accommodation of workers, recorder's offices, etc.

The St. George Temple was built by free-will offerings and by appropriations from the tithings of the people. In one year, specifically the year 1875, over one hundred and twenty-three thousand dollars were expended in the work, and the total cost of the completed building was considerably more than five hundred thousand dollars. The structure was practically finished by the close of 1876. Some parts were dedicated on January 1, 1877, so as to permit of certain ordinance work to be done before the dedication of the building as a whole, which event occurred on the sixth of April following. At the preliminary dedicatory service, January 1, 1877, twelve hundred and thirty persons were in attendance. Music, some of which had been specially composed for the occasion, was rendered by the choir, and dedicatory prayers were offered by members of the Council of the Twelve as follows: by Elder Wilford Woodruff in the basement story; by Elder Erastus Snow in the main room of the story next above the basement; by Elder Brigham Young, Jr., in the room designated as the sealing room. Addresses were delivered by Elders Erastus Snow, Wilford Woodruff, and by President Brigham Young.

Baptisms for the dead were first administered in the St. George Temple on January 9, 1877; and endowments for the dead were begun two days later.

Proceedings incident to the dedication of the Temple as a whole began on the 4th of April, 1877, and terminated on the sixth, the last day's assembly being held in connection with the annual conference of the Church, which conference had been appointed to be held at St. George, in view of the dedication. On the fourth and fifth of the month general assemblies were held in the Temple during both forenoon and afternoon, each session marked by the rendition of special music and by inspired addresses from the Church leaders. At ten in the morning on Friday, April 6th, the general conference was opened in the Temple. The presiding officers of the several quorums occupied the stands exclusively allotted. There was but little in the way of special addresses, two days having been devoted to the work of instruction and preliminary preparation. The dedicatory prayer was offered by Daniel H. Wells, Second Counselor in the First Presidency of the Church.[3]

The Logan Temple

Scarcely had the St. George Temple been finished and

---

[3]The St. George Temple was closed for extensive remodeling and exterior additions in 1974-75. Following a ten-day public preview in October 1975, the temple was rededicated in services held November 11 and 12, 1975, under the direction of President Spencer W. Kimball.

opened to the sacred ordinances for which it had been built, when another House of the Lord was begun by the Latter-day Saints, this at Logan in the northern section of the long-time Territory and present State of Utah. The St. George Temple was dedicated on the 6th of April, 1877; the Logan Temple was begun on the 19th of September in the same year.

The city of Logan is the county seat of Cache county and the distributing center for the rich and beautiful Cache valley, a valley that has won for itself the distinguishing name of the Granary of Utah. Logan is sixty-six miles on a straight line from Salt Lake City, and one hundred and two miles as the railway runs. The Temples of St. George and Logan are therefore three hundred and thirty-six miles apart in a direct line. Logan is prominent in the valley by virtue of its commanding situation; it occupies the delta and adjoining terrace built by the mountain stream that flowed from the canyon into old Lake Bonneville, and commands a view of the entire valley with the majestic mountain-wall in the background. The Temple occupies a position of prominence in the city, situated as it is upon one of the higher terraces locally known as the Bench, and visible from practically all points in the great valley. The grounds comprise an entire city block of eight acres; and the Temple stands in the northeast quarter of this block.

The site of the Logan Temple was dedicated on May 17, 1877, under the direction of the Presidency of the Church and the Council of the Twelve Apostles. There were in attendance the full First Presidency, composed of President Brigham Young and his counselors, John W. Young and Daniel H. Wells; also John Taylor, president of the Council of the Twelve; Orson Pratt and other members of that Council, together with a large concourse of people. The dedicatory prayer was offered by Elder Orson Pratt, after which Counselor John W. Young broke the ground and threw out the first spade-full of

earth; in this ceremonial moving of the soil he was followed by Counselor Daniel H. Wells and President John
Taylor. Brief addresses were delivered by President
Brigham Young and by Elders Daniel H. Wells and John
Taylor. The remarks of Brigham Young, expressive of
the purpose for which temples are built and of the un-
selfish spirit in which the work was to be prosecuted, were
as follows:

"We have dedicated this spot of ground upon which we expect to
erect a temple in which to administer the ordinances of the House of God.
Into this house, when it is completed, we expect to enter to enjoy the
blessings of the Priesthood and receive our anointings, our endowments
and our sealings; and the brethren will be sealed to brethren to continue
the links and make perfect the chain from ourselves to Father Adam. This
is the object of the temple which we are about to commence building at
this place. We require the brethren and the sisters to go to with their might
and erect this temple; and from the architect to the boy who carries the
drinking water to the men that work on the building, we wish them to
understand that wages are entirely out of the question. We are going to
build a House for ourselves and we shall expect the brethren and sisters,
neighborhood after neighborhood, ward after ward, to turn out their proportion of men to come here and labor as they shall be notified by the
proper authorities.

"This may be called a temporal work, but it pertains to the salvation
of ourselves as well as our friends who have passed behind the veil, and
also the generations who are to come after us. We can carry this temple
forward with our labor without any burden to ourselves if our hearts are
in the work and we will be blessed abundantly in doing so. We will be
better off in our temporal affairs when it is completed than when we commenced, and than we would be if we did not build it. The time we enjoy
is the Lord's, but we have permission to direct its use according to our
good pleasure. When the brethren come to work on this temple they may
expect to be blessed of the Lord according to their faith.

   *   *   *   *   *   *   *

"We pray for you continually that you may be blessed. I feel to bless
you according to the power and keys of the Holy Priesthood bestowed
upon me and my brethren with me, heart and hand, and all the Saints
feel to say 'Amen.' Feel to bless each other, feel to do the work of the
Lord and dismiss the narrow, contracted, covetous feelings that are so
interwoven with the feelings of our natures. It seems hard to get rid of
them but we must overcome them and unite ourselves together in the holy
order of God that we may be Saints of the Most High, that our interests,
our faith and labors may be concentrated in the salvation of the human
family.

"Brethren and sisters, try to realize these things. Awake and lay these things to heart. Seek the Lord to know His mind and will and when you ascertain it also to have the will to do it. God bless you. Amen."

On Monday, May 28, 1877, the work of excavation was begun. Workmen were supplied by wards of the Logan Temple District, which at that time comprised the Cache, Box Elder, and Bear Lake Stakes of Zion. Besides giving of their time and energy,—gifts known as labor donations,—the people contributed freely of cash, livestock, merchandise, and farm produce, and their contributions were supplemented by liberal appropriations from the general Church funds. Truman O. Angell, Jr., was the architect. Rock-laying began on July 20, 1877, on what was known as the extension—a building eighty feet by thirty-six feet in area and twenty-three feet high, lying immediately north of the Temple proper and connected therewith; this has been used since the completion of the Temple for engine room, office, reception, and assembly rooms, thus corresponding to the Annex of the Temple in Salt Lake City.

On September 19, 1877, the corner stones were laid under the immediate direction of John Taylor, president of the Council of the Twelve. President Taylor laid the south-east corner stone and Franklin D. Richards offered the dedicatory prayer thereon. The south-west corner stone was laid by Edward Hunter, Presiding bishop of the Church, and the dedicatory prayer thereon was offered by his counselor, Leonard W. Hardy. The north-west corner stone was laid by George L. Farrell, president of the High Priests' quorum of the Cache Stake of Zion, and the accompanying prayer was offered by Moses Thatcher, of the Council of the Twelve. The north-east corner stone was laid by Albert P. Rockwood, one of the First Council of the Seventy, and the accompanying prayer was offered by Horace S. Eldredge, another member of the First Council of the Seventy.

The Temple as it stands is one hundred and seventy-

one feet long, ninety-five feet wide, and eighty-six feet
high at the square, with an octagonal tower at each corner
one hundred feet high, and a large square tower at each
end. The tower at the west end is one hundred and
sixty-five feet, and that at the east one hundred and seventy feet high. In this feature of the east tower being
higher than that at the west the Logan Temple resembles
the greater structure at Salt Lake City. Massive buttresses strengthen the walls, and the masonry is of the
best. As to architecture, the Temple may be described as
belonging to the castellated style.

The rock used in the building was brought from the
mountain quarries near by, and is a very hard, compact,
dark-colored silicious limestone, locally called fucoid rock
from its content of fossilized marine plants known as
fucoids. A more typical limestone was used for the
arches and for the uprights and lintels of doors and windows, this material being susceptible of a better dressed
surface than was possible with the silicious rock. Water-
tables, string-courses, and the caps of battlements and
towers, consist of a light buff sandstone, brought from
quarries near Franklin, Idaho. As the rock used in the
walls is of diversified color the entire exterior has been
painted in buff.

The lumber used in the building was obtained from
Logan canyon and was prepared at the Temple saw-mill,
which had been specially installed for the purpose. An
interesting sidelight is thrown on the spirit of earnestness
with which the people went about this work of temple
building, by the fact that even the saw-mill was ceremo-
nially dedicated when first put in commission. All the
lumber used was selected, and, as nearly as possible, was
chosen so as to be free from defect. The principal vari-
eties are red pine for the heavier work and white pine for
such interior construction as stands and altars. The frame-
work of the roof is of the best red pine, and is of inge-
nious construction, spanning a distance of ninety-five feet

without under-pinning. At first the roof was covered with sheet-metal, but this proved unsatisfactory because of leakage due to fractures resulting from variations in temperature; and the old but efficient style of shingle roof was finally substituted. The workmanship throughout is high class; indeed it is said that after nearly thirty years not a door has been known to sag or a wall to crack. The total cost of the Temple when completed was approximately seven hundred thousand dollars.

The building has five full stories. The basement story is occupied by the font room and adjoining dressing rooms. In common with the practise followed in Latter-day Saint Temples generally, the font is supported on twelve oxen of cast-iron which stand in a well beneath the general level of the floor. From the basement level rise at intervals of a few feet a number of rooms used in ceremonial work. Thus, about eight feet above the basement floor is the room corresponding to the Lower Lecture Room, four feet higher one corresponding to the Garden Room, and five feet higher one corresponding to the World Room, and yet ten feet higher a room corresponding to the Upper Lecture Room or Terrestrial Room, as already described in connection with the Temple at Salt Lake City. The rest of the space in the first and second stories is occupied by offices for the president of the Temple, the recorders and other officials, library room, etc. The third story is occupied by what is known as the C Room, which corresponds to the Celestial Room elsewhere described. As in other Temples this is the most splendidly finished of all the large rooms. Connecting with this room on the east side are three small apartments used in the sealing ordinances.

The fourth floor is wholly occupied by the main assembly room with its vestries and ante-chambers. The assembly room itself is one hundred and four feet long by ninety-five feet wide, and the ceiling is thirty feet high. At the east is a large elevated platform with stands or pulpits reserved for the officers of the Melchisedek Priesthood, and at the west is a corresponding platform with stands devoted to the officers of the Aaronic Priesthood. The auditorium is occupied by reversible seats, allowing the audience to face either way according to the nature of the services ·at any time,—whether conducted by the Higher or Lesser Priesthood. This room provides for the comfortable seating of fifteen hundred people. The fifth floor comprises detached rooms in the east and west towers. There are no rooms in the main body above the assembly room on the fourth floor already described.

The Logan Temple was seven years in building. On May 17, 1884, the structure was dedicated to the service of the Lord and immediately thereafter was opened for sacred ordinances. The dedicatory services lasted three days, that is to say, services were held on each of two days following the official dedication, and on these later days the dedicatory prayer was read to the assembly. The ceremonies and services attending the dedication were held in the large assembly room on the fourth floor, and the seating capacity of the great auditorium was taxed to the utmost at every meeting. President Brigham Young had died before the laying of the corner-stone, and the building of the Temple had been prosecuted at first under the administration of the Council of the Twelve, which, on the dissolution of the First Presidency becomes the presiding council of the Church, and later under the direction of the new First Presidency. On the day of the dedication the prayer was offered by President John Taylor, after which his Counselors, Elders George Q. Cannon and Joseph F. Smith, made addresses, and they were followed by Elders Wilford Woodruff and Lorenzo Snow of the Council of the Twelve Apostles. A brief address was then delivered by President John Taylor, after which the stirring Hosanna shout was rendered. Benediction was pronounced by John Smith, the Presiding Patriarch.[4]

---

[4]For assistance in compiling data relating to the Logan Temple the writer is indebted to the presiding officer, President William Budge, and his associates.

The Manti Temple

Before construction work had been begun on the Logan Temple, preparations were in progress for the erection of another House of the Lord. Manti, the chief city of Sanpete County, situated about one hundred and four miles southerly from Salt Lake City in a direct line, and one hundred and thirty miles by rail, was selected as the place of this new sanctuary. In a circular issued by the First Presidency and the Council of the Twelve, October 25, 1876, the boundaries of the Manti Temple district were specified, as the following shows:

"We feel led to say to the Latter-day Saints throughout these mountains, let us arise and build temples unto our God at such places as He shall designate, into which we and our children can enter and receive those blessings that He has in store for us. Let the Bishops of the settlements in Washington, Kane, Iron, Piute, Beaver, Millard, Sevier, Sanpete and Juab counties call the people of their wards together and ascertain from them how much each one is willing to do in labor and means, monthly, quarterly, and annually, toward the erection of a Temple at Manti, Sanpete County."

Let it not be forgotten that at this time the people were putting forth strong efforts to complete the temple at St. George, and were taking preliminary steps toward the erection of that at Logan; and throughout this period the greatest temple of all was in course of construction at Salt Lake City. Yet, notwithstanding the weight of these duties, which many would call tasks if not burdens, the call of authority was heard directing another great undertaking of the kind.

As to the location of the precise site on which the Manti Temple should stand, a decision had been reached in a council of the authorities held at Ephraim, June 25, 1875, and the spot known as the Manti Stone Quarry had been reserved for the purpose. The spot so designated is the termination or point of a hill, which in turn appears as the spur of a low range of hills, marked by the outcrop of a well stratified and evenly bedded deposit of oolite. This is a granular rock, the separate particles of which are minute spheroids consisting of concentric layers of calcium carbonate; the stone appears under a lens not unlike fish-roe, hence the name oolite, literally meaning egg-stone. The selection of this spot on which to found the temple meant that the structure would literally be built upon the rock,—upon rock in place, upon an unbroken and undisturbed terrane. The temple was to consist of stone found at the spot, cut and shaped for beauty and service. The material is admirably adapted for the purpose; readily quarried, easily tooled, and withal attractive both in texture and color. The Manti oolite is of uniform grain and of a fine cream color. It has been used extensively for the erection of some of the more pretentious residences in Salt Lake City and, moreover, is the material of the Annex to the Salt Lake Temple, and of the window-facings and other trimmings of the great granite structure.

The site at Manti was dedicated April 25, 1877. In the presence of many of the general authorities of the Church and hundreds of other people, President Young, standing at the south-east corner of the temple lot, broke ground and dedicated the site by solemn service, he himself offering the prayer.[5] He then gave brief instructions as to further procedure, emphasizing the fact that the temple was to be built by the labor of the people and as a free-will offering, and that work thereon was not to be made a means of profit. His address, so clearly illustrative of the peculiar regard with which the Latter-day Saints invest the great commission they hold to build temples unto the Lord, follows:

"We now call upon the people, through the several bishops who preside in this and the neighboring settlements, for men to come here with teams and wagons, plows and scrapers, picks and shovels, to prepare this ground for the mason work. Let this work be commenced forthwith; and as soon as possible we shall expect from 50 to 100 men every working day throughout the season to labor here.

---

[5]For this prayer, see "Latter-day Saints' Millennial Star," Vol. XXXIX, No. 24, June 11, 1877.

"We intend building this temple for ourselves, and we are abundantly able to do it; therefore no man need come here to work expecting wages for his services. The neighboring settlements will send their men, and they can be changed whenever, and as often as, desirable; and they can get credit on labor tithing or on donation account for their services, and we expect them to work until this temple is completed without asking for wages. It is not in keeping with the character of Saints to make the building of temples a matter of merchandise.

"We want to rear this temple with clean hands and pure hearts, that we, with our children, may enter into it to receive our washings and anointings, the keys and ordinances of the holy Priesthood, and also to officiate in the same for our fathers and mothers and our forefathers who lived and died without the gospel, that they with us may be made partakers of the fruits of the tree of life, and live and rejoice in our Father's kingdom. The gospel is free, its ordinances are free, and we are at liberty to rear this temple to the name of the Lord without charging anybody for our services.

"We call upon the sisters also to render what assistance they can in this matter. They can do a great deal by way of encouraging their husbands and sons, and also by making clothing of various kinds for them, and in otherwise providing for them while they are working here.

"Now, Bishops, if any person should inquire what wages is to be paid for work done on this temple, let the answer be, 'Not one dime.' And when the temple is completed, we will work in God's holy house without inquiring what we are going to get, or who is going to pay us, but we will trust in the Lord for our reward, and he will not forget us. 'Behold the fowls of the air (says the Savior) for they sow not, neither do they reap, nor gather into barns; yet your heavenly Father feedeth them. Are ye not much better than they?'

"Let this work be commenced without delay. Building cannot be performed here in the winter, as in St. George. The rearing of this temple will have to be done in the milder portions of the season, when the air is free from frost.

"God bless you, brethren and sisters; we hope and pray that you will be inspired to perform this work with honor to yourselves and glory to God. This is the work of the latter days that we are engaged in, and this is the way that Zion is to be built up. We will continue our labors at home, and we will carry the gospel to all the nations of the earth, to the whole house of Israel, and the good work of redemption and salvation will continue until all is completed, and Jesus presents the kingdom to the Father. Amen."[6]

The beginning of excavation was marked by a further ceremony of prayer. We read that at 8 a.m., April 30, 1877, about one hundred people assembled upon the tem-

---

[6]"Latter-day Saints' Millennial Star," Vol. XXXIX, No. 24, June 11, 1877, p. 373.

ple site where all knelt while prayer was offered, after which the men and horses entered upon the work of preparing for the foundation of the great structure. The peculiar location required the construction of terraces or other form of graded ascent leading from the level of the valley to the temple hill. By December, 1878, four terrace walls were completed in the rough, and by April following the excavation for the foundation was ready. The terrace structure has been substituted by a uniform slope with a retaining wall below.

On April 14, 1879, the corner-stones were laid. President Young, under whose direction each of the temple sites in Utah had been selected and work thereon begun, had passed from earth; and a new First Presidency had not been inaugurated at this time. The presiding authority in the Church was the Council of the Twelve Apostles, of which Council John Taylor was president. On the day named a large body of people assembled near the temple site and, forming in procession, moved to the south-east corner of the grounds. There, after appropriate preliminaries of singing and prayer, an address was delivered by Elder Erastus Snow, one of the Twelve, Wm. H. Folsom, the architect-in-charge, laid the south-east corner-stone, and Elder Lorenzo Snow of the Council of the Twelve offered the prayer thereon. This being regarded as the chief corner-stone, it was designated as the record stone. In a cavity previously prepared, Church publications and other literature were deposited and sealed up before the stone was officially laid. Bishop Edward Hunter, the Presiding Bishop of the Church, laid the south-west stone, and his counselor, Leonard W. Hardy, pronounced the prayer. Elder F. W. Cox, president of the High Priests' quorum of the Sanpete Stake, then laid the north-west stone, and Elder Canute Peterson, president of the stake, offered the prayer. Elder Horace S. Eldredge of the First Council of the Seventy, laid the north-east stone, and his associate in that Council, Elder John Van Cott, pronounced the dedicatory prayer. The services were witnessed by approximately four thousand people.

From the laying of the foundation stones to the completion of the building, the work progressed without serious hindrance. As it stands, the structure is one hundred and seventy-one feet in length, and ninety-five feet in extreme width. From the top of the first water-table to the square the height of the building is seventy-nine feet; the water-table is three feet above the ground. The walls are three and a half feet thick at the base with buttresses four feet in thickness, and both walls and buttresses narrow as they rise. At the square the walls are three feet and the buttresses two feet six inches. The main front of the building is toward the east, as is the case with all existing temples; nevertheless, the doorways most commonly used and the entrance from the Annex are at the west. The foundation on the east end abuts against the hill; and this end of the structure is seen in its entirety by those only who climb the hillside to a commanding position. A tower at the east rises to the height of one hundred and seventy-nine feet; the tower at the west end is ten feet lower. Each of these towers is thirty feet square at the base. The grade or ground-level surrounding the Temple is a little over sixty feet higher than that of the street at the foot of the hill on which the building stands. The drive-way at the east end is at the elevation of the short flights of steps which rise to the doorways on the level of the main assembly room on the top floor.

Adjacent to the main structure and connecting therewith is the Annex building, one hundred feet in length, forty feet in width, and of but one story. In this building is installed the apparatus for heating, and herein also are provided reception rooms, offices, and an assembly room for preliminary services. The Temple is furnished with its own water supply from perennial springs situated in the hills at a distance of a little over a mile.

In the interior the rooms are practically counterparts

of those already described in connection with other Temples. The main assembly room on the upper floor has a seating capacity for over fifteen hundred persons. The estimated cost of the building as it stood ready for dedication was one million dollars.

Dedicatory services were set for May 21, 1888. From accounts published at the time it is plain that the interest in the great event was intense. Thus we read:

> "From an early hour on the 21st of May people began to assemble on the hill east of the Temple, at which admission was to be gained, and by 9:30 the grounds were black with people. The day was lovely, the threatened rain of the night preceding having passed away. As for two days before, all the roads leading to Manti were clouded with incoming teams, each loaded with living freight bound for the dedication."[7]

President John Taylor who, as the presiding officer of the Council of the Twelve Apostles had directed the laying of the corner-stones, and who afterward became the President of the Church, had died in July, 1887. Again The Church of Jesus Christ of Latter-day Saints was without an organized First Presidency of three, and at the time of the dedication of the Manti Temple, the Council of the Twelve was the presiding quorum[8] of the Church. Wilford Woodruff was at this time the president of the Council of the Twelve.

The services began at 11 a. m., by which time the great room was filled to its utmost capacity. The principal feature, of course, was the dedicatory prayer, which was offered by Elder Lorenzo Snow of the Council of the Twelve. Addresses were delivered by the Presiding Patriarch of the Church, by several of the Council of the Twelve Apostles, and by other prominent brethren in the Priesthood. On account of the large numbers desiring to

---

[7] See "The Dedication of the Manti Temple," "Latter-day Saints' Millennial Star," Vol. L, No. 25, June 18, 1888, p. 386.

[8] For this peculiar usage of the term quorum, designating a council or organized body and not specifically a majority of such body, see "Standard Dictionary" wherein we read under "Quorum," "Mormon Ch. A council or an organized body of the priesthood; as, an Elders' quorum; the quorum of the First Presidency."

attend, services were repeated on the two days following,
May 22 and 23. On each of these occasions the dedicatory
prayer was read, hymns and anthems were rendered and
addresses given by speakers chosen by the presiding
authorities. On the first day the actual services occupied
five hours, and over seventeen hundred people attended.
Many of the Saints testified to remarkable manifestations
of Divine power which they witnessed on this grand and
solemn occasion.

"On the first day, just as Professor Smyth was concluding the volun-
tary—a selection from Mendelssohn—a number of the Saints in the body
of the hall and some of the brethren in the west stand heard most
heavenly voices singing. It sounded to them as angelic, and appeared to
be behind and above them, and many turned their heads in that direction
wondering if there was not another choir in some other part of the building. There was no other choir, however. * * *

"Some of the Saints saw the spirit of Presidents Young and Taylor,
J. M. Grant, and others in the Temple, and the heads of some of the
speakers were surrounded by a halo of heavenly light during the services.
The saints enjoyed a spiritual feast extending through the three days, and
many shed tears of joy while listening to the testimonies and admonitions
of the servants of God. There can be no question but that God has
accepted the Manti Temple at the hands of His Saints and will bless all
who have in any degree assisted to build it, or who, not having the means
to assist, have said in their hearts, 'I would have helped if I could.' "[9]

Work on the grounds has been carried on of late
years, to the greater beautification of the site. A magnificent stairway has been constructed from the grade
of the street to the level of the Temple threshold. This
stairway is twenty feet in width with retaining walls on
either side, connecting with large square pillars at each
landing. The steps have a tread of twelve inches and a
rise of six, and of these there are one hundred and twenty-
five. There are nine landings between top and bottom,
each six feet wide. The top of the stairway connects
directly with the roadway surrounding the Temple. The
stairway, its walls and pillars, are all constructed of

[9]"Latter-day Saints' Millennial Star," Vol. L. No. 26, June 25, 1888, p. 405.

cement; and cement walks encircle the building.[10] Scattered over the lawn which occupies the slope on the west are attractive trees and shrubs; each of these is planted in a hole excavated for the purpose in the solid rock. The soil for shrubs, grass, and flowers is foreign to the place.

On May 28, 1888, the Manti Temple was opened for ordinance work and from that time to the present this work has been in progress without interruption except that incident to the regular recess periods each year.[11]

---

[10]See illustrated description of the stairway and other approaches to Manti Temple published in the "Deseret Evening News," December 28, 1907, under the caption, "Manti Has Biggest Cement Stairway in the Country." In a letter to the author, Lewis Anderson, the present president of the Manti Temple, vouches for the correctness, of the data given.

[11]For assistance in compiling data regarding the Manti Temple the writer is indebted to the presiding officer of the Temple, President Lewis Anderson, and his associates.

CHAPTER XI

Conclusion

As set forth in the preceding pages, The Church of Jesus Christ of Latter-day Saints proclaims the need of Temples at the present time, reared and dedicated to the service of the Most High; and affirms that upon the Church has been placed the commission to build and maintain these sanctuaries, and to administer therein the saving and exalting ordinances of the Gospel for both living and dead.

This labor has already attained a magnitude at once impressive and surprising. Ordinances of baptism with accompanying confirmation, ordination in the Priesthood, and sealing both in the relation of husband and wife and in that of parents and children, as solemnized in the Temples of the current dispensation, already number many millions; and the continuation of the work is marked by unabated zeal and devotion.

The Gospel of Jesus Christ is given for the salvation of human-kind; its requirements apply alike to the living whose blessed privilege it is to hear its glad tidings while in the flesh, and to the dead who may accept the truth in the spirit world. The genius of the Gospel is that of altruism unbounded; its power to save extends beyond the portals of death. As the vicarious work for the dead can be done only in sanctuaries specially devoted thereto, there will be an ever-present need for Temples so long as there are souls awaiting this ministry.

The present is the age of greatest import in all history, embodying as it does the fruition of the past and the living seed of the yet greater future. The present is the dispensation of fulness, for which the dispensations of bygone centuries have been but preliminary and preparatory. The saving and sanctifying labor incident to modern Temples surpasses that of the Temples of earlier times as the light of the full day exceeds the twilight of the dawn.

The authority of administration in the Temples of Solomon, Zerubbabel, and Herod, was that of the Lesser or Aaronic Priesthood; for the Higher or Melchisedek Priesthood, otherwise known as the Holy Priesthood after the order of the Son of God, had been taken from Israel with Moses. The temples of the present are administered under the greater authority. The importance of the distinction between these two orders of Priesthood may warrant a further consideration in this place. That the two are essentially separate and distinct is made plain by Paul in his epistle to the Hebrews:

"If therefore perfection were by the Levitical priesthood, (for under it the people received the law,) what further need was there that another priest should rise after the order of Melchisedek, and not be called after the order of Aaron?

"For the priesthood being changed, there is made of necessity a change also of the law."[1]

The apostle emphasizes the superiority of the Priesthood named after Melchisedek by affirming that Jesus Christ was a High Priest of that exalted order.[2] This Priesthood was held and exercised by the patriarchs in turn from Adam to Moses. Aaron was ordained to the priest's office, as were his sons; but that Moses held superior authority is abundantly shown.[3] After Aaron's

[1]Hebrews 7:11, 12.
[2]See Hebrews 5:6, 10; 6:20; compare Psalm 110:4; see also Genesis 14:19.
[3]Consider the Lord's rebuke to Aaron and Miriam, Numbers 12:1-8.

death his son Eleazar exercised the authority of High Priest of the Lesser Priesthood; and even Joshua had to ask of him counsel and instruction.[4]

From the ministry of Moses to that of Christ the Lesser Priesthood alone was operative upon the earth, excepting only the instances of specially delegated authority of the higher order such as is manifest in the ministrations of certain chosen prophets, Isaiah, Jeremiah, Ezekiel and others. It is evident that these prophets, seers, and revelators, were individually and specially commissioned; but it appears that they had not the authority to call and ordain successors, for in their time the Higher Priesthood was not existent on earth in an organized state with duly officered quorums. Not so with the Aaronic or Levitical Priesthood, however, for the courses or quorums of that order were continued until the time of Christ. The last to hold and exercise the authority of the Aaronic Priesthood under the old or Mosaic dispensation was John the Baptist, who was specially commissioned. The matter is thus set forth in a modern revelation:

"Now this Moses plainly taught to the children of Israel in the wilderness, and sought diligently to sanctify his people that they might behold the face of God;

"But they hardened their hearts and could not endure his presence, therefore the Lord in his wrath (for his anger was kindled against them) swore that they should not enter into his rest while in the wilderness, which rest is the fulness of his glory.

"Therefore he took Moses out of their midst, and the Holy Priesthood also;

"And the Lesser Priesthood continued, which priesthood holdeth the key of the ministering of angels and the preparatory gospel;

"Which gospel is the gospel of repentance and of baptism, and the remission of sins, and the law of carnal commandments, which the Lord in his wrath, caused to continue with the house of Aaron among the children of Israel until John, whom God raised up, being filled with the Holy Ghost from his mother's womb;

"For he was baptized while he was yet in his childhood, and was ordained by the angel of God at the time he was eight days old unto this power, to overthrow the kingdom of the Jews, and to make straight the

---

[4]See Numbers 27:18-23.

way of the Lord before the face of his people, to prepare them for the coming of the Lord, in whose hand is given all power."[5]

The Higher or Melchisedek Priesthood was restored through the personal ministry of Jesus Christ, and remained with His apostles and in the Church under their administration, but was again lost as the great apostasy progressed.

The Holy Priesthood in its fulness has been restored in the present age,—not alone the lesser functions of deacon, teacher, and priest, which constitute the distinctive offices of the Aaronic order including the Levitical, but the higher authority as well—that of the elder, the seventy, the patriarch, the apostle, and the high priest.[6]

---

[5]Doctrine and Covenants 84:23-28; read the preceding verses 14-22.

[6]"*The Aaronic Priesthood* is named after Aaron, who was given to Moses as his mouthpiece, to act under his direction in the carrying out of God's purposes respecting Israel (Exodus 4:14-16). For this reason, it is sometimes called the Lesser Priesthood; but though lesser, it is neither small nor insignificant. While Israel journeyed in the wilderness, Aaron and his sons were called by prophecy and set apart for the duties of the priest's office. (Exodus 28:1.)

"At a subsequent period of Israel's history, the Lord chose the tribe of Levi to assist Aaron in the priestly functions, the special duties of the Levites being to keep the instruments and attend to the services of the tabernacle. The Levites thus chosen of the Lord were to take the place of the first-born throughout the tribes, whom the Lord had claimed for His service from the time of the last dread plague in Egypt, whereby the first-born in every Egyptian house was slain, while the eldest in every Israelitish house was hallowed and spared. (Numbers 3:12-13, 39, 44-45, 50-51.) The commission thus given to the Levites is sometimes called the *Levitical Priesthood;* (Hebrews 7:11.) it is to be regarded as an appendage to the priesthood of Aaron, not comprising the highest priestly powers. The Aaronic Priesthood, as restored to the earth in this dispensation, comprises the Levitical order. (Doctrine and Covenants 107:1.) This priesthood holds the keys of the ministering of angels, and the authority to attend to the outward ordinances, the letter of the gospel; (Doctrine and Covenants 107:20.) it comprises the offices of deacon, teacher, and priest, with the bishopric holding the keys of presidency.

"The greater or *Melchisedek Priesthood* is named after the king of Salem, a great High Priest of God (Genesis 14:18; Hebrews 7:1-17.) before his day it was known as 'the Holy Priesthood, after the order of the Son of God, but out of respect or reverence to the name of the Supreme Being, to avoid the too frequent repetition of His name, they, the Church, in ancient days, called that Priesthood after Melchisedek.' (Doctrine and Covenants 107:2-4.) This priesthood holds the right of presidency in all the offices of the Church; its special functions lie in the administration of spiritual things: comprising as it does the keys of all spiritual blessings of the Church, the right 'to have the heavens opened unto them, to commune with the general assembly and Church of the First Born, and to enjoy the communion and presence of God the Father, and Jesus the Mediator of the new covenant.' (Doctrine and Covenants 107:8, 18-19.) The special offices of the Melchisedek Priesthood are those of apostle, patriarch and evangelist, high priest, seventy, and elder." The "Articles of Faith," XI:13-15.

The Temples of today are maintained and the distinctive ordinances pertaining thereto are administered under the authority of the Higher of Melchisedek Priesthood, the greatest and highest commission ever conferred upon man. The Divine prediction voiced by Malachi is in process of rapid fulfilment. Elijah the prophet has been sent to earth and he has committed to the Church that power and authority by which the vicarious service in behalf of the dead was inaugurated. Through his ministration the hearts of the fathers are turning toward the children, and the hearts of the children toward the fathers, and this in preparation of the approaching advent of our Lord, the Christ.[7]

---

[7]See Malachi 4:5, 6; also pages 69-72, this book.

Appendix I

The Great Temple At Salt Lake City—Interior*

The Temple Annex: While there are four doorways leading into the temple directly from the outside, the usual entrance is through the building known as the annex. Under ordinary conditions, patrons entering the temple use the annex, though on rare occasions of special convocations of the priesthood many have passed through the outside portals.

The annex can be entered from three locations, one directly off North Temple Street, another through a passageway running from the Main Street entrance, and the third connecting with the Church parking plaza. The outer room or lobby of the annex, which is entered first, is modestly, yet attractively furnished, and is graced with plants and flowers to enhance the atmosphere of peace and serenity one feels immediately upon entering the annex. Within the annex there is an inner lobby which includes a recommend desk by which all who enter the temple must pass. The well equipped office rooms include those of the temple presidency, matron, and recorder, as well as areas for clerical personnel who handle the extensive work of registration and recording.

The main area of the annex, however, is the chapel. This occupies the full south end of the annex on the ground level and has a seating capacity for 400 persons. At the south end of the chapel is a large mural, 34 feet

*Since James E. Talmage prepared the original text for *The House of the Lord* the interior of the Salt Lake Temple has been remodeled and renovated to meet current usage. The material in this appendix, written by Wm. James Mortimer, patterned after the material written by Dr. Talmage in Chapter VIII, reflects the status of the Temple in 1968.

in height, depicting Jerusalem and the Mount of Olives. At the north of the chapel is a raised platform furnished with an attractive pulpit, a large electronic organ, and benches to accommodate seating for 30 people. Temple patrons are seated in the chapel prior to registration for temple sessions. The chapel is also used for appropriate temple meetings and special gatherings.

At the extreme north end of the chapel is another massive mural, in full view of those seated on the benches. Both murals are the work of the Salt Lake artist Harris Wiberg. The mural at the north depicts the Risen Lord instructing his disciples before his ascension into heaven. One can feel through this painting the Lord himself instructing his disciples, "Go ye therefore, and teach all nations, baptizing them in the name of the Father, and of the Son, and of the Holy Ghost: . . ." (Matt. 28:19.)

From the chapel, temple patrons are invited to proceed down stairways or elevators at the east of the annex to continue the registration process. These semi-subterranean rooms in the lower part of the annex are adjacent to the north wall of the temple and provide access to the main structure.

Included on this lower level are rooms or areas for typing, suitcase storage, children's nursery, kitchen and dining facilities for temple workers and patrons, separate dressing rooms for men and women temple workers and patrons, instruction rooms for brides and for grooms, temple clothing and linen areas, study rooms for temple workers, laundry facilities, ordinance rooms, and the building control center utilized by maintenance personnel.

The Baptistry: Occupying the central third of the entire first floor of the north side of the temple is the baptismal room, in which stands the great font. The room is floored with white marble, and a ten-inch wainscot of the same material extends along each wall, with grained woodwork above. The walls are virtually a succession of double doors, of which the lower half is of paneled wood, and the upper of pebbled glass. Each doorway is arched, and carries a large semi-circular transom with a central aperture occupied by an open grill of metal. Of these doors there are five pairs on the north and six on the south, and two pairs on the east. There are 12 fluted pilasters around the walls, each extending from floor to ceiling.

The baptismal font is, of course, the most prominent feature of the room. To provide for the font, a depression or well to a depth of three feet has been placed in the ceiling of the basement. This well, tiled with marble, is circular and is surrounded by a low marble wall. In this depression stand 12 life-sized oxen, of cast iron, with bronzed bodies and bronze horns. The oxen face outward in groups of three and support the massive font.[1] The font is of cast iron with a durable and attractive fiberglass liner in gold and blue. It is elliptical in form, of ten and six feet in its longer and shorter axes respectively, and four feet deep. Its capacity is over 500 gallons of water. The rim is reached by a short flight of steps, with balustrade and top-rail of iron. Five inside steps at either end provide for descent into the font. Facilities for constantly recirculating, filtering, chlorinating and renewing hot and cold water in the font are adequate and efficient, and due attention has been given to ventilation and sanitary requirements throughout.

The landing at the top of the steps on the west end of the font expands into two small platforms, one at either side; these are enclosed by extensions of the balustrades. On the south side is a small table for the use of the recorder, and on the north are seats for the witnesses whose presence is essential at every baptism performed in behalf of the dead.[2]

---

[1]Compare with the "molten sea" in the Temple of Solomon, I Kings 7:23-26; II Chron. 4:3-5.

[2]See Doctrine and Covenants Section 128.

The placing of the baptistry on the lower or basement floor was not a matter of mere convenience. Baptisms performed within the temple are in behalf of the dead, and the symbolism of the font location is set forth by authority:

> The baptismal font was instituted as a simile of the grave, and was commanded to be in a place underneath where the living are wont to assemble, to show forth the living and the dead. (D&C 128:13.)

On the north of the baptistry are spacious and convenient dressing rooms used by the brethren, and on the south are equally appropriate dressing rooms for the sisters. Provision is also made for rooms where certain ordinances of anointing are performed. In these ceremonies only women administer to women, and men to men.

The Creation Room: On the east side of the lower corridor of the temple are two assembly rooms. The first of these is about 40 to 45 feet, and is finished with plainness. Murals on the walls are subdued in tones, and depict scenes representative of the creation of the earth. The seats are comfortably cushioned, typical of those in the various lecture rooms of the temple. Provision is made for 301 persons. This room is used for preliminary instruction purposes, and may be called for convenience the Creation Room.

The Garden Room: In striking contrast with the room last described is the room on the south, entered from the Creation Room by an arched doorway hung with portieres. While of about the same size as the room described, and seated to accommodate the same number of persons, in all its appointments it is of more elaborate design. Ceiling and walls are embellished with oil paintings to represent clouds and sky, with sun and moon and stars; the latter showing landscape scenes of rare beauty. There are sylvan grottoes and mossy dells, lakelets and brooks, waterfalls and rivulets, trees, vines and flowers, insects, birds and beasts, in short, the earth beautiful—as it was before the Fall. It may be called the Garden of Eden Room, for in every part and appurtenance it speaks of sweet content and blessed repose. There is no suggestion of disturbance, enmity or hostility; the beasts are at peace and the birds live in amity. In the center of the south wall is a platform and an altar of prayer, reached by three steps. The altar is upholstered in velvet, and on it rests the Holy Bible.

The Grand Stairway starts near the south end of the lower east corridor of the temple. It is provided with a stately newel post and a massive balustrade, both of solid cherry wood, and finished in white and gold. This stairway comprises 35 steps with three landings, and at its top is the upper corridor, running 40 feet north and south. At the south end of the corridor is an art window in rich colors, elliptical in form, about ten feet in height, depicting the expulsion from Eden. It is of special significance in the journey from the Garden Room below to the symbolical room which will next be described.

The World Room: Leading off to the west from the first landing below the top of the grand stairway is a side corridor nine feet wide and 15 feet long. At either end the corridor terminates in an arch way. The room to which it leads is of equal size with those below, 40 by 45 feet. It is carpeted richly, and is seated in the usual way. At the west end is an upholstered prayer altar, on which are placed in readiness for use the Holy Scriptures. Near the altar is a stairway leading to a small waiting room adjoining the elevator landing.

The walls are entirely covered with scenic paintings and the ceiling is pictured to represent sky and cloud. The earth scenes are in strong contrast with those of the Garden Room below. Here the rocks are rent and riven; the earth-story is that of mountain uplift and seismic disruption. Beasts are contending in deadly strife, or engaged in murderous attack, or already rending their prey. The more timorous creatures are fleeing from their ravenous

foes or cowering in half-concealed retreats. There are
lions in combat, a tiger gloating over a fallen deer,
wolves and foxes in hungry search. Birds of prey are
slaying or being slain. On the summit of a rugged cliff is
an eagle's eyrie, the mother and her brood watching the
approach of the male bird holding a lambkin in his
claws. All the forest folk and the wild things of the mountain are living under the ever-present menace of death,
and it is by death they live. The trees are gnarled, misshapen, and blasted; shrubs maintain a precarious root-
hold in rocky clefts; thorns, thistles, cacti, and noxious
weeds abound; and in one quarter a destructive storm is
raging.

The scenes are typical of the world's condition under
the curse of God. Nevertheless there is a certain weird
attractiveness in the scenes and in their suggestiveness.
The story is that of struggle and strife; of victory and
triumph or of defeat and death. From Eden man has
been driven out to meet contention, to struggle with difficulties, to live by strife and sweat. This chamber may
well be known as the room of the fallen world, or more
briefly, the World Room.

The Terrestrial Room: From the north-west corner of
the room last described is a large door-way leading into
another room, lofty, spacious, and beautiful. Its general
effect is that of combined richness and simplicity. Following the elaborate decoration of the World Room, this is
restful in its soft coloring and air of comfort. The carpet
is a light shade of blue. The walls are of pale blue, the
ceiling and woodwork are white with trimmings in gold.
At the west end is a large mirror framed in white and
gold. The chairs, which provide seating for 300, are upholstered to harmonize with the floor-covering. From the
ceiling hang two massive crystal chandeliers.

An upholstered altar stands near the east end of the
room, with copies of sacred writ in place. In this room
lectures are given pertaining to the endowments and

emphasizing the practical duties of a religious life. We may, for convenience, designate it the Terrestrial Room. At the east end is a raised floor of two levels reached by two steps to each level across which springs an arch of 30 feet span. The arch is supported by five columns between which hangs a silken portiere in 24 sections. This is the Veil of the Temple.

The Celestial Room: From the room last described to the one now under consideration the passage leads through the Veil. This is a large and lofty room about 60 by 45 feet in area and 34 feet in height, occupying the northeast section of the building on this floor. In finish and furnishings it is the grandest of all the large rooms within the walls. If the last room described could be considered typical of the terrestrial state, this is suggestive of conditions yet more exalted; and it may appropriately be called the Celestial Room. The west end is occupied wholly by the Veil and a mirrored wall. The east wall is in part taken up by five large mirrors and a mirrored door, 13 feet high; the central section of each is three feet eight inches wide, and the side sections each three feet in width. Along the walls are 22 columns in pairs, with Corinthian caps. These support entablatures from which spring ten arches, four on either side and one at each end. The ceiling is a combination of vault and panel construction elaborately finished. Massive cornices and beams separating the ceiling panels are richly embellished with clusters of fruit and flowers. The color scheme of the walls is soft brown relieved by the light tan of the fluted columns and by abundant trimmings in gold. Eight chandeliers with shades of richly finished glass hang from the ceiling, and each of the 22 columns holds a bracket of lights in corresponding design. A newel-post at the east bears a flower-cluster of colored globes with an artistic support in bronze. The floor is covered by a heavy carpet and the movable furniture is all of rich yet appropriate design. At the east is a short flight of stairs leading into a sealing room.

Each of the three arched-window recesses in the north
is framed by draped curtains of silk, which in material
and design match the Veil. An arched doorway at the
north leads to the sealing room annex to be later described.
On the south side are four pairs of double doors in
position and size symmetrically corresponding with the
windows on the north. The portal at the south-west opens
directly into the upper corridor at the head of the grand
stairway already described; each of the three other portals
is fitted with sliding doors, and opens into a separate
room slightly raised above the floor of the large room,
and reserved for special ceremonial work more specifically
described in the following paragraphs.

Sealing Rooms: The first of the three small rooms at
the south of the Celestial Room is about 10 by 13 feet
in the square with a semi-circular recess five feet deep
on the south side. This room is raised two steps above
the main floor. In the wall of this recess is a bay art
window of stained glass, representing with effective and
impressing detail the resurrected Prophet Moroni delivering the plates of the Book of Mormon to the youthful
seer, Joseph Smith. It is a fitting symbol of the actuality
of communication between the dead and the living; and
it is to ordinances pertaining to this relationship that the
room is devoted. This is one of the temple's sealing rooms.
The west wall is occupied by a large mirror. In the
center stands a richly upholstered altar finished in white
and gold. The altar is six by three feet six inches at its
base and two feet six inches in height. Here kneel in
humble service the living proxies representing deceased
husbands and wives, parents and children. The only
other furniture consists of chairs for the officiating elder,
the witnesses, and persons waiting the ordinances at the
altar.

The easterly room of the three is in size and shape a
counterpart of the last described. Its finishing, however,
is in brighter tone; the altar and chairs are tastefully

upholstered, and the walls are of light tint. Mirrors extend from floor to ceiling on the east and west walls. This sealing room is typical of those in the temple used for the living. Here is solemnized the sacred ordinance of marriage between the parties who come to plight their vows of marital fidelity for time and eternity, and to receive the seal of the eternal priesthood upon their union. Here also are performed the ordinances of sealing or adoption of living children by their parents who were not at first united in the order of celestial marriage.[3] On the south side of this room is a door with transom and side panels of jeweled glass in floral design, leading into a reception room which is provided for the accommodation of parties awaiting the sealing ordinance. This room connects on the west by a short passage with the sealing office, and this in turn opens upon the upper corridor at the head of the grand stairway.

Sealing Annex: Because of the great numbers who come to the temple for the sealing ordinances, both for themselves and for the dead, a special series of rooms have been constructed at the north of the Celestial Room for the convenience of temple patrons. These rooms are furnished in a manner typical to those sealing rooms already described. These rooms are used for sealings of the living and the dead, as are other rooms throughout the temple which are designed for this purpose. In all, there are 14 sealing rooms in the temple.

The Holy of Holies: The central of the three small rooms at the south side of the Celestial Room is, among the smaller rooms of the temple, by far the most beautiful. Yet its excellence is that of splendid simplicity rather than of sumptuous splendor. It is raised above the other rooms and is reached by an additional flight of six steps inside the sliding doors. The short staircase is bordered by hand-carved balustrades, which terminate in a pair of

---

[3]See p. 88.

newel-posts bearing bronze figures symbolical of innocent childhood; these support flower clusters, each jewel blossom enclosing an electric bulb. On the landing at the head of the steps is another archway, beneath which are sliding doors; these doors mark the threshold of the inner room of Holy of Holies of the temple, and correspond to the inner curtain or veil that shielded from public view the most sacred precincts of tabernacle and temple in the earlier dispensations.

The floor is of native hard-wood blocks, each an inch in cross-section. The room is of circular outline, 18 feet in diameter, with paneled walls, the panels separated by carved pillars supporting arches; it is decorated in blue and gold. The entrance doorway and the panels are framed in red velvet with an outer border finished in gold. Four-wall niches, bordered in crimson and gold, have a deep blue background, and within these are tall vases holding flowers. The ceiling is a dome in which are set circular and semi-circular windows of jeweled glass, and on the outer side of these, therefore above the ceiling, are electric globes whose light penetrates into the room in countless hues of subdued intensity.

On the south side of this room, opposite the entrance doorway, and corresponding in size therewith, is a window of colored glass depicting the appearance of the Eternal Father and his Son Jesus Christ to the boy Joseph Smith. The event here delineated marked the ushering-in of the dispensation of the fulness of times. The scene is laid in a grove; the celestial Personages are clothed in white, and appear in the attitude of instructing the boy prophet, who kneels with uplifted face and outstretched arms. Beneath is inscribed the scripture through which Joseph was led to seek Divine instruction:

"If any of you lack wisdom, let him ask of God, that giveth to all men liberally, and upbraideth not; and it shall be given him." (James 1:5.)

And below:

"This is my beloved Son, hear Him."

This room is reserved for the higher ordinances in the priesthood relating to the exaltation of both living and dead.

Dome Room: Near the landing of the granite stairway in the southeast tower on the fourth floor is the entrance to the large Dome Room, 39 by 44 feet. On the south side are three oval windows. In the center appears a large dome, 51 feet in circumference at its base and seven feet high. This is set with 17 jeweled windows and may be readily recognized as the ceiling of the Holy of Holies already described as a prominent feature of the second floor. In each of these windows electric bulbs are placed, and it is from these the room below derives its beauty of ceiling illumination and coloring. The walls are hung with portraits of Church authorities. No specific ordinance work belongs to this room. At the northwest corner this room opens into a hall or corridor 75 feet long, eight feet wide throughout the first 15 feet of its extent, and 10 feet wide for the rest of its course. From this corridor rooms open on either side.

The Prayer Room: This is the first room on the south side of the corridor, west from the Dome Room. It is 31 by 13 feet and is lighted by one oval window. The furniture consists of an altar for prayer, chairs, and a table.

The Council Room of the Twelve Apostles: This room lies to the west from the last described, on the south side of the corridor. This is 28 by 29 feet, and has two oval windows on the south. It is furnished with 12 upholstered chairs, other chairs for recorders or clerks, a desk, table, and an organ. On the walls are seen portraits of latter-day apostles now living, and also the First Presidency and Patriarch. Adjoining this chamber is an ante-room 14 by 21 feet.

The Council Room of the Seventy: Entrance to this room is from the corridor near its westerly termination. The room is 28 by 14 feet, and has one oval window on the south side. This chamber is reserved for the use of the First Seven Presidents of the Seventies, or more accurately stated, the First Council of the Seventy. It is furnished for its purpose with seven chairs of a kind, an extra chair for the recorder or clerk, and a table.

The Council Room of the First Presidency and the Twelve Apostles: This room is situated on the north side of the corridor, and with its ante-room occupies the greater part of that side. The main room is 40 by 28 feet. In the center is a prayer altar of white wood upholstered in blue velvet. Twelve large upholstered chairs are arranged in a semi-circle around the altar. The rest of the circle is occupied by a table, behind which are chairs of the same kind for members of the First Presidency of the Church, and another chair for the Patriarch to the Church. These pieces, with desk, table, chair for the use of the recorder, and a small electric reed organ, constitute the essential furniture of the room; all additional pieces are decorative. The walls support several fine paintings, including original canvases showing landscape scenes of interest in the history of the restored Church.

The ante-room to this chamber is 16 by 14 feet. On the north side is seen a commemorative window of colored glass presenting in the central panel a splendid picture of the finished Temple, above which appears the sacred inspiration, "Holiness to the Lord." Each of the side panels presents an escutcheon with scroll and inscriptions.[4]

The Main Assembly Room: With its vestries and the end corridors, this room occupies the whole of the fifth floor, and is 128 by 80 feet in area, and 36 feet in height. A commodious gallery extends along both sides, and but for the space occupied by the stands, includes the ends. At either end of this great auditorium is a spacious stand—a terraced platform—a multiple series of pulpits.

---

[4]See p. 113.

The two are alike as to finish and furniture; a description of one will serve for both.

The stand comprises four terraces, the lowest of which is one foot above the floor, while each of the other three has a rise of two feet. On each of the lower three terraces is a settee or dais eighteen feet long; the upper terrace is furnished with three upholstered chairs for the seating of the president and his two counselors. On each terrace is a central lectern, with smaller pulpits of corresponding design on either side. All the woodwork on these terraced platforms is hand carved, and is finished in white and gold.

The upper stand at either end of the room is covered by a canopy, supported by columns, and bearing on its front the designation of the order of priesthood to which the end is devoted. The stand at the west end is inscribed "Aaronic Priesthood," and the one at the east, "Melchisedec Priesthood." It will be remembered in connection with the description of the temple exterior that the towers at the east rise to a greater height than do those at the west. It is now seen that this difference is in accordance with the graded orders of priesthood, stationed within, the higher at the east and the lesser at the west.

Flanking the official stands at either end of this auditorium are seats for officials in the priesthood not directly called to officiate in the services of the day. The gallery and the wings of the stands are furnished with chairs permanently placed in position. The chairs belonging to the body of the auditorium may be placed in position to face the stand in which the priesthood officiating on the occasion belongs.

This great room is finished in white and gold. In the rear of each stand are commodious vestries with entrances on either side. In each corner of this imposing auditorium is a spiral stairway leading to the gallery; the stairway is of graceful design with hand-carved embellishments.

The Upper Floors: Above the level of the main assembly

room with its accessories there are no rooms. The next floors have elevator landings at the west and a cross-corridor connecting the two corner towers at both the east and west ends of the temple. The next landing is on a level with the roof of the temple, above which are only spires and finials.

The Four Granite Stairways: In each of the four corner towers is a stairway leading from basement to roof, each and every step of solid granite. The stairs are attached to a central column of granite four feet in diameter, and every step is set and anchored to withstand for ages any and all ordinary loosening by time. In each of these four corner stairways there are 177 steps, a total of 708 in all. Each step is six feet long with an insert of three inches at either end; at the narrow end each step is five inches wide, and at the other end 20 inches; the steps present a projecting tread of one inch and a half. There are broad landings at convenient intervals in the long spiral. Each complete step weighs over 1700 pounds, and the aggregate weight of the granite in the four stairways is over one and a quarter million pounds. On each floor is a cross corridor ten feet in width, running north and south, connecting the tower stairways. At the west end of the structure are two commodious elevators running in separate shafts of granite from basement to roof. At first hydraulic lifts were installed, but these have been replaced by automatic electric elevators.

Be it remembered that the temple has been built not for the present alone. In structure it is stable and of the best construction skill and devotion could achieve. In the interior its appearance is strictly in keeping with the stability of the walls and in harmony with the impressive and imposing appearance presented without. I no part is there evidence of hurried plan or careless execution. Even the attic rooms and muniments—but seldom used—are well and fully furnished.

However, the temple is not beautified throughout with

equal elaboration. There has been no lavish nor unnecessary expenditure in embellishment. The predominating intent has been that of appropriateness. There are many rooms of plain design, furnished in but simple style; there are others in which no effort has been spared nor cost considered to secure the essentials of grandeur and sublimity. In no part is there a hint of incompleteness; nowhere is there a suggestion of the excessively ornate. Every room has been planned and constructed for a definite purpose, and both finished and furnished in strict accordance therewith. Within this, the greatest temple of the present dispensation, there is no mere display, no wasting of material, no over-ornamentation. The temple has been planned and built as was believed to be most appropriate to

The House of the Lord.

Appendix II

Temple Block*

Marvelous as was the achievement of the people in rearing the great Temple, and particularly so in the commencement of the work under conditions that appeared so generally unfavorable, the undertaking becomes even more remarkable when we take into consideration other building-work carried on while the Temple was in course of erection. Not only were three other Temples begun and completed during this period, but meeting-houses were reared in all the various wards and stakes, and other structures of yet greater capacity were erected for assemblies of the Church in general. The buildings constructed on Temple Block in Salt Lake City represent in and of themselves great undertakings when considered in the light of circumstances prevailing at the time. Among such buildings are the existing Tabernacle; the structure long since removed and now referred to as the Old Tabernacle, and the Assembly Hall.

It is interesting to know that the first shelters erected for public gatherings within what is now Salt Lake City were boweries; among these the Old Bowery is distinctively named and known. On the 31st of July, 1847—but one week after the arrival of the pioneers in the valley of the Great Salt Lake, a detachment of the Mormon Battalion,[1] which had just reached the settlement, or as it

---

*Improvements and additions to Temple Square in Salt Lake City have been made since the original material in Chapter IX was written by Dr. Talmage. This appendix material written by Wm. James Mortimer is patterned after the original Talmage text and reflects Temple Square as it is in 1968.

[1]The Mormon Battalion was a body of five hundred men furnished by the migrating people on demand of the general government to assist in the war between the United States and Mexico. The Battalion was mustered into service in July, 1846, and formed part of the forces commanded by General Stephen F. Kearney. The main part of the Battalion marched from Fort Leavenworth to Santa Fe, and arrived in southern California during January, 1847. A detachment from this band, comprising those who had become disabled while on the march, had wintered at Pueblo; this body reached Salt Lake Valley in July, 1847, but a few days after the entrance of the Pioneers.

was even then called, the city, built for the accommodation of worshipping assemblies a bowery of pole and brush. This in time was superseded by a yet larger structure of the kind, one hundred feet by sixty feet, which came to be known in local history as the Old Bowery. It consisted of posts set up at convenient intervals around the sides of a quadrangle, the tops of the posts being joined by poles held in place by wooden pegs or lashed in position by rawhide thongs, and upon this skeleton-roof, willows, evergreens, sagebrush, and other shrubs were piled, resulting in a covering which was a partial protection from the sun, though but a poor barrier against wind and rain.

The Old Tabernacle: At first this building was known as the Tabernacle; since the erection of the present building bearing that name, the earlier structure has come to be known as the Old Tabernacle. It was one hundred and twenty-six feet in length by sixty-four feet in width, and occupied the site of the present Assembly Hall in the south-west corner of Temple Block. For its day and time it was a large and pretentious building. As to its seating capacity, we read that at the time of its dedication during the April conference of 1852, there were twenty-five hundred persons present at one session. Its ceiling was arched, and was supported without pillars. Many of the posts and poles of the Old Bowery entered into the construction of the Old Tabernacle.[2]

The Tabernacle: The building now so known was distinctively designated the New Tabernacle at the time of its construction. It was begun in July, 1864, and was so far advanced as to permit the holding of the general conference beneath its roof in October, 1867. This remarkable structure was planned and erected under the direction

---

[2]Descriptions of the Old Tabernacle and accounts of the proceedings incident to its dedication and opening for public use appear in the "Deseret News" of that time, April, 1852. Reprints in part appear in the "Latter-day Saints' Millennial Star." Vol. XIV, Nos. 22 and 23, July 24th and 31st, 1852. These accounts comprise also synopses of the minutes of the general conference of the Church for that year and include the dedicatory prayer.

of President Brigham Young. For it no claim of architectural beauty is asserted; the general appearance is that of a huge inverted bowl resting on pillars. It is in truth a vast elliptical dome supported at the edge by massive sandstone walls and buttresses. The buttresses measure nine feet in width or depth and three feet in thickness. The space between the buttresses is occupied by doors, windows, and walls; the doors open outward, thus affording ready means of exit. The building measures two hundred and fifty feet in length and one hundred and fifty feet in width at the center. The ceiling is seventy feet from the floor in the middle; and from the ceiling to roof the distance is ten feet. A capacious gallery, thirty feet wide, extends along the inner walls and is broken at the west end only, where it gives place to the grand organ and the seats reserved for the great choir. In contrast with the usual methods of construction this enormous gallery is not continuous with the walls. At intervals of twelve to fifteen feet great beams connect the gallery with the wall buttresses, but between these beams the gallery is set forward two and one-half feet from the inside of the walls and the open spaces are guarded by a high railing. It is believed that the surprising acoustic properties of the building are due in part to this feature of construction; the great dome is, in fact, a colossal whispering gallery, as the hundreds of thousands of visitors who have inspected the building know. When it is emptied save for the few, the fall of a pin dropped at the focal point of the ellipse near one end of the building may be heard at the corresponding point near the other end. The convenient seating capacity of the building, including that of the gallery, is nearly nine thousand, though under conditions of crowding, congregations much larger than this have assembled.

At the west end is the rostrum, including the pulpit. The rostrum rises in tiers or terraces, affording accommodations for Church officers of different grades in authority. On either side of the terraced rostrum are platforms for seating other bodies of priesthood or special guests. The rostrum area is so erected that it can be dismantled for placement of a large platform to accommodate such events as symphony concerts, pageants, dramatic offerings, or other public performances in keeping with the spirit of the tabernacle. Behind the rostrum area, rising on either side to the level of the gallery, and occupying the space in front of the great organ, is the choir space, seated to accommodate approximately 375 singers.

The great organ in the Tabernacle is generally admitted to be one of the best instruments of its class ever built. At the time of its construction it was the largest organ in this country and the second or third largest in the world. One of the many surprising features connected with the instrument lies in the fact of its having been constructed by local artisans. The woodwork, including pipe and mechanical equipment, was originally built completely of native material. The organ occupies a floor space in excess of 39 square feet, while the towers in front reach a height of 48 feet. Major remodelings of the organ took place in 1885, 1901, 1915, 1926, 1940, and 1948, until now there are 189 sets of pipes totaling 10,814 individual pipes. Many of the original pipes and much of the original casing are still in the organ. All of the cherished qualities have been retained, and in addition the dynamic range and tone color variety, the warmth, and the brilliance have been greatly extended. Ten of the original pipes built by Joseph Ridges who constructed the organ in the pioneer wilderness of Utah in 1867 are still in use, these being some of the large visible wooden pipes in the front.

In size and proportions the organ comports with the great building in which it is installed; while in tonal quality and mechanical equipment it is of an order of excellence corresponding to the other appointments of this splendid auditorium.

The domed roof is constructed on the principle of lattice-work support, and is self-sustaining throughout its entire extent, there being no pillars between ceiling and floor. The roof-work is of wood, and at the time of its construction the beams and trusses were held together by wooden pegs and rawhide thongs. These materials were used instead of nails from necessity rather than from choice; nails were obtainable only as new supplies were brought in by prairie wagons, and the cost of the long haul precluded their use. While at present there are many larger roof-spans in the great buildings of the country, most of the more recent structures are of steel; and it is doubtful if ever there has been made a more stable structure of its kind consisting wholly of wood.

The Assembly Hall: In the south-west corner of Temple Block stands the Assembly Hall, a substantial structure designed for congregations of smaller size than those requiring the great Tabernacle auditorium. During the summer of 1877 the Old Tabernacle, about which so many pleasant memories had clustered, was removed to make room for the new building. The Assembly Hall was begun in the year named, and, though meetings were held in the unfinished structure, it was not until 1882 that the building was ready for dedication. The edifice is one hundred and twenty by sixty-eight feet, including the extreme recesses. The walls are of granite from the quarries in Cottonwood canyon.

The Information Center and Museum: Of interest to many visitors on Temple Square is the historic museum and information center located in the southeast section of the square. This building was first opened August 4, 1902 and was known as the "Bureau of Information and Church Literature." The building marked the beginning of guided tours for visitors on Temple Square, which has been a great aid to missionary work of the Church. In 1904 the building was remodeled and enlarged, and since then has been added to for the comfort and convenience of those visiting Temple Square. Herein are preserved many important relics and artifacts of early Church history and of life in Salt Lake valley as experienced by the early pioneers. Important murals and paintings are also housed in the building.

The Visitors' Center: Of recent construction on Temple Square is the attractive Visitors' Center, which, in a relatively short period of time, has become one of the most popular tourist attractions in the city, and a valuable missionary tool. This three-story granite structure stands in the northwest corner of Temple Square, and includes ample space for special exhibits and displays, and theaters for film presentations.

Visitors to Temple Square are conducted through the center by guides who donate their time. Various phases of the restored gospel are discussed, and the visitor has an opportunity to see and hear the message of truth proclaimed by The Church of Jesus Christ of Latter-day Saints.

The lower floor of the building includes special rooms where the visitors, at their leisure, can view dioramas, witness coordinated sight and sound presentations, enjoy attractive paintings and murals, and operate various self-controlled display devices which explain the gospel message and the programs of the Church.

In all, this facility is a valuable aid to Church missionary efforts, both within the surrounding area, and among those who come to Temple Square as tourists or visitors.

General Service Plant: It is of interest to note that the buildings on the temple block are supplied with steam and electric power from an independent plant situated near the middle of the city block immediately west of Temple Square. From this plant subterranean tunnels lead to the several buildings connected therewith. The main tunnel is six feet six inches in height, by five feet six inches in width; through this run all pipes for steam, water, and cooling purposes, and in addition full equipment for electric service. The diverging branch tunnels are each six feet six inches by four feet. The entire length of the tunnel system is over 1,400 feet, and the tunnels are constructed of reinforced concrete with walls six inches thick.

Prior to 1911 the temple was supplied with heat and light from its own boilers and dynamos within the old temple annex, but the service plant afterward met these needs. Originally the service plant was owned and operated by the Church, but it is now operated by a private utility firm.

Appendix III

Other Temples of The Church*
by William James Mortimer

The detailed description of the great temple at Salt Lake City, and lesser descriptions of the other temples in Utah serve to illustrate the common purpose and plan for temples and temple work in these latter-days. The Church will continue to erect new temples as its membership grows and as increased work for the dead merits these important edifices.

Brief descriptions will here be offered of the temples thus far constructed or announced.

Hawaii Temple

The first temple to be built by the Church off the U. S. mainland was at Laie, Oahu, Hawaii. Amid the beauty and tropical grandeur of this island paradise, it is fitting and appropriate that a House of the Lord be found.

President Joseph F. Smith, sixth President of the Church, went to the Hawaiian Islands when he was just a lad of 15 to do missionary work. He developed a life-long love for the people of the islands, and in 1915 returned as President of the Church to dedicate and set apart a site for a temple in which the people of the

---

*These temples have been built by The Church since James E. Talmage wrote the original text.

South Pacific might participate in the sacred ordinances performed in these holy houses.

On Thanksgiving day, November 27, 1919, members of the Church gathered from the islands of the Pacific and from the body of the Church in the United States, and met in the completed temple to dedicate it to the Lord. President Heber J. Grant who had succeeded President Smith offered the dedicatory prayer.

Alberta Temple

In 1887 members of the Church settled in the Province of Alberta in Western Canada. The town of Cardston was named after the leader of the pioneer group, Charles Ora Card, who later donated to the Church an eight-acre block.

On July 27, 1913, President Joseph F. Smith dedicated this block as a building site for a temple, and on the following November 9, ground was broken for construction of another House of the Lord.

Work was delayed because of the First World War which raged in Europe from 1914 to 1918. Canada, as part of the British Empire, was seriously involved in the war.

The temple was completed for the most part in 1921, but it was not dedicated until August 26, 1923, with President Heber J. Grant offering the dedicatory prayer.

Arizona Temple

Latter-day Saints were among the early settlers of Arizona, and pioneer colonies were established by them in many areas. To serve the needs of Church members in Arizona, and also the Lamanites and Spanish-speaking members of the Church, President Heber J. Grant dedicated the site for a temple on November 28, 1921.

The temple site consists of 20 acres in Mesa, only a few miles from Phoenix. Ground was broken on April

25, 1923. Like the Hawaii and Alberta temples, the building has neither spires nor towers. In general appearance it has a terraced effect.

Beautiful flowers and stately trees, flourishing in the warm Arizona climate, make the temple and its surrounding grounds an attraction for travelers from many parts of the world. It was dedicated by President Heber J. Grant on October 23, 1927.

Idaho Falls Temple

The Idaho Falls Temple occupies a beautiful site along the Snake River. Ground for the temple was broken on December 19, 1939, and the cornerstone was laid on October 19, 1940, by President David O. McKay, then a counselor to President Heber J. Grant.

The building is constructed of reinforced concrete. The outside walls are faced with white cast stone and stand in beautiful contrast to the green of the lawns and shrubbery. Many of the interior walls are faced with marble, much of which was imported from Europe.

The building was dedicated on September 23, 1946 by President George Albert Smith, eighth President of the Church.*

Los Angeles Temple

Completion of the Los Angeles Temple marked a significant chapter in the history of the Church. Comparable in size and facilities only to the Salt Lake Temple, this structure stands as a sacred memorial to the faith of the Latter-day Saints.

For many years the saints in Southern California had looked forward to the time when they might have a tem-

---

*On April 15-16, 1975, for the first time in the history of the Church, a temple was rededicated. The Arizona Temple was rededicated at seven services, following several months of extensive remodeling and exterior additions.

ple in their midst. Their hopes were brightened on March 6, 1937, when President Heber J. Grant announced the purchase of a 24 acre temple site on Santa Monica Boulevard.

Construction of the temple was delayed by World War II, but following the war, ground was broken in September, 1951, by President David O. McKay, and the cornerstone was laid on December 11, 1953, in impressive ceremonies by President Stephen L Richards of the First Presidency. Dedication of the building came on March 11, 1956, by President David O. McKay.

The building is constructed of reinforced concrete, faced with a light colored cast stone. Surmounting the tower is a statue representing Moroni with a trumpet, announcing to the world the glad tidings of the restored gospel.

Swiss Temple

The first temple on the European continent was truly a dream fulfilled for faithful members of the Church in Europe. The announcement to build the temple near Berne, Switzerland, was made by President David O. McKay in July, 1952, at the completion of his first tour of the European missions. President McKay officiated at the groundbreaking services in August, 1953, and actual construction work began in October of that year. The cornerstone was laid on November 13, 1954, by President Stephen L Richards of the First Presidency.

Dedication of the temple began on Sunday, September 11, 1955, with President David O. McKay officiating. Members of the famed Mormon Tabernacle Choir had been on an extensive tour of Europe, and were then present to participate in the dedicatory services which continued through September 15.

Two dedicatory sessions were held each day to accommodate the large number of saints from throughout the countries of Europe and America who attended the dedication. President McKay repeated the dedicatory prayer at each of the sessions, and then with Sister McKay, and the general authorities who were present, participated in the first ordinance work of the temple on Friday, September 16, 1955.

New Zealand Temple

Significant steps forward in temple building came in 1958 when in that one year, two new temples in opposite parts of the world were completed and dedicated by President David O. McKay.

The first was the New Zealand Temple at Hamilton, which was dedicated on April 20, 1958. The second was the London Temple in Great Britain which will be described later.

Missionary work among the Polynesians in the South Pacific had begun in 1851, and many had traveled the long distances to the Hawaii Temple since its dedication in 1919. However, these people mostly of humble means found it increasingly difficult to travel to Hawaii, and so in 1954 their pleas were honored by the First Presidency who announced that somewhere in the South Pacific an additional temple would be constructed.

Location of a site was a difficult decision, but President McKay made a personal trip through the South Pacific in January and February of 1955 visiting many areas and bringing hope and inspiration to many members of the Church who had never before seen their Prophet.

After his return, President McKay recommended to the Council of the Twelve that the temple be built at Hamilton, New Zealand, where a Church college was already under construction, and where the spiritual and educational atmosphere seemed ideal. Work went forward immediately, and many faithful saints gave much in time and means to complete the edifice for dedication by President David O. McKay beginning April 20, 1958.

Two dedicatory sessions were held each day for three days. Following the temple dedication President McKay also dedicated the seven-million-dollar Church college nearby.

London Temple

The second temple to be dedicated by President David O. McKay in 1958 was the imposing structure at Newchapel Farm, Lingfield, England, some 26 miles south of London. This was the fourth temple to be dedicated by President McKay as President of the Church.

Negotiations for the temple site had begun in the early 1950's and President McKay inspected the proposed spot during his tour of missions in 1952. The property, a 32-acre estate known as Newchapel Farm, was purchased in 1953, and dedicated as a temple site by President McKay on August 10, 1953. While he was in Europe for the Swiss Temple dedication, President McKay returned to England and officiated at the groundbreaking services on August 27, 1955. The cornerstone was laid on May 11, 1957 by Elder Richard L. Evans of the Council of the Twelve. Completion of the construction came in mid-1958, and plans were made for open-house tours of the building starting August 16, 1958. Officials had anticipated that perhaps 50,000 visitors might come, but when more than 80,000 came, the viewing dates had to be extended from August 30 to September 3. The first of the dedicatory sessions was held Sunday, September 7, and continued twice daily with some 12,000 persons participating.

Oakland Temple

In his 92nd year, President David O. McKay presided at the dedication of the Oakland, California Temple, exhibiting faith and vigor far beyond the expectation of his years.

President McKay's interest in the Oakland Temple

dated back to 1934 when he visited the site as one of the general authorities. He recommended purchase of the temple site in 1942. Site dedication and groundbreaking took place May 26, 1962, with President McKay again participating. The cornerstone was laid Saturday, May 25, 1963, by President Joseph Fielding Smith of the Council of the Twelve. President McKay dedicated the temple on November 17, 18, and 19, 1964.

Ogden Temple

The Ogden Temple in Weber County, Utah, was dedicated in six sessions January 18, 19, and 20, 1972, under the direction of President Joseph Fielding Smith. Services were held in the Celestial Room, with closed-circuit television to other areas of the temple and the nearby Ogden Tabernacle. The temple is on the same block as the tabernacle in downtown Ogden, Utah's second most populous city. Groundbreaking ceremonies were held September 8, 1969, and the cornerstone was laid September 7, 1970.

Provo Temple

Dedicatory services for the Provo (Utah) Temple were held February 9, 1972 at 2 and 7 p.m. The services, held in the Celestial Room, were televised by closed circuit to other areas of the temple as well as the 22,000-seat Marriott Special Events Center and other locations on the Brigham Young University campus. More than 70,000 persons attended, in the single largest temple dedication meetings in the history of the Church. President Joseph Fielding Smith presided; the dedicatory prayer was read, at his request, by President Harold B. Lee, first counselor in the First Presidency. Groundbreaking ceremonies were held September 15, 1969, and the cornerstone was laid May 21, 1971.

Washington Temple

The Washington Temple, built in Kensington, Maryland, in a heavily wooded area not far from the U.S. capital, is the sixteenth temple of the Church. The architectural design follows the spired concept of the Salt Lake Temple. President David O. McKay announced plans for the temple November 15, 1968; President Hugh B. Brown of the First Presidency dedicated the site in December 1968. Ten dedication services were held November 19, 21, and 22, 1974, under the direction of President Spencer W. Kimball. The Washington Temple district covers most of the eastern half of the U.S. and eastern Canada.

Sao Paulo Brazil Temple

At an area general conference in South America in February and March 1975, President Spencer W. Kimball announced plans for a temple in Sao Paulo, Brazil, to be built on a 1.5-acre site previously purchased by the Church. He noted the steady growth of the Church in South America; as of 1975 there were approximately 140,000 members there, with more than 40,000 of them in Brazil. Membership in South America had increased almost 500 percent in the past decade.

Tokyo Japan Temple

On August 9, 1975, at an area general conference in Tokyo, Japan, President Spencer W. Kimball announced plans for a temple to be built there, to serve the more than 65,000 members in Asia. It will be built on a half-acre site now occupied by mission offices in the Minato-Ku section of the city.

Seattle Washington Temple

Announcement was made in late 1975 that a temple

will be built in Seattle, Washington, to serve some 170,000 members in Washington, Oregon, northern Idaho, Alaska, and British Columbia. Construction is expected to begin in late 1976 and to be completed sometime in 1978.

Mexico City Temple

On April 3, 1976, plans were announced for a temple to be built in Mexico City. The structure, to be completed in about three years, will feature a modern adaptation of Mayan architectural styles.

Index

Aaron, and sons see God on Sinai, 18; and sons set apart, 23.

Ahaz, king of Judah, robs temple, 7; King, removes altar of Temple, 35.

Ahimelech, maintains service of the shewbread, 24.

Aholiab, son of Ahisamach, 19.

Alberta Temple, the, 224; site dedicated for, 224; dedication of, 224.

Alpha and Omega, inscription on Salt Lake Temple, 150.

Altar of sacrifice, 3.

Amulek, speaks of repentance, 60.

Anderson, James H., article on Salt Lake Temple, preface.

Angell, Truman O., architect for Salt Lake Temple, 119.

Angell, Truman O. Jr., architect for Logan Temple, 184.

Annex, Salt Lake Temple, 152.

Antiochus Epiphanes, King, plunders Temple of Zerubbabel, 43.

Apostles, gather at Far West temple site, 104.

Arizona Temple, the, 224; site dedicated for, 224; dedication of, 225.

Ark of the Covenant, in ancient tabernacle described, 4; brought into Solomon's Temple, 6; contained the sacred tables of stone, 16; set up in City of David, 25.

Ark of God, passes to Philistines, 24.

Assembly Hall, on Salt Lake Temple block, 169, 173, 220.

Atonement, of Christ was a vicarious offering, 66.

Authority, essential to a temple, 10, 11; to labor in behalf of the dead, 69; is characteristic of the Holy Priesthood, 87.

Babylonians, subdue kingdom of Judah, 8.

Balshazzar, King, is slain, 36.

Baptism, by water an essential ordinance, 60; of the Holy Spirit, 60; for the dead, a temple ordinance, 75; of universal application, 75.

Baptistry, of Salt Lake Temple, 154.

Beth Elohim, Hebrew for House of the Lord, 1.

Bezaleel, son of Uri, 19.

Book of Mormon affirms temple erected by Nephites, 9.

Bowery, old, on temple block, 169.

Brown, Hugh B., directs groundbreaking for Provo Temple, 230; directs groundbreaking for Washington D.C. Temple, 231.

Cannon, George Q., offers prayer at capstone ceremony, 126.

Carthage Jail, Joseph and Hyrum martyred in, 109.

Celestial Glory, the, 81.

"Celestial Marriage," a term in use by LDS, 85, 88.

Christ, as a "lamb without blemish," 67; atoning death of, terminated Mosaic Law, 93; reveals self in Kirtland Temple, 101; atonement of, was a vicarious offering, 54, 66.

Church of Jesus Christ of Latter-day Saints, marked by manifestations of divine power, 11; provides early for a temple, 11; possesses Holy Priesthood, 14; has divine commission to build temples, 14; stands alone in practice of temple ministration, 53.

Confirmation, follows baptism for the dead, 78.

Council Room of Twelve Apostles in Salt Lake Temple, 164.

Cowdery, Oliver, Elijah appears to, 70; testifies of Christ's appearance in Kirtland Temple, 101.

Cox, F. W., lays Manti Temple cornerstone, 191.

Cyrus, King, issues royal decree on building of temple, 40.

Dallin, C. E., sculptor of Angel Moroni, 147.

Darius, King, issues decree on building temple, 41.

Day of burning yet awaits fulfillment, 70.

David, King, desired a temple, 5; erects the Third Tabernacle, 25; ark set up in the City of, 25; desires to build temple, 26; lays on Solomon a solemn charge to build temple, 27.